CHRIST WITHOUT BORDERS

CHRIST WITHOUT BORDERS

Jacob Parappally, MSFS

ORBIS BOOKS
Maryknoll, New York 10545

Founded in 1970, Orbis Books endeavors to publish works that enlighten the mind, nourish the spirit, and challenge the conscience. The publishing arm of the Maryknoll Fathers and Brothers, Orbis seeks to explore the global dimensions of the Christian faith and mission, to invite dialogue with diverse cultures and religious traditions, and to serve the cause of reconciliation and peace. The books published reflect the views of their authors and do not represent the official position of the Maryknoll Society. To learn more about Maryknoll and Orbis Books, please visit our website at www.orbisbooks.com.

Copyright © 2024 by Jacob Parappally

Published by Orbis Books, Box 302, Maryknoll, NY 10545-0302.

Material in Chapter 6, "The Different Christologies of Asia," originally appeared in "Gesu in Asia: cristologie nella teologia asiatica," in *Teologia in Asia*, edited by M. Amaladoss and R. Gibellini. It is used here with the kind permission of Editrice Queriniana, Brescia.

All rights reserved.

No part of this publication may be reproduced or transmitted in any form or by any means, electronic or mechanical, including photocopying, recording, or any information storage or retrieval system, without prior permission in writing from the publisher.

Queries regarding rights and permissions should be addressed to: Orbis Books, P.O. Box 302, Maryknoll, NY 10545-0302.

Manufactured in the United States of America

Library of Congress Cataloging-in-Publication Data

Names: Parappally, Jacob, 1953– author.
Title: Christ without borders / Jacob Parappally, MSFS.
Description: Maryknoll, NY : Orbis Books, [2024] | Includes bibliographical references and index. | Summary: "Approaches the mystery of Christ through Indian experiences and perspectives"— Provided by publisher.
Identifiers: LCCN 2024007831 (print) | LCCN 2024007832 (ebook) | ISBN 9781626985919 | ISBN 9798888660478 (epub)
Subjects: LCSH: Christianity—India. | Christianity and culture—India. | Christianity and other religions—India. | Multiculturalism—Religious aspects—Christianity.
Classification: LCC BR1115.C8 P38 2024 (print) | LCC BR1115.C8 (ebook) | DDC 275.4—dc23/eng/20240319
LC record available at https://lccn.loc.gov/2024007831
LC ebook record available at https://lccn.loc.gov/2024007832

Contents

Introduction ix

1. One Jesus, Many Christologies 1
The Emergence of Many Christologies 2
Paradigm Shifts in Christology 4
Contextual Christologies 11
Christologies of Liturgy and Piety. 13

2. The Emergence of Various Christologies 16
A Universal Quest and a Particular Answer 18
The Contextual Christologies in the New Testament 19
Normative Christologies in Christian Tradition 21

3. The Mystery of Christ in Our History. 44
The Search for Understanding the Mystery of Christ 46
An Advaitic Intuition into the Mystery of Christ. 48

4. Christographies and Christologies 53
The Christologies of the Insiders and
    the Christographies of the Outsiders 54
Futile "Quests" for the Historical Jesus and
    the Christographies 58
Contemporary Christographies 64
Contemporary Christologies 69

5. The Challenge to Discover Christ within Cultures 89
Christ's Relation to Cultures 90
Christ within Cultures 98
Christ and Culture: Nondualistic Relationship 100
Discovering Christ within Cultures 102

v

vi *Contents*

6. **The Different Christologies of Asia**....................105
    "What do you have to do with us, Jesus of Nazareth?" 105
    Chinese and the Other East Asian Faces of Christ 107
    Jesus of the Indian Subcontinent 112
    Jesus of Asian Women 119

7. **Jesus of the Poor and the Christ of Religion** 121
    What Are the People Saying about Jesus?..................122
    What Is God Saying about Jesus? 123
    Would the Real Jesus Speak Up? 124
    The Suffering Jesus of the Poor 126
    The Christ of Religion 130

8. **Rejection and Reception of Christ in India** 134
    Rejection of Jesus, the Word,
        by the Anti-Christian Apologists 135
    Jesus, a Guru for Moral Transformation...................137
    Jesus, the *Satyagrahi*, the Prince of Nonviolence............137
    Jesus, the Perfect Yogi, the Ideal Sannyasin or Ascetic........138
    Jesus, Incarnate Son of God 140
    Jesus, the Unique Incarnation 142

9. **The Newness of Jesus Christ** 144
    Toward a Meaningful Indian Christology: Problems 146
    Toward a Meaningful Indian Christology: Prospects 147

10. **Christ beyond Chalcedon:**
    An Indian Interpretation of the Meaning of Christ 151
    Upadhyaya's Theological Method 152
    Upadhyaya's Christological Reflections 154
    An Appraisal of Upadhyaya's Approach 166

11. **The Suffering Christ of the Subcontinent.** 171
    Christic Identification and Identity in the Early Church 172
    Christic Identification in the Indian Context 176
    Christ, the Suffering God of the Subcontinent 182

12. **Christ of Christian Faith in Dialogue**
    with Islamic Faith 189
    Sectarian Christologies' Influence
        on the Islamic Understanding of Jesus 192

Contents vii

Christian Response to the Islamic Understanding
of Jesus Christ and a Triune God 193

13. **Christ beyond Postmodernism** 202
Postmodernism's Challenge to Christology 203
Postmodernism's Insight into the Mystery of Jesus 209
Jesus beyond Postmodernism 211

14. **From Christology to Christophany:
Panikkar's Liberating Vision of Christ** 217
A Critique of Traditional Christology 218
Christophany: A Disclosure of Christ 226

Index 233

Introduction

India encounters Jesus Christ beyond all dogmas about him. This was shown in the past by various authors when they wrote about the "unknown Christ of Hinduism,"[1] "the unbound Christ of Hinduism,"[2] "the acknowledged Christ of the Indian Renaissance,"[3] and so on. Indian thinkers and mystics criticize the Christian preoccupation with dogmas and doctrines about Jesus Christ that do not let the mystery of Christ be experienced by those who do not share the Western Christian worldview. Raimon Panikkar is right in asking whether Indians or other people of Asia should first go through a "circumcision of the mind" by accepting Jewish, Greco-Roman, and Mediterranean imagery of Jesus and then try to understand him in those alien categories of thought.

In Asia broadly and India particularly, thousands of people experience Jesus Christ beyond the boundaries of the church and its dogmas. They have discovered the mystery of Jesus Christ through their own worldview and express it through their own forms of thought. Do they not contribute something more to the knowledge of Christ that surpasses understanding and enlarges the traditional

---

[1] Raimon Panikkar, *The Unknown Christ of Hinduism* (Bangalore: ATC Publications, 1982).

[2] Stanley J. Samartha, *The Hindu Response to the Unbound Christ of Hinduism* (Madras: CLS Publications, 1974).

[3] Madathilparampil M. Thomas, *The Acknowledged Christ of the Indian Renaissance* (Madras: CLS Publications, 1970).

Christian understanding of the mystery of Christ? Jesus Christ is the mystery of God in history. As the one who transcended history, it must be admitted that no dogma, however constitutive it is for our Christian faith, can exhaust the mystery of Christ. Even the most celebrated Chalcedonian Formula does not claim to have said everything that can be said about the mystery of Christ.

Dogmas express only the minimum about the mystery that is revealed through the Scriptures. They are necessary to preserve the content of faith experienced and shared by the apostolic community. Now questions are raised in diverse cultures that encounter the mystery of Jesus Christ with or without the knowledge of any dogmatic formulations about him, whether the content of the dogmas itself is limited because they have taken into account only the Jewish and the Hellenistic worldviews in the beginning of their formulations. Those first disciples who were Jews would not have been able to go beyond proclaiming Jesus a prophet, "mighty in deed and word" (Lk 24:19), the expected Messiah, "the Son of Man," after their encounter with the risen Lord because their worldview and their belief systems provided only such categories. Even if they knew for certain that the experience of the risen Lord was different from what they were speaking about him, they had no terminology to express it. Thanks to the Hellenistic worldview, which some of them had access to through their education or through the Hellenistic context in which they lived because they were in the Diaspora situation, they could better express that experience through the titles "Son of God" and *Kyrios*.

A new culture, a new language, and a worldview different from the original worldviews in which the gospel was proclaimed could contribute to the understanding of the inexhaustible mystery of Christ. Therefore, the content of faith expressed by dogmas may not be a set of truths but symbols of truth that are meant to lead the believer to surrender to the reality communicated through them.

Introduction   xi

Now the question is: Have we said everything about the mystery of Christ that can be articulated about this mystery that surpasses all understanding? Have we really understood what "the fullness of revelation in Jesus Christ" is? Should we not take the experience of those who encountered the reality of Christ informed and enriched by their own cultures and language seriously to expand our vision of Christ? Can some Indian insights into the mystery of Christ complete what is lacking in the traditional proclamation about Jesus Christ? These insights are not strangers to the Christian tradition but have been neglected or abandoned in the course of time for the sake of more appealing, easier ways, which were convenient for the church.

The Indian Worldview and Christological Thinking

The Christic experience and the consequent transformation of persons and societies is possible only if the insight into the mystery of Christ is made available in a way that is meaningful to persons who are confronted by the gospel. However, there are individuals and groups who respond to the message of the gospel even if it is presented in a foreign idiom and language. The spread of the Christian message on all continents and the subsequent growth of the church are examples of such an acceptance of Jesus Christ. But the life-giving message of the gospel remained in these isolated groups without much impact on the larger society because these groups of Christians remained as exclusive groups and insulated themselves from any influence from the surrounding cultures. This is true of the Indian context of Christian proclamation. The vast majority of the people of the Indian subcontinent remained unaffected by the revelation of God in Jesus Christ.

The history of Christological development includes many attempts to overcome the one-sided understanding of Christ. The easiest solution was to deny either the humanity of Jesus or his divinity. They emphasized either the historical dimension of his personhood or his transhistorical dimension. Some emphasized the cosmic Christ or the immanent Christ as the center of the believer's being. Such mutually exclusive positions and theological opinions have narrowed and sometimes distorted the image of Christ.

In the unique, specific, decisive, and historical existence of Jesus Christ as the final and full revelation of God, when received within the Hebrew worldview, he was seen as the Messiah, the fulfillment of Hebrew prophesies. The Jewish expectation of the messiah had to undergo a lot of transformation to become the Messiah of the apostles' experience after his resurrection. He was understood as the one who leads everyone to the eschatological fulfillment of history.

If the Hebrew worldview of history begins with God and ends with God, the flow of history to its God-intended finality has been thwarted by humans' misuse of their freedom. This usurpation of God's sovereignty by playing God by way of directing the world to a different and self-destructive course is a sin from which humans are to be saved. In Jesus Christ, the world is brought back to its God-given course of liberation. Jesus, unlike other humans, is the God-intended human, the God-become-human. In his total freedom, by submitting to God's plan in total obedience, Jesus redirects history from its perverse course to its eschatological finality, as God determined before the foundation of the world (Eph 1:3).

In this worldview, history becomes especially important. The history of humans and their world becomes the history of God Himself. It is a neat scheme where everything falls in line. But questions remain: how does an experience of God, humans, the world, and their relationship become meaningful in a culture in which reality cannot be understood and explained in terms of a linear history that has a beginning and an end? A worldview that provides meaning for human and world history as having

Introduction xiii

its beginning and end in God does not make any sense to those billions of people who do not share this view of history as having a beginning and an ending. In the Indian worldview, time is cyclic. It has no beginning or end. It goes on and on.

In the Indian worldview, what is transhistorical is more important and more liberative than what is historical. Whatever is of this world is nothing compared to the absolute reality that transcends this world. Anything historically limited is only one dimension of reality, and therefore it is a symbol of reality. In this worldview, history moves in a cyclical order, and it is a misery to go through this cycle until final liberation is obtained. The final liberation, then, is a release from the cycle of birth and rebirth.

One of the greatest intuitions of the Indian mind is that the absolute and the world are distinct but not separate. They are not one but also not two; it is *Advaita* (not one–not two). Everything that exists is radically related. In this worldview, the encounter with the absolute is not outside oneself but is an experience within. Since the absolute and the relative are inseparable—not one and not two—one cannot speak of an objective encounter with a reality outside of oneself, even with the absolute reality. Rather, one speaks of a subjective, transformative experience that changes one's vision of everything that exists. Any objectification of such an experience is for the sake of communicating it to others who have not yet received such an experience. The articulation of such an intense existential experience can only be through symbols and metaphors that can evoke a similar experience in others who are graced to experience it. Therefore, the revelation of the mystery of the absolute, the world, and humans is not from the outside, as it were, but a discovery from within.

Christ without Borders articulates theological insights into the mystery of Christ from Indic experiences of Jesus Christ that go beyond Christological dogmas expressed in Greek categories of thought. How does a historical existence—like that of Jesus, who was encountered after his death as the one who is the beginning and end of everything that exists, as the one beyond space and time—fit within the Indian worldview? Does the Western obsession with the historical reality of Jesus reduce him to the status of a mere sage or social reformer or, at the most, rank him as one among the founders of the world's numerous religions, contrary to the apostolic experience of him after his resurrection? What is meaningful in one worldview cannot be translated into another worldview without robbing it of its all-encompassing meaningfulness. In this case, the mystery of Jesus Christ must be re-visioned in the Indian worldview for Christ's own sake and for the sake of all who are graced to encounter him.

I would like to express my sincere thanks to Fr. Edward Philips at Maryknoll, and to the whole team at Orbis, including Rev. Dr. Thomas G. Hermans-Webster, Maria Angelini, Nancy Keels, and Robert Ellsberg.

1

One Jesus, Many Christologies

Jesus is One, but Christologies are many. The plurality of Christologies emerging on the theological horizon can be confusing. However, the presence of a variety of Christologies is not a new phenomenon. Any critical reader can find different Christologies in the New Testament itself. The Christology of Mark is different from that of Matthew, Luke, or John. Paul's Christology has a distinctive character of its own, for Paul is not interested in what had happened in Palestine. His Christology emerges from his existential encounter with Jesus on the road to Damascus. The New Testament contains other Christologies, too.[1]

Yet the diversity of Christological spotlights blends with the blinding light of the Easter proclamation that "Jesus is Lord." There is such a unity in diversity that the fusion of various Christologies ought not to lead to confusion.[2] They all highlight one or another dimension of the mystery of Jesus according to the catechetical needs of the community, all while "Jesus Christ is the same yesterday and today and forever" (Heb 13:8).

---

[1] See R. de Menezes, "Christology of Catholic Epistles," *Jeevadhara* 27 (1997): 81–106.

[2] See James D. G. Dunn, *Unity and Diversity in the New Testament* (London: SCM Press, 1993), 56–59, 216–231.

The Emergence of Many Christologies

The post–New Testament era witnessed a proliferation of Christologies. The wide spectrum of Christologies extended from one extreme to the other: from Docetism, which denied Jesus's real humanity, to Arianism, which held that Jesus was an exalted creature. In the ensuing confusion, the Council of Nicaea (325 CE) reaffirmed the orthodox faith of the church. Jesus is the Logos, "light from light, true God from true God, begotten not made, one in being with the Father." But the controversies would not end there. Jesus provokes discussion, for he is both a mystery and a revelation. As in his time in Palestine, he continues to be an enigma even today.

The Alexandrian theologians stressed Jesus's divinity at the cost of his humanity. The Antiochenes counteracted with an overstress on his human dimension. In 451 CE, the Council of Chalcedon put an end to these controversies by precariously balancing both humanity and divinity in the hypostatic union "without confusion, without separation, without division." This seemed to be an achievement par excellence. Chalcedon tried to define (*de-finire*: to mark limits) the mystery. Defining the undefinable seemed necessary. Why not, if incarnation itself is just that?

From then on, any Christological reflection had to be a restatement of the Chalcedonian Formula. No theologian could escape the danger of heresy if he or she went beyond Chalcedonian Christology. As a result, no serious Christological development took place during the fifteen centuries between Chalcedon and Vatican II. Whatever be culture, language, or philosophy of a particular people, Christology had to be in the formula and idiom of Chalcedon to be orthodox.

In the recent past, however, some began to think of Chalcedon as not the end but only the beginning of Christological development. Karl Rahner articulated this view, saying, "The clearest formulations, the most sanctified formulas ... are not the end but the beginning, not the goal but the means, truths which open the way to the—ever greater—Truth."[3] Faithfulness to the content of faith articulated by the Chalcedonian Christology calls for its meaningful interpretation in a different context by a different generation of committed Christians. The new Christologies emerging both in Catholic and Protestant theological circles in various parts of the world are an indication of this commitment to interpret the meaning of the Christ event in response to various contexts.

The theological climate created by Vatican II also contributed to the growth of a variety of Christologies. Christologies that have emerged include liberation Christology, Black Christology, and feminist Christology. Transcendental Christology, inclusive Christology, pluralists' Christology, and even a bullock-cart Christology versus a helicopter Christology continue the expansion.[4] Various tribal Christologies, national Christologies, and the Christologies of oppressed groups like that of the Dalits (the discriminated castes in India) are in the making.

What are we to conclude about such a bewildering variety of new or contextual Christologies? Are they all referring back to the living Christ of apostolic experience, the unique self-communication of God in history? Or are they relativizing the definitive, decisive, irrevocable, and all-surpassing offer of

---

[3] Karl Rahner, *Theological Investigations*, vol. 1 (London: Darton, Longman & Todd, 1961), 149.

[4] According to S. J. Samartha, a helicopter Christology is a "Christology from above" that attempts to land on the religiously pluralistic Asian terrain raising missiological noise and theological dust, making it difficult for the people to hear and see the descending divinity. But a bullock-cart Christology is a Christology from below, moving along "with a steady pace, even when the driver sometimes falls asleep." See Stanley J. Samartha, *One Christ—Many Religions: Toward a Revised Christology* (Maryknoll, NY: Orbis Books, 1991), 115–116.

God's salvation in and through the person of Jesus? Do contextual Christologies adversely affect the mission of proclaiming Jesus Christ as the unique savior of humankind? Or do they enhance a more meaningful and relevant proclamation of the person and message of Jesus Christ to which people can freely respond from their own existential life situations?

Paradigm Shifts in Christology

As we have already mentioned, the plurality of contextual Christologies is not a new phenomenon. One can find them in the New Testament as well as throughout Christian tradition. But the wide range of Christologies that have emerged in the recent past or are still taking shape in different contexts is something new. It should be no wonder, then, that some are alarmed by these new developments. They are apprehensive of the consequences of this pluralism. But they fail to observe the paradigm shifts in Christology that took place after Vatican II that, in turn, contributed to the development of many Christologies.

From Alexandrian to Antiochene Christology

Before Vatican II, the Alexandrian Christological model or paradigm obviously determined much of Christian life and praxis. This model overstressed the divinity of Christ. Every attribute of God, both scripturally revealed and philosophically postulated, was Christ's as he is God: majesty, glory, transcendence, perfection, power, omniscience, and so on. There might have been many reasons for the predominance of this model of Christology over the Antiochene. Powerful personalities like Cyril of Alexandria, Athanasius, and others championed its cause. Whatever the reason for its origin and survival, the image of Christ presented by this school determined possible types of ecclesiology, liturgy, ministry, missiology, and religious life[5] on through to Vatican II. Based on the Alexandrian paradigm of Christology, ecclesiology envisioned a pyramidal structure of the church with a powerful hierarchy representing the divine Christ to rule the laity. The liturgy purported to reenact the heavenly liturgy with elaborate rubrics, ornate and heavy vestments, and solemn chant using an ancient language. The priesthood was understood mainly in terms of cultic functions for the people but often distanced from the people. The driving force of mission was an exclusive understanding of salvation in and through Christ and the church.

After Vatican II, a shift in the Christological paradigm could be observed. The shift has been from an Alexandrian Christology to an Antiochene. It was a shift from a Christology "from above" to a Christology "from below," from a one-sided emphasis on the divinity of Christ to the humanity of Christ. The influence of the Antiochene Christological paradigm can be seen in the Second Vatican Council's understanding of the Catholic Church as the people of God who are served by the hierarchy, in the renewal of liturgy for a more meaningful and participatory celebration of the divine mysteries in the various life situations of the people using their own language, in understanding of priestly ministry as for the building up of the community, in the church's attitude of openness and respect toward other religions, and in the renewal of religious life. Such a change from a pre–Vatican II understanding of the church's life, attitudes, and commitments was possible because of a revision of Christian life and praxis that envisioned Jesus, the human, as the paradigm of life. Obviously, there was no public proclamation of a paradigm shift in Christology, but the aim of the council to clarify the church's response to the global context demanded it.

---

[5] See R. L. Schebera, "The Effects of Christology on Religious Life," *Sisters Today* 50 (1978): 226–230.

A paradigm shift in Christology was taking place already before the Council. It was Jesus, the Human, who caught the imagination of the modern youth in their existential quest for meaning. It was Jesus, the Human, in whom the oppressed and the dehumanized could find a liberator who was involved in their struggle to achieve liberation. Jesus, the Human, revealed a compassionate God whose kingdom transcends the boundaries of the church and, therefore, makes dialogue with other religions and movements for human liberation an imperative. The new challenges and a belated recognition of the importance of the differences of the contexts called for a variety of Christologies.

A paradigm shift from the Alexandrian to the Antiochene model made it possible to respond to such needs. Perhaps the exigency of the contexts itself forced a paradigm shift. Many have not observed this paradigm shift or have not accepted it, so the mushrooming of contextual Christologies and the other changes in Christian life and practices have created much confusion and apprehension in their minds. This is understandable, but the tendency to discredit and condemn the emergence of contextual Christologies escapes our comprehension.

Is it not obvious that a living faith in Christ cannot be reduced to a mere repetition of old Christological formulas, however orthodox they may be? This does not mean that we abandon the shared Christ experience of the community. The "once and for all" reality of the Christ event is the content of our shared faith experience. Rather, it calls for an existential response to the question "Who do you say that I am?" *here* and *now*. An authentically existential, meaningful, and grace-filled response to this fundamental question cannot but be contextual. Contextual Christologies, whether well-articulated or not for other contexts, are expressions of a vibrant Christian community that takes its commitment to the person and mission of Christ seriously. An absence of such Christologies may be a sign of an indifference to Christ or to the context in which he is encountered. It may also reveal the laziness of those who are content with following a literal orthodoxy. Faith is not faith if it is not manifested in a commitment that expresses that faith (Jas 2:18–19).

The paradigm shift from Alexandrian to Antiochene Christology has been an internal affair of the church that changed and is changing perspectives and praxis of Christian life. In the recent past, a new paradigm shift in Christology has emerged: a shift from Christocentrism to theocentrism. This affects the church's understanding of herself vis-à-vis other religions and the church's mission in a world of plurality of religions that claim to offer different means of salvation.

From Christocentrism to Theocentrism

The new paradigm shift in Christology is more unsettling than the previous one. Some even consider this paradigm shift to be a "Copernican revolution" in theology. According to this position, God is the center and not Christ. They hold that Jesus was not proclaiming himself but God and his kingdom. Therefore, it is legitimate to center one's belief on God and not on Christ. Christ can be the normative or one among the many different ways to God.

It is also held that such a shift of the center allows us to understand God's presence and revelation in other religions, opening the way to dialogue in a multireligious society. This paradigm shift is observed by some in *Unitatis redintegratio* and *Nostra aetate* of Vatican II. According to S. J. Duffy, "These texts relativize Roman Catholicism and Christianity, and they mark a shift from ecclesiocentrism to christocentrism to theocentrism."[6] Vatican II reaffirmed the universal salvific will of God (1 Tim 2:4), which would not leave the extra-Christian religions without providing them the means of salvation. So, the council had no hesitation to

---

[6] Stephen J. Duffy, "The Galilean Christ: Particularity and Universality," *Journal of Ecumenical Studies* 26 (1989): 161.

8   *Christ without Borders*

recognize in other religions the "seeds of the Word" (AG 11, 15) and the reflection of "a ray of that truth that enlightens all peoples" (NA 2). Hence, the emergence of a theocentric Christology that goes beyond the exclusivist Chalcedon was inevitable.

A realigned Christology, though faithful to the intentions of Chalcedon, needed to be "one not based on the wooden interpretation of Chalcedon that generated all triumphal and tragic 'onlys' that damaged so many—the *only* Savior, the *only* religion, the *only* church."[7] Some theologians encouraged by the openness of the council to recognize God's presence and activity in other religions began to consider Christianity as the extraordinary way of salvation and other religions as the ordinary ways. Their overriding concern was to show that God's revelation and salvation remain always and everywhere available to human beings because God is love and God desires the salvation of all. Before the historical incarnation in Jesus, this salvation must have been available to all, and even after the incarnation it is available to those who do not accept Jesus for whatever reason. However, everyone is saved in and through the saving mediation of Jesus Christ. Following the Greek Patristic tradition this position holds that by the fact of creation through the Word (John 1:4) and by the fact of the incarnation all are included in Christ. While an exclusive Christocentrism affirms that salvation is possible only with an explicit acceptance of Christ as only savior, an inclusive Christocentrism affirms that Christ is constitutive of salvation even if some do not recognize Christ's function of mediation. Rahner's "anonymous Christianity" presupposes an inclusive Christocentrism.

Theocentric Christologies move beyond both exclusive and inclusive Christocentrism in a wide spectrum. Some hold a moderate theocentric position that considers that God's love and grace extend to all, but Jesus Christ remains the normative way to God and means

---

[7] Duffy, "The Galilean Christ," 160.

One Jesus, Many Christologies 9

of salvation. But he is neither the exclusive nor the constitutive way to salvation. For some, even if Jesus Christ is not explicitly accepted as the norm, if kingdom values are accepted and lived, then there is an implicit acceptance of Christ. An extreme position of theocentric Christology considers Jesus Christ to be neither the normative nor the constitutive mediator of salvation. Jesus Christ is one among many mediators and saviors. This position acknowledges the incomprehensibility of God and the inability to make judgment about religious traditions and savior figures. It is called the pluralistic approach.[8] "It affirms that there is no point from which we affirm that Jesus Christ is the constitutive or even normative way of salvation."[9] According to this position, Jesus and the other names are both to be taken seriously for a globally responsible, correlational dialogue among religions.[10] For P. F. Knitter, who champions the cause of a pluralistic Christology, this approach is imperative if religions are to realize their responsibility toward the "religious other" and the "suffering other."[11]

In the context of dialogue among peoples in terms of their common responsibility toward building up a just and humane world by cooperation not only in the fields of economics and ecology but also in the spheres of culture and religion, the second paradigm shift in Christology may be very appealing to some. No doubt, at its best this approach can present a fascinating vision. But it

---

[8] John Hick proposes a theocentric nonnormative Christology in his writings. See John Hick, *God and the Universe of Faiths* (London: Macmillan, 1981); *The Metaphor of God Incarnate* (London: SCM Press, 1993); Paul F. Knitter, *No Other Name?* (London: SCM Press, 1985), proposes a theocentric Christology.

[9] J. Peter Schineller, "Christ and Church: A Spectrum of Views," *Theological Studies* 37 (1976): 565.

[10] See Paul F. Knitter, *Jesus and the Other Names: Christian Mission and Global Responsibility* (Maryknoll, NY: Orbis Books, 1996).

[11] Knitter, *Jesus and the Other Names*, 3.

may not energize one for a significantly transforming mission. Normally, an integral vision and a universal mission can flow only from a transforming encounter with the ultimate in and through a particular and concrete person or event. And what lies behind the missionary motivation is the conviction that such a person or event is unique, decisive and has a universal significance. Inherent in such an experience is the urge as well as the urgency to communicate with others. There may be many reasons for the missionary zeal of some persons belonging to a particular religion or ideology to convert others, some with noble and some with ignoble intentions. But in the question of sharing one's religious experience, "the one thing necessary" is the commitment and conviction that what one believes and experiences along with a particular faith community is something unique, liberating, and universally valid for everyone. Therefore, the use of "love language"[12] to express the reality that gives ultimate meaning to one's life cannot but be exclusive. It is impossible for such people to stand outside their faith experience and propose the possibility of a market of soteriologies or savior figures from which anyone can select. Hence, the claim of the pluralists that there are many saviors and mediators, with Jesus Christ as only one among them, is not the confessional statement of a believer but a comparative statement of a philosopher of religions. And as such it may have an academic value but not the transformative value necessary for global responsibility or for any authentic dialogue that are the avowed intentions of the champions of this position.

---

[12] Referring to the exclusive statements in the New Testament concerning the uniqueness of Jesus Christ, "one and only Savior," Knitter comments that they are not the analytical language of the philosophers but the enthusiastic language of the believers, not of the scientists but the lovers. He refers to Krister Stendhal who considers all religious language as "love language, caressing language." See Knitter, *No Other Name*, 185.

Contextual Christologies

The death of a monolithic Christology was necessary for the true resurrection of many authentic contextual Christologies. As mentioned earlier, the paradigm shift from Alexandrian to Antiochene Christology occasioned it. Though late, the contextual Christologies found recognition in the official catechetical text in preparation for the Holy Year 2000 composed by the Theological Historical Commission appointed for this purpose. The text affirms that the Catholic Christological vision is characterized:

> 1. by its emphasis on the humanity of Jesus, which is leading to the discovery and affirmation of his divinity and as the model of full human realization; 2. by dialogue with the contemporary world. which gives rise to a multiplicity of interpretative approaches to the mystery of Christ; 3. by the demand for inculturation, which produces a variety of contextual Christologies particularly suited to the cultural conditions of the different regions of the Church; 4. by an orientation to existential-practical demands, which orientation tends to harmonize orthodoxy and orthopraxy.[13]

This document quotes *Gaudium et spes* 44 and reiterates that the church appeals to every people's capacity to express the message of Christ according to the particular genius of a culture, and that the genuine incarnation of the good news takes place in a particular culture.[14] Since the message of Jesus cannot be separated from the person of Jesus, this attitude of the church as expressed in the council's document seems to encourage contextual Christologies.

---

[13] *Jesus Christ: Word of the Father: The Savior of the World,* Official Catechetical Text by the Theological-Historical Commission for the Great Jubilee Year 2000, trans. A. Walker, Indian ed. (Mumbai: Pauline Publications, 1997), 40–41.

[14] *Jesus Christ: Word of the Father,* 47.

12 *Christ without Borders*

No wonder then, the Official Catechetical Text on Christology calls our attention to the inculturated Christologies that are emerging in the Philippines, India, Bangladesh, Papua New Guinea, Korea, China, Taiwan, Tribal Australia, and Japan, as well as in some African countries. In spite of certain setbacks,[15] it is evident that contextual Christologies will continue to emerge and develop with or without official sanction because Jesus Christ continues to affect the lives of human beings in and through particular contexts in which they live, move, and have their meaning system.

It is the Christian experience and belief that Jesus Christ is the answer to the fundamental questions about the life and destiny of all human beings. However, every culture articulates these fundamental questions differently because their view of life and way of life are different. Jesus Christ, being human and divine, can be understood as the answer to the vexing questions of human life only if the genius of a culture understands what it means to be human and divine according to their own experience and thought patterns. As B. Cooke puts it, "If we are to consider Jesus as the fulfillment of what 'human' is all about, that consideration is governed by what it means to be human for us in a definite cultural context at a particular point in history."[16] Therefore, diverse cultures would understand and express the mystery of Jesus differently. Within the same culture itself, official doctrine, folk recollection, official and popular ritual, art, and iconography would present him differently.[17] The contextual Christologies present the infinite richness of the mystery of Jesus that cannot

---

[15] See Georg Evers, "The Excommunication of Tissa Balasuriya: A Warning to Asian Theologians," *Jeevadhara* 27 (1997): 212–230.

[16] Bernard Cooke, "Jesus of Nazareth, Norm for the Church," *The Catholic Theological Society of America: Proceedings of the Forty-Ninth Annual Convention* 49 (1994): 27.

[17] Cooke, "Jesus of Nazareth, Norm for the Church," 27.

be reduced to a few dogmas and doctrines, however valuable and sublime. Though Jesus is one, there can still be many contextual Christologies.

Christologies of Liturgy and Piety

The emergence of various contextual Christologies is a hopeful sign that Jesus Christ continues to affect the texture of life in various cultures. The impact of contextual Christologies can be seen in some of the theological writings, literature, art, architecture, hymns and poems, music, and dance of post–Vatican II origin. Many of the emerging contextual Christologies, however, have not made much impact on liturgy and popular piety. For example, one may find that the paradigm shifts have not affected the Christology celebrated in the liturgy of the Eastern churches. The Christ celebrated in the liturgy is the glorious and triumphant Christ of the heavenly Jerusalem. But there is an obvious influence of the paradigm shift in the liturgical celebration of the Western Church. At least in some way, Jesus, the human, and his ministry find a place in some of the prayers of the liturgy.

The Christology of popular piety remains unaffected by the paradigm shifts whether in the East or the West. While discussing the contrast between Jesus in historical exegesis as well as in theological reflection and Jesus in popular piety, F. Schüssler Fiorenza comments, "In short, for Catholic Christians, the interpretation of Jesus takes place through more sources than historical research. Jesus is mirrored in the lives of the saints, proclaimed in paradigmatic Gospel stories, and is actualized in the liturgical calendar commemorating the key mysteries of his life."[18]

---

[18] Francis Schüssler Fiorenza, "The Jesus of Piety and the Historical Jesus," *The Catholic Theological Society of America: Proceedings of the Forty-Ninth Annual Convention* 49 (1994): 94.

The eternal and preexistent Christ, the glorious Christ who is enthroned at the right of the Father yet present in various ways in the believing community—especially in the Eucharist and other sacraments—is worshiped in the liturgical celebrations.

The Nicene Creed itself gives importance to a transcendental Christology in which "the faithful are told next to nothing, save that he was born and died."[19] However, the genius of popular piety develops its own Christologies in which divinity and humanity, the Logos and the Flesh, the "above" and the "below" and "the heavenly and the earthly" enter into a union but not always according to the Chalcedonian Formula without confusion or change, without division or separation. The popular expressions of such Christologies—for example, "infant Jesus," "Christ the King," "Sacred Heart," and so on—may engender devotion but are not always free from superstitious beliefs and practices. Though the Christian faith affirms that Jesus is the only mediator (1 Tim 2:5), for popular devotion he becomes one among many mediators.

Certainly, Jesus occupies the place of prominence as a super saint, but still a saint who can be bypassed for the sake of others who are thought to be more accessible for bestowing particular favors. The official document on Christology suggests the need for proper catechesis to purify popular devotions from all exaggerations and superstitions. From time to time, from culture to culture, ordinary believers would continue to create their own popular Christologies dyed with the color of their culture and life.

The vital circle of liturgy and contextual theologies may not be very evident in our times. The official attitude to the process of inculturation in liturgy often appears to be one step forward and two steps back. Such an attitude is understandable in a situation created by paradigm shifts. But the contextual Christologies can

---

[19] Geza Vermes, *Jesus the Jew* (London: SCM Press, 1986), 15.

fully emerge and challenge the believers to deeper commitment to the person and mission of Jesus Christ only if the vital interaction between inculturated liturgy and contextual theologies is encouraged.

The repetition of literal orthodoxy or the acceptance of a monolithic Christology may serve the purpose of uniformity with regard to what one believes as member of a believing community. But the living faith in Jesus Christ as the absolute meaning of one's life and sharing of that experience in various cultures will bring forth a plurality of Christologies. Therefore, the dialogue between the Christic experience communicated through the Christologies of the New Testament and tradition and the Christic experience of the believing community expressed through the contextual Christologies and popular devotions will always continue.

It is a fact that many are not comfortable with a plurality of Christologies. It may be due to our fear of abandoning orthodoxy that we cling to a monolithic Christology. Chalcedon provides such a Christology. It gives the security that one needs in matters of belief. But the Christian faith is not a matter of private luxury. It is a living faith that has to be shared in a meaningful way so that the living Christ of one's experience can be encountered by others. The transforming encounter with Christ leads a person to confess the identity of the one whom he or she encountered using the genius of a particular culture and language. Moreover, there may be as many personal Christologies as there are believers, rarely articulated but authentically lived. Hence, the plurality of Christologies—instead of relativizing the Christ event—manifests the infinite richness of the mystery that cannot be exhausted by any human logos. Jesus Christ is one—yesterday, today, and forever—but there can be many Christologies.

2

The Emergence of
Various Christologies

The word of God is unbound (2 Tim 2:9). God's Word finds expression in infinite ways in the world. Above all, this claim is true in the unique expression of the Word in Jesus Christ. He transcended everything that bound him, even death. The early theologians of the church interpreted Jesus Christ as the Messiah of Jewish expectations as well as the fulfillment of the hope cherished by the Gentiles of all times. Ignatius of Antioch (d. 110 CE), for example, proclaimed Jesus Christ as the "ground for hoping that [all of humanity] may be converted and win their way to God." Further, he affirmed that Jesus was "our common name and common hope."[1]

The followers of Jesus Christ believe that he is indeed the common name and common hope meant for the whole of humanity. They encounter him as the Way, the Truth, and the Life. They experience him as the beginning and the end of their lives and, therefore, the ultimate meaning of their lives. They confess him as the Lord of history and the universe who lived and died at a particular time in history and yet is alive after his death, leading all

---

[1] Ignatius of Antioch, "Epistle to the Ephesians," in *The Apostolic Fathers*, J. B. Lightfoot, ed. and trans. (Christian Classics Ethereal Library online), 10.1; 1.2.

to the fullness of life. He is the alpha and the omega, the beginning and the end.

Yet something that is bound up with this transforming experience of Jesus Christ must be shared. It must be proclaimed in a meaningful way so that the same Jesus Christ can be encountered by people of all cultures and languages. In the multireligious society of the Roman Empire, the early church found creative ways to theologize and proclaim the universal significance of Jesus Christ. When the Roman Empire accepted Jesus Christ as its Lord and Savior, Christianity became a monoreligious culture with little challenge to its claims about Jesus Christ from outside. It had to face internal challenges regarding interpretations of the person of Christ expressed through various heresies. The Christological heresies were the inadequate ways of interpreting the mystery of Christ proclaimed by the New Testament witnesses. The dogmas formulated in the early councils responded to these challenges from within.

The strongest challenges to a monoreligious Christian culture came from Islam and, later, from religions that the West encountered in the colonial era. Colonizers could not find Christ's presence in the religions of their colonial subjects, as doing so would have hampered their claims to military, religious, and cultural superiority. With their absolute and exclusive claims about Christ and Christianity, they reduced Christ to a tribal God and Christianity to a sect. Yet, if everything is Christified through creation and incarnation (John 1:9, 14), colonial exclusivist separations of Christ and later reductionist comparability of the incomparable stand as affronts to the Christic experiences of believers. Some Christians still live in a Eurocentric monoculture utopia, scuttling the process of an effective and meaningful proclamation of Christ in multireligious and multicultural societies of Asia. In the name of preserving orthodoxy, some prevent the working of the Spirit as the Spirit unfolds the truth and the richness of the mystery of Christ in every age and every culture.

18   *Christ without Borders*

For those who are seriously committed to the proclamation of Jesus Christ such that all people of Asia can encounter him as the ultimate meaning of their life, it is imperative that they proclaim him in a language meaningful to the people of various cultural, religious, socioeconomic, and political contexts of the world. What makes any Christology normative is that it is founded on the totality of scriptural witness about who Jesus Christ is; what he has accomplished for humans through his life, death, and resurrection; and what the content of the symbols of faith about him in the Christian tradition communicate. Such a normative Christology can become meaningful and relevant only when it takes seriously the context of its articulation. An authentically Christian Christology that is meaningful for its context can, then, emerge when those who find the ultimate meaning of their lives in Jesus Christ systematically reflect on the situation within which the people seek salvation or liberation and how and why Jesus Christ is the Lord and Savior who brings about the true liberation from situations of misery and bondage.

A Universal Quest and a Particular Answer

The quest for meaningfulness is another way of expressing the fundamental human desire for wholeness and harmony. There is an existential experience of dissatisfaction and consequent restlessness stemming from fears and anxieties about life and ultimate questions about life. How one perceives the present situation of uncertainty and existential angst and the desire for wholeness or liberation are determined by one's religious, cultural, social, and economic context.[2] It is an undeniable fact that the Weltanschauung— worldview—of a particular people determines what they consider

---

[2] Karl-Heinz Ohlig, "What Is Christology?," *Theology Digest* 43, no. 1 (1996): 15.

The Emergence of Various Christologies   19

to be ultimately significant for their lives. This is evident in how people of different cultures and traditions experienced and articulated the significance of Jesus Christ for their lives.

For the earliest believers, Jesus of Nazareth raised the most fundamental question with which a human person can be confronted; the question of identity (Mt 16:15). Today, it is another way of articulating the same question that human beings ask themselves concerning the meaning of their lives. The ultimate answer to the question, therefore, affects the totality of the person who encounters Jesus. Paul's Damascus encounter is a typical case. Here, the questioner was Paul and not Jesus. Whether in Caesarea Philippi or on the road to Damascus, it is not the question that is important but the answer. In both cases, the answer is "from above." The answer is a gift. It is given to the individual person in a particular context, even though the quest for meaningfulness is universal.

The Contextual Christologies
in the New Testament

Confronted with the resurrection experience, the apostolic community struggled to express the content of their experience. In the light of the resurrection, they began to understand Jesus in a new light. It was a difficult task. They had no terminology to express this mystery. At the same time, they found themselves deeply involved in the mystery of the risen Jesus. He is the one with whom they had shared their life during his ministry. But he is also different. This *difference* made all the difference in their lives. They had no words to articulate it. So, their understanding of the person of Jesus is expressed in some of the confessional formulas of the NT. The struggle of apostolic community to proclaim him as Messiah or Christ immediately after the resurrection experience was that the political expectations related to the Messiah were not fulfilled in Jesus. He is the Messiah or Christ but not according to the expectations of the Jewish people. Though each of the evangelists, Paul, and other authors of the NT have their own ways of communicating in a systematic manner that Jesus is the fulfillment of their expectations, there is no real systematic reflection on the person of Jesus Christ. However, the catechetical need of the community and the challenges they had to face in proclaiming the reality of the risen Jesus determined the NT Christologies.

One of the initial attempts was to confess Jesus a prophet. We cannot take it for granted that it was so obvious that he was a prophet, mighty in word and in deed. He was killed as a criminal. For the Jews, he was accursed by God as he was hanged on a tree (Deut 21:22). But the resurrection experience was so compelling that from the initial confession as a prophet they began to proclaim him as the future Messiah or the Christ (Acts 3:20). They had to concede to the fact that the political expectations associated with the Messiah were not fulfilled in him. So only in the future would he be the Messiah; it was a future Christology. But a further reflection on the experience of the resurrection confirmed that he is the expected one; so he must be confessed as the Christ. In order to make such a proclamation that he is the Christ, they needed to change, first of all, their mindset about the kingdom that Christ would come to establish. They did change. The experience they had of the risen Jesus was so overwhelming that, in its blinding light, the shades of an illusory political kingdom they had expected gradually vanished. He became more important for them than their vision of the kingdom. So, they proclaimed that he is the Messiah, but his kingdom is not of this world. In their proclamation, they moved from a future Christology to a present Christology. At resurrection, Jesus is indeed Christ.

Was he Christ before resurrection? Their answer was affirmative. They were raising a question about the Christhood of the historical Jesus of Nazareth. In the beginning of this reflection, they affirmed that at baptism by John he was Christ. The theophany at the baptism scene is an expression of this faith affirmation (Mk 1:9ff.; Mt 3:16–17). Was he Christ before baptism? The infancy narratives of Matthew and Luke, though couched in Midrashic language, affirmed that he was Christ from the moment of conception in his mother's womb. John takes this line of Christological reflection further when he proclaims that he is the Logos, who was with God from the beginning (John 1:1). Thus, he will not only be the future Christ, but he is also the present Christ of resurrection, the past Christ of baptism and of conception, and even the preexistent Christ. The NT reflections on the person of Jesus reached their climax in the Gospel according to John. All that we need to know about Jesus for our salvation seemed to have been communicated that we "may believe that Jesus is the Christ, the Son of God" (John 20:31).

Normative Christologies in Christian Tradition

The question "Who is Jesus Christ?" was raised only in the context of his significance to his followers. The believers experienced him as the ultimate meaning of their lives. In him they experienced a complete transformation of their lives from alienation to communion, fragmentation to wholeness, meaninglessness to meaningfulness, death to life. "Only those who receive Jesus soteriologically can speak the confession that Jesus is the Christ."[3] Therefore, in the Christian tradition the identity of Jesus Christ was of utmost importance, so normative Christologies developed due to the responses of particular peoples to their soteriological concerns. Therefore, it is important to see the various normative Christologies of the Christian tradition to understand the process of their development and to recognize the legitimate need to

---

[3] Ohlig, "What Is Christology?," 15.

22   *Christ without Borders*

develop a normative Christology in the context of one's life. It is also imperative for those who are committed to Christ in India/ Asia to develop a normative Christology or Christologies in their particular contexts.

Normative Christology of Jewish Christianity

In the Jewish worldview, the existential human situation had a beginning and would have an end. All of life is historically oriented. Therefore, history is not only important, but the whole drama of Yahweh's intervention in the creation takes place on the stage of history. Each human being has to play his or her role in history. Since history has a beginning from Yahweh, he also will bring about its eschatological fulfillment. In this linear understanding of history which moves toward its final fulfillment, human beings realize that they have reversed the process of this movement of history by not playing their part according to God's plan, His law. The corruption of history was a result of the misuse of human freedom by taking the one-way road to self-destruction and the destruction of others and the world. Thus, the history of suffering and guilt form the background of Old Testament yearning for Yahweh's redemptive intervention in history. All Jewish expectations centered around the coming God's reign to set right the course of history, which was ravaged by the evil powers—whether human or diabolic—causing dissatisfaction, restlessness, sickness, and meaninglessness in life. God's reign brings about wholeness by "God's being with us" (Emmanuel) or by Yahweh's presence in history as the savior (Yehoshua or Jesus).

The Jewish Christians, with the background of the Jewish expectation for the definitive intervention of Yahweh in history, could clearly recognize the fulfillment of their expectations in the person and mission of Jesus. They identified him as the expected Messiah, the "Son of Man" who would come at eschatological times as a Son of David to set right the history by transforming it from a destructive history to salvation history. Jesus is enthroned as "Son of God" for these transformative functions. Jesus's complete surrender to the Father by his obedience to him, his fulfilling of his Father's will by his preaching and death on the cross were considered significant events that brought about salvation. So, every kingdom-centered action of Jesus became salvific and therefore significant to the lives of those Jewish Christians who accepted him as Lord and savior. In Jesus they encountered not only the ultimate meaning of history but also the ultimate meaning of their own lives as they realized that they were participating in the fulfillment of history in its God-given pattern. Jesus was believed to be the alpha and omega of history—and therefore its center and meaning. God's lordship dawned in Jesus. Jesus was also designated "Son of God," in the Jewish sense of kingly enthronement as "Son of God." In his historical function, Jesus appeared as 'son of God.'[4] His historical life of obedience to his Father—even to his death on the cross—and his deeds of power over sickness, evil spirits, and nature aside from his power to forgive sins are the signs that a new course of history of God's reign has begun with him. Thus, he is absolutely significant in the experience and articulation of a Jewish Christian as one's personal savior and the savior of history.

Normative Christology of the Hellenistic Christians

If the Jewish worldview had a historical orientation, the Hellenistic worldview had a cosmocentric orientation. What we call Hellenistic culture was a complex mixture of various cultural traditions of the Roman Empire, which had their unity in Greek thought and language. In the context of the Hellenistic culture, the cause of human experience of frustration and meaninglessness in life

---

[4] Ohlig, "What Is Christology?," 15.

was interpreted differently, and consequently the understanding of liberation from this situation was also different. What caused misery in the human situation was not any criminal misuse of freedom and the consequent corruption of history but the lack of right knowledge, the limitations of their beings as finite, as being mortal, and the fact of being caught up in the evil matter. Each person as a microcosm suffered from the limitations of being that hindered his or her full integration into the macrocosm of which the human person was a part. Hence liberation consisted also in acquiring true knowledge to extricate oneself from imprisonment in matter and in securing immortality, thus becoming deified.

In this context of Hellenistic culture, Jesus Christ would be significant only if he could be the mediator of true liberation from the limitations of human predicament—indeed, humanness itself. Therefore, Hellenistic Christology developed as an answer to Hellenistic soteriological concerns. In this Christology, Jesus Christ was seen as the mediator between the microcosm and macrocosm, matter and spirit, finite and infinite, relative and absolute. In the Greek philosophical tradition, Logos had the function of mediation between those pairs of polarities. It was, therefore, easier for the Greek Fathers to show that Jesus Christ was the Logos that brings about this mediation.[5] Apologists like Justin, Theophilos of Antioch,

---

[5] Influenced by the Platonic idea of the world as the image of the perfect idea of the world, Philo considered that this perfect image as the Logos and the biblical understanding that human beings are the image of God would then mean that they are the image of the image or Logos (*eikon eikonos*). So Philo could say, "The Image of God is the Logos through whom the whole universe was framed." The Logos has two dimensions, according to Philo. The Logos, as thought in God or as unuttered, preexistent Word, the Logos *endeathetos,* and which is uttered and through which the world comes into being, the Logos *prophorikos.* The synthesis of Logos, *dabhar,* and also *Sophia* achieved by Philo provided the needed new meanings to the Christ symbol in the new context of the Hellenistic world.

and Athenagoras could make use of the symbol, Logos, to interpret the meaning of Christ as Logos incarnate.[6] Justin, for example,

As there are similarities between the Philonic Logos and Johannine Logos, there are also differences. The Johannine Logos that becomes flesh (John 1:4) is not only not an ideal and personified Logos that Philo's syncretism provided, but a real preexistent and personal one. However, the Christ symbol would not have been interpreted by the Johannine community in terms of the Logos if this was not somehow present in the cultural context of the community, providing new meaning to their experience of Christ, the symbol of God. The logos-Christology of the prologue of John influenced the interpretation of the symbol Christ leading to orthodox doctrinal statements about the divinity of Christ—sometimes, even, at the cost of orthopraxis. Since the symbol *is* and *is not* the reality, if we stop at the *is* dimension of the symbol and articulate dogmas and doctrines based on it eclipsing the *is not* dimension, the vision of the reality becomes blurred and confused. Most of the Christological controversies have their origin in the metaphysical understanding and elaboration of the *is* dimension of the symbol Christ. Faith seeking understanding often sought the help of metaphysics to explain the plausibility and intelligibility of the faith claims by "locating them with in the interpretation of being itself." Since metaphysics can deal only with the *is* dimension of the symbol, leaving the *is not* dimension, it gives the illusion that everything about the reality is expressed. Such an approach has dangerous consequences both in practical life as well as in the vision and encounter of reality. It leads to a maximalist's reading of the dogmas, arrogant exclusivism, and stark absolutism. Dogmas stifle. Symbol liberates. The liberating capacity of the symbol emanates from its *is not* dimension. The Logos-symbol expresses the *is not* aspect of the reality of the symbol Christ. When logos-symbol was ontologized by Arius its symbolism was ravaged. The church's reaction to Arian heresy as expressed in the Council of Nicaea (325 CE)—using ontological categories like *ousia, homoousios,* etc.—was necessary to preserve the content of the apostolic faith but deprived the symbol of its power to evoke transforming vision and encounter.

[6] J. N. D. Kelly, *Early Christian Doctrines,* 5th ed. (London: A&C Black, 1989), 95–101.

26 *Christ without Borders*

considered Logos as Logos *spermatikos* (seeds of Logos), which united human beings to God to explain who Christ was. For him, the same Logos that was the source of relation between God and human beings and gave them the awareness of God become incarnate.[7]

Incarnational Christology fit well with the Hellenistic soteriological expectations of deification. Jesus Christ, being both divine and human—preexisting as Logos (John 1:1; Phil 2.6), as the Lord, as the Son of God, and as Son of Man of earthly existence—could fulfill the soteriological need because he is "Word became Flesh" (John 1:14). He is the *enanthropesis* of the divine Logos, according to Origen. Chalcedon's (451 CE) Christological Formula—that Jesus Christ, one person in two natures "without confusion or change, without division or separation, perfect in humanity and perfect in divinity"[8]—could adequately express the significance of Jesus Christ in Hellenistic Christianity's cultural context.

In incarnational Christology, the very incarnation itself was soteriological. Though the historical death and resurrection of Jesus was also considered redemptive, emphasis was on the fact of liberation brought about by incarnation. For example, Clement of Alexandria says, "The Word ... became man so that you might learn from man how man may become God."[9] Christ bestows immortality as well as knowledge. Thus, human beings are deified by incarnation. According to J. N. D. Kelly, "Clement's soteriology issues in a Christ mysticism in which the Lord's passion and death have little or no redemptive part to play."[10] Athanasius affirmed that the Word became human that we might be made God.[11] Hellenistic

---

[7] Justin Martyr, *Apologia* I.5.4.8; *Apologia* II.10.1; 13.4.

[8] Joseph Neuner and Jacque Dupuis, eds., *The Christian Faith: In the Doctrinal Documents of the Catholic Faith*, 5th ed. (Bangalore: TPI, 1992), nos. 614, 615.

[9] Kelly, *Early Christian Doctrines*, 184.

[10] Kelly, *Early Christian Doctrines*, 184.

[11] Henry Bettenson, *The Early Christian Fathers* (London: Oxford University Press, 1956), 384.

The Emergence of Various Christologies 27

Christology, with its incarnational soteriology, responded to the quest for significance experienced and articulated in the Hellenistic cultural milieu. Though not divorced from the Jewish Christian Christological concerns, Hellenistic Christology was conditioned by Hellenistic worldview. In the Hellenistic context, the Christology that was most meaningful brought thousands to encounter Jesus's mission command but only if it proclaimed Jesus and his message in a language that was not alien to the peoples of these contexts.

Normative Christologies in the Syrian Christian Tradition

The cultural contexts of both Western Syria and Eastern Syria determined the soteriological concerns as well as the Christologies of the Syrian Christian tradition. Western Syria had a Semitic heart but a Hellenistic mind. Aramaic was the language of ordinary people. The educated spoke Greek and articulated their thought in Hellenistic categories. With Antioch as its cultural center, it developed a Christology different from that of East Syria because of its specific cultural context. Here, there was an organic synthesis of Hebrew and Greek worldviews. The ontological categories of thought inherited from the Greeks were used to express historical concerns. The Jewish Christian soteriology of historical fulfillment was indeed the liberation of human nature from the predicament of finiteness and imperfections. Imperfections were believed to be caused by the misuse of human freedom, leading to acts that are wicked and sinful. Therefore, liberation from the limitations of human nature involved liberation from the sinful state of human beings. Jesus Christ is significant in this context only if he is able to bring about an ontological transformation as well as moral regeneration of human beings. In fact, this belief that Jesus Christ was fulfilling this expectation of human beings for an integral liberation triggered the Christological reflections of many Antiochene theologians like Diodore, Theodore of Mopsuestia, John of Antioch, and others.

The Hellenistic idea of God's absolute transcendence and the monolithic monotheism of Judaism[12] probably influenced their initial reluctance to accept an incarnational Christology with its full implications. Instead of a Logos-*sarx* Christology of the Alexandrians, they preferred a Logos-*anthropos* Christology that would safeguard the transcendence of the Logos and the autonomy of the human being. Who Jesus was and what he did were to be significant only if his life and death proved acceptable to God. Jesus's life of obedience to the Father even unto death proved his response to his vocation by God. His resurrection from the dead verified that God had approved and accepted his person and mission. Jesus became Son by his surrender to the Father, or sonship was conferred on him by the Father. So, in the beginning, West Syrian Christology moved in the direction of adoptionism. For Paul of Samosata, who championed the adoptionist Christology, "Jesus Christ and the Word are other and other (*allos kai allos*).... The Word is ... from above; Jesus Christ the man is from below."[13] God adopted the human Jesus through Logos so that human beings could attain integral liberation by following him.

Arius attempted an integration of Hellenistic incarnational Christology and Antiochene adoptionist Christology. He was trained in Antiochene theology but worked as a priest in Alexandria. He proposed a Christology that safeguarded the transcendence of the absolute of Hellenistic Christianity and the strict monotheism of the Jewish Christian tradition. At the same time, he found a place for Jesus in the scheme of God's intervention in history for human liberation. Jesus was the embodiment of the created Logos and was given the honorific title "Son of God." It was an ingenious idea. No wonder, then, that he could take along almost half the

---

[12] Roch A. Kereszty, *Jesus Christ: Fundamentals of Christology*, J. Stephen Maddux, ed. (New York: Alba House, 1995), 189.

[13] Anastasius, *Adversus Haereses* IV.18.4–5; Kereszty, *Jesus Christ: Fundamentals of Christology*, 189.

number of believers of his time to his side as they found this Christology very attractive.

Adoptionism and Arianism faced the question of soteriological concerns of Antioch and Alexandria intelligently but heterodoxically. They suggested an artificial synthesis of traditions for their intellectual satisfaction without recognizing the paradox of God's revelation in Jesus Christ, "a stumbling block to the Jews and folly to the Gentiles" (1 Cor 1:23). They were not faithful to the apostolic tradition, so the Council of Nicaea (325 CE) had to affirm that salvation in Jesus Christ was significant only if Jesus Christ was the preexistent Logos, one in being with the Father (*homoousios*), begotten, not made. After the Council of Nicaea, the Syrian theologians abandoned the adoptionist Christology and began to expound the Logos-*anthropos* Christology differently. They were at variance in explaining the type of presence of Logos in Jesus but were unanimous in affirming that he was fully human like any other human being with a rational soul. If not, he had no significance for humanity.

Theodore of Mopsuestia insisted that salvation consisted in the restoration of the authentic humanity that was the work of Christ the man in his life, death, and resurrection because he had been "one of us, who came from out of our race" and our nature.[14] Both the Antiochene and the Alexandrian traditions were in agreement that the very purpose of incarnation was the salvation of humankind. For both of these traditions, the validity of the Christological doctrine depended on its congruence with the salvific work of Jesus. It was common to their understanding that salvation was achieved when human beings could receive immortality and impassibility. But in their Christological doctrine they differed.

---

[14] Jaroslav Pelikan, *The Christian Tradition: A History of the Development of Doctrine: 1. The Emergence of Catholic Tradition (100–600)* (Chicago: University of Chicago Press, 1971), 235–236.

30 *Christ without Borders*

Following the theological reflections of Theodore, Nestorius insisted that Logos indwelt in the man Jesus as in the temple, interpreting John 2:9, where the man Jesus was referred to as the temple that could be destroyed but would be raised up. He supported his argument with Colossians 2:9: "In him [the man who was assumed] the whole fullness of deity dwells bodily."[15] For Nestorius, if Jesus was really human, and indeed he was, there could only be an empirical union between Logos and the human Jesus, and therefore divine predicates could not be attributed to the human Jesus. It was the opposite side of the Alexandrian view.

The Logos-*sarx* Christology of Apollinaris (d. 390) insisted that Jesus had only one nature, the Logos replacing the human soul and mind. According to him, "The divine energy fulfills the role of the animating spirit and of the human mind."[16] Cyril of Alexandria insisted on the one subject of incarnation, the Logos. Both divine and human predicates had the same subject. But in the Antiochene theological reflection, any unity that destroyed the distinction between human and divine would make salvation through Christ impossible. "As a complete human being, Jesus can be held up as a pattern for his followers."[17] Though the Councils of Ephesus (431 CE) and Chalcedon (451 CE) condemned the extreme Antiochene position, they had integrated some of its concerns into their doctrines.

West Syrian Christological tradition that opposed the Chalcedonian Formula of "the hypostatic union of two natures in one person" moved in the direction of monophysitism. Eutyches (d. 448) as its spokesman seemed to have asserted that the Lord before the union was of two natures, but after the union, he was of one nature (monophysis). After the Council of Chalcedon, the Alexandrian ideas spread, especially among the monks in Western Syria.

---

[15] Pelikan, *The Christian Tradition*, 252–253.

[16] Kelly, *Early Christian Doctrines*, 292.

[17] Linwood Urban, A *Short History of Christian Thought* (New York: Oxford University Press, 1986), 82.

The anti-Chalcedonian party installed Peter the Fuller, a Greek, as the patriarch of Antioch in 470. He was driven out later but again assumed office until his death in 488. His successor, the Syrian Philoxenus, was the most virulent opponent of Chalcedon. In 512 another opponent of Chalcedon—the Greek monk Severus of Pisidia—became the patriarch of Antioch. He was considered to be the father of moderate monophysitism.[18] Fierce opposition to the Chalcedon council and to Leo's Tome, considering them godless, blasphemous, and unorthodox by successive Antiochene patriarchs because it spoke of two natures in Christ, led the West Syrian church to settle down with monophysitism. This monophysitism in Christological thinking was expressed in its liturgical life.

The original theological tradition of West Syria was inherited by the East Syrian tradition. East Syria had a unique Christian tradition "which retained relative autonomy in comparison with the Greek West and had virtually no contact at all with the still more distant Latin West."[19] It had developed an "archaic" Christology in opposition to the Jewish charges that the Christians were worshipping an ordinary man as God. Aphrahat, the Persian sage (d. c. 345) affirmed the Christian faith against Jewish opponents. For him, Jesus was God (*Alaha*) and Lord (*Marya*). In his instructions he told his people, "But it is certain for us the Jesus, our Lord, is God (*Alaha*), Son of God (*Bar Alaha*) and king, prince, light of light, creator (*Barē*) and counsellor and leader and redeemer and shepherd and gatherer and gate and pearl and lamp; and with many names is he named."[20] Aphrahat introduced the Syrian term

---

[18] W. de Vries, "The Reason for the Rejection of the Council of Chalcedon by the Oriental Churches," in *Christ in East and West*, P. Fries and T. Nersoyan, eds. (Macon, GA: Mercer University Press, 1987), 9.

[19] Aloys Grillmeier, *Christ in Christian Tradition*, vol. 1, 2nd rev. ed. (Oxford: Mowbrays, 1975), 214.

[20] Aphrahat, *Demonstrationes* XVII.2; Grillmeier, *Christ in Christian Tradition*, 215.

32 *Christ without Borders*

kyana almost in the same sense of Greek *physis* to explain Christ's manner or condition of being as God and human, preexistent, humiliated and finally exalted. In him we can also find the presence of a spirit Christology which is a decisive character of Eastern Christology. Ephrem the Syrian (d. 373) also used the term *kyana* in his hymns, sometimes meaning the unity of the person and at other times meaning two natures.[21] However, after Chalcedon, the East Syrian church adopted the Nestorian Christological formulas at the Council of Seleucia Ctesiphon in 486 CE. Though the founder of the East Syrian Christology, Babi the Great (d. 628),[22] praised Leo for eliminating the teachings of Dioscorus of Alexandria through the Council of Chalcedon, Katholikos Iso'yabb III rejected the Chalcedonian Formula because it proclaimed the unity of the *hypostasis* in Christ. According to Elias of Nisibis (975–1049), the East Syrians in Persia rejected the teachings of the heretic Cyril and the formula of Chalcedon forcibly effected by the emperor as they found these teachings blasphemous.[23]

Christology was determined by the doctrine of the Trinity. Those who opposed Chalcedon, whether the monophysites of West Syria or the Nestorians of East Syria, affirmed that the Chalcedonian Formula did violence to the Trinitarian dogma by confessing two natures in Christ. According to them, "The doctrine of hypostatic union, even in the form adopted at Chalcedon, compromised the relation of the divine hypostases within the Trinity and threatened the impassability of Logos and therefore of the entire Godhead."[24]

---

[21] Ephrem, *Hymn* 10.3; 11.9; Grillmeier, *Christ in Christian Tradition*, 335.

[22] Geevarghese Chediath, *The Christology of Mar Babai the Great* (Kottayam: Oriental Institute, 1982).

[23] Grillmeier, *Christ in Christian Tradition*, 12.

[24] Pelikan, *The Christian Tradition: A History of the Development of Doctrine,* 268.

The Emergence of Various Christologies   33

It was the anthropological significance of Christ that was at stake in the fourth and fifth centuries' debate about Christ. The question was about the origin and destiny of human being, the two transcendent poles of human existence in history upon this earth.[25] Those who found in Jesus Christ their origin and destiny affirmed that he was God. Whatever diluted divinity was unacceptable to them, even the affirmations about his true humanity. The Greek Christianity's reverence for tradition, the close link between "the faith believed in the divine liturgy, taught in theology and confessed in dogma" greatly influenced the life and thought of the Orient.[26]

Syrian Christian tradition both in its monophysite or Nestorian orientation continued to hold the significance of Christ for human salvation understood in terms of deification through configuration with Christ. Deification through mystical union with God was main theme of the writings of Dionysius the Areopagite, which influenced the Syrian tradition from the sixth century onward. According to Dionysius, the Eucharist was the main sacrament of deification. Eucharist itself was defined as "a participation in Jesus, the communion of the most divine Eucharist."[27] Such communion permitted one to share in "the most perfect form of deification" and "enabled him to ignore any but the most basic demands of the body and to grow, by means of this sublime deification, into a temple of the Holy Spirit."[28] Thus, the Syrian tradition saw the significance of Jesus Christ as the mediator of this deification,

---

[25] Paulos Mar Gregorios, "The Relevance of Christology Today," in *Christ in East and West*, P. Fries and T. Nersoyan, eds. (Macon, GA: Mercer University Press, 1987), 100.

[26] Pelikan, *The Christian Tradition: A History of the Development of Doctrine*, 341.

[27] Pelikan, *The Christian Tradition: A History of the Development of Doctrine*, 346.

[28] Pelikan, *The Christian Tradition: A History of the Development of Doctrine*, 346.

34 *Christ without Borders*

which was effected through the participation in the Eucharistic celebration.

Along with the influence of Cyril on the Christological thinking of West Syria, his Eucharistic theology also found wide acceptance. Salvation was mediated through the Eucharistic body of Christ. Cyril wrote that every week when they celebrated the Eucharist, Christ came among them both visibly and invisibly: invisibly as God, visibly as being again in body, allowing them to touch his holy flesh, in the *homologia kai anamnesis* of his death and resurrection.[29] The monophysite tradition received an intense religious fervor from the dynamic faith of Cyril, who affirmed that every Eucharist is a reincarnation of Logos whose flesh is given to the communicant. In fact, "The key to Cyril's Christological interpretation of sacramental theology lay in his emphasis upon the lifegiving power conveyed by the sacraments, especially the Eucharist."[30]

In the Nestorian tradition of East Syria, too, the Eucharist was of first importance. Before Nestorius, Theodore of Mopsuestia had already expounded a Eucharistic theology with the doctrine of real presence and sacramental transformation of bread and wine into the body and blood of Christ by the descent of the Holy Spirit, who changes them into "the power of spiritual and immortal nourishment."[31] In his *Book of Heracleides*, Nestorius insists that "what we receive in the Eucharist is his body and blood which are of one substance with ours, so that thereby we are made to share in his resurrection and immortality."[32] It is obvious that when a tradition sees the significance of Jesus Christ only in his

---

[29] Henry Chadwick, *History and Thought of the Early Church* (London: Variorum Press, 1982), 155.

[30] Pelikan, *The Christian Tradition: A History of the Development of Doctrine*, 237.

[31] Pelikan, *The Christian Tradition: A History of the Development of Doctrine*, 237.

[32] Chadwick, *History and Thought of the Early Church*, 157.

mystical role for the individual believer's deification or immortality, Christ's significance in his prophetic role for the wholeness of the society and the world would be neglected. Eucharistic celebration, which provides the means for the transformation of human beings to make them worthy to participate in the impassable and incorruptible nature of God, would become the only and real concern of Christian existence.

Normative Christology in the Latin Tradition

As Jewish, Hellenistic, and Syrian Christian traditions had their culturally conditioned soteriological concerns, the Latins had their own. Hence, their soteriological concerns determined their understanding of the significance of Christ. Though the gospel was proclaimed in Rome in the first century itself, it did not develop its own theology as it was under the influence of Hellenism and Hellenistic theology. But in the second century with the resurgence of the Latin language and thought in North Africa, the Latins began to develop their own theology. In their cultural tradition the humans and the world were under the divine law (*ius divinum*), which had established an order (*ordo*). Through misbehavior, sacrilege, and rebellious actions, humans have destroyed this order.[33] Therefore, the existential situation of misery and meaninglessness was interpreted by the Latins as disorder caused by offenses against the divine order. The divine legal power needed to be reestablished to bring about order. In this cultural context Jesus Christ could be significant only if he would mediate salvation by reestablishing the order in the name of God by his atoning death.

For Augustine of Hippo (d. 430), the most prominent representative of the Latin tradition, the original order was destroyed by the original sin of Adam. So human beings became

---

[33] Ohlig, "What Is Christology?," 18–19.

"corrupt, vitiated, lost and dead" and they had no power to reestablish the order. Jesus Christ, being God and man, could pay for human guilt and reestablish the order. In this new Christology, the Hellenistic Christological categories were used for a different soteriological purpose, while Hellenistic Christology's understanding of the ontological transformation of humans and the world by the fact of incarnation itself had little relevance for the Latin Christology. The soteriological concern of the Latins was juridical restitution, justification, and redemption from guilt because of the sins committed by human beings. Jesus, the Godman could pay for the human guilt as demanded by the just judge, the righteous God. Pope Leo I expressed this Roman understanding in his Tome to *Flavius*, which became a part of the Chalcedonian Formula. He wrote,

> And, in order to pay the debt of our fallen state, the inviolable nature was united to one subject to suffering so that, as was fitting to heal our wounds, one and the same "mediator between God and men, the man Christ Jesus" (*I Tim. 2.5*) could die in one nature and not in the other. The true God, therefore, was born with the complete and perfect nature of a true man; He is complete in His nature and complete in ours.[34]

For Leo, the destroyed order could be restored only by the God-man who could conquer the devil, the author of sin and death. In fact, on the cross, according to Leo, the devil was tricked, as the devil thought that he was victorious over this human being who died on the cross without realizing that it was the Godman who could not be subdued by sin and death. By his claim for the soul of Christ who was sinless, the devil forfeited his right over the souls all sinners and thus they are saved from his domination.[35]

---

[34] Neuner and Dupuis, *The Christian Faith*, 164–165.

[35] Urban, *A Short History of Christian Thought*, 110.

The Emergence of Various Christologies 37

According to Pope Gregory the Great (540–604), God deceived Satan by baiting the hook of Christ's deity with the worm of his humanity.[36] The Roman concern for lawful rights and legal restitution in the understanding of soteriology reached its extreme when Gregory the Great declared that the devil must be given his due. What Paul wrote, "You are brought by a price" (1 Cor 6:20), was understood as referring to a price paid to the devil who had legal rights over human beings who freely sold themselves to the devil. Gregory says, "God in his goodness would restore us again to freedom. There was a kind of necessity for Him not to proceed by way of force, but to accomplish our deliverance in a lawful way. It consists in this, that the owner is offered all that he asks as the redemption price of His property."[37]

While Athanasius considered that the demons existed in the external world needed to be defeated by the crucified Christ, Augustine explained the power of Satan both in the outside world and within human beings. Only Christ, both divine and human, could accomplish this task of legal battle and rescue human beings and establish the lost order. Thus, Latin Christology, according to Ohlig, used the categories like two natures, divine and human, for a soteriological schema quite different from Logos-*anthropos* Christology and soteriology. The divine and the human natures were no longer soteriological terms but Roman legal titles, juridical conditions to make adequate payment or atonement for our guilt and effect the restoration of the order.[38]

With the Christianization of Europe, the Latin interpretation of soteriology was internalized, and later it was spread through missionary enterprises in the colonial era. In the Middle Ages, Anselm of Canterbury (1033–1109) and Thomas Aquinas

---

[36] Urban, *A Short History of Christian Thought*, 110; Gustaf Aulen, *Christus Victor* (London: SPCK, 1931), 68–70.

[37] Gregory the Great, as quoted in Aulen, *Christus Victor*, 65.

[38] Ohlig, "What Is Christology?," 19.

(1225–1274) gave new explanations to justification through satisfaction but the basic Roman legal framework remained unaffected. Anselm rejected the idea of paying a price to the devil and proposed a positive way of atonement through the perfect sacrifice of Christ in his classic book *Why God Became a Man* (*Cur Deus Homo*). In the context of the feudal society of his time, Anselm expounds his Christology based on the Latin justification Christology. According to Anselm, God's honor and the moral order of the universe had been degraded by human sins. God's *mercy* could forgive this, but his *justice* would not allow this. Without proper satisfaction or the voluntary payment of debt the original order cannot be restored. No human being could provide proper satisfaction as all were born in sin, so Jesus Christ—the Godman, who was sinless and immortal—freely offered himself as an oblation and satisfied God's justice so that God's love could flow and restore human beings and creation.

Peter Abelard (1079–1142) criticized the classical Latin theory of satisfaction as well as Anselm's theory of Christ's atoning sacrifice. For him we are transformed by the infinite love of God manifested through the incarnation of the Son. Only Martin Luther (1483–1546), in his theory of atonement, integrated Abelard's view. However, Anselm's understanding of atonement continued to have its influence in the theological reflection of the succeeding centuries with various modifications.

Thomas Aquinas modified Anselm's theology of satisfaction by expounding that God could have forgiven human beings without due satisfaction, but it was most fitting for him to demand it.[39] According to Aquinas, more than the sinlessness of Christ, who had beatific vision from his mother's womb, the greatness of the love of Christ expressed in his passion and suffering was the direct principle of satisfaction.[40] The later Western Christian tradition,

---

[39] *Summa Theologiae* III.1.2a.2.
[40] *Summa Theologiae* III.Q8.a3; Q68, a1.

whether Catholic or Protestant, followed without many changes the Leonian, Augustinian, Anselmian, and Thomistic theologies of satisfaction or atonement, which the Roman system of juridical worldview had culturally conditioned. The Latin Christology with its predilection for understanding and explaining the significance of Christ in terms of legal categories like justification, satisfaction, or restitution for the offense against divine order influenced all of Western theology until present times. How does this theological understanding of the Cross reveal God? The subject of the death on the cross is the second person of the Trinity or God himself. It is God who becomes human—and it is God who dies as a human on the cross. He was murdered by crucifixion by the systems of oppression and injustice created by the inhumanity of humans. His crucifixion would continue till the end of time and as long as humans misuse and abuse their God-given freedom to become authentically human. The atonement theologies of the Latin tradition were influenced by the sociocultural contexts of their times. They were considered legitimate and valid at that time and were produced by great and saintly theologians. However, with the evolution of the religious consciousness of the human mind and with a critical understanding of the philosophical, sociocultural, and political perspectives that influenced the articulation of such theological positions, they may not be that meaningful and evocative in the various contexts of our present times as they were understood and spiritualized by the believers of the Middle Ages.

A Normative Christology in the Asian Context

Asia is a continent of many religions and worldviews. There cannot be one normative Christology for the entire land mass of diverse cultures and contexts, but one can reflect on those elements that are fundamental to all various Christologies of Asia. All the religions in Asia admit that humans need liberation from the situation of misery and wretchedness. They offer philosophical or religious

40 *Christ without Borders*

explanations for the situation of misery or misfortune and the way in which one can experience liberation from this situation. They concern themselves with the questions of ultimate concerns of life and life-after. The basic concern of liberation from this world of misery overrides the interest in the transformation of this world. The prophetic dimension of the religions and their capacity to create a new world give way to an apocalyptic vision that lulls the spirit in their struggle to face misery and misfortune in their lives. The poor are fed on the hopes for a better life hereafter. A normative Christology for Asia must, therefore, address not only the ultimate liberation but also liberation from sociocultural, economic, and political oppression and injustice. The rich and the powerful continue to maintain the structures and systems of domination bequeathed to them by the colonizers and have become agents of neocolonialism even at the cost of their own national interests.

In most Asian countries a rich minority controls the means of production as well as political power, condemning the vast majority to abject poverty and exploitation. Most of the countries in Asia have become victims of international militarism and the arms race at the cost of socioeconomic development and friendly relationships with neighboring countries.[41] The quest of people all over Asia is for an integral liberation. Perhaps, like the Syrian Christology that made a synthesis of the Hellenistic and Jewish-Christian soteriological concerns, a normative Asian Christology must synthesize the soteriological concerns of the Asian religions and the quest for a historical liberation of the poor and the marginalized, who form the majority of the people of Asia.

The fundamental question that the normative Christologies of the Jewish, Hellenistic, Syrian, and Latin Christian traditions

---

[41] Franklyn J. Balasundaram, *The Prophetic Voices of Asia*, part 1 (Bangalore: ATC, 1993), 8–14.

The Emergence of Various Christologies   41

raised was about the role of Jesus Christ in liberating humans from the situation of misery and misfortune. They were clear about their situation of misery from which they needed liberation. In encountering Jesus Christ, they experienced the liberation they were searching for, so they articulated their Christology—who the person of Jesus Christ is—from the perspective of their liberation experience. Similarly, the normative Christology in the Asian context emerges from the experience of liberation from historical and cosmic bondage through Jesus Christ.

The sufferings that make human life miserable in this world are caused by ignorance (*avidya*) according to Hinduism, and by desire (*tanha* or *trshna*) according to Buddhism. There are complex religio-philosophical systems that analyze the various aspects of these root causes of misery and misfortune and propose ways and means to liberate oneself from this situation. Most such systems suggest that one can liberate oneself from the situation of suffering and reach the ultimate liberation. A few others may suggest that God's grace is needed for the ultimate liberation. Are humans themselves responsible for their own suffering and the sufferings of others, or are they like puppets in the hands of a puppeteer who controls their destiny? The emphasis of these religions seems to be that the situation of suffering is given or destined by the supreme reality or the whole structure of humans is such that they desire what they are not and what they have not and end up in their own misery.

Does Jesus Christ offer anything new to the poor of Asia that the religions of Asia cannot give? Is he just another apocalyptic visionary or a true prophetic missionary? Can Jesus address the quest for ultimate liberation and questions of poverty? The fundamental Christian kerygma is that Jesus Christ is Lord and Savior. But the question is how to proclaim this kerygma meaningfully in the Asian context. A normative Christology of Asia needs to be the articulation of the Christic experience of the people in a way that it proclaims Jesus as the one whom the poor and the oppressed can encounter as their historical liberator and as the Christ, the Logos, whose presence is "known" or "unknown" in the religions of Asia. How does Jesus Christ as the self-emptying of God respond to the situation of suffering in the Asian context, whatever the cause of suffering?

Is Jesus Christ just another God competing with a myriad of gods and goddesses of the Asian continent for supremacy? Can we discover what God has said about Jesus from the history of his people, from their struggles, from their hopes and frustrations? What God has said about his Son must be heard in unheard of ways and must be seen in hitherto unseen ways that we do not force God to reveal only through the familiar framework of our minds. It is simply letting God be God. The religion of his time could not recognize in him the revelation of God because he had failed to fit into their understanding of God. So the Christology of the Asian context must reveal the *radical newness* of God's self-revelation in Jesus Christ as well as the voice of God breaking the silence from below, in the voice of the voiceless and the sigh of the oppressed.

Asia can only respond to a God who reveals himself from within its own context—probably the Christology of the kenotic Christ that God opted for and to which all humans could respond if they make themselves free from the false values of their systems and structures. It overcomes the temptation of Christians to present Jesus Christ in a triumphalist way and as an alien God to the cultures and religions of Asia.

A normative Christology for any culture must be in continuity with the living tradition of the church expressed through the Scripture, traditions, worship, way of lived faith, practice of charity, and so forth. The various Christologies in the New Testament show how difficult it was for the disciples to articulate their experience of the risen Lord. The Christologies of the Jewish, Greek, Syrian, and Latin Christian traditions show the development of normative

The Emergence of Various Christologies   43

Christologies as the reflection on their Christic experience as the answer to the quest for liberation, understood from the context of their religio-cultural context. A normative Christology for Asia needs to remain in continuity with these living traditions that form the totality of the Christian articulations about the mystery of God revealed in history.

The *newness* of the revelation in Jesus Christ is that he is God's self-communication in a way hitherto unknown to humans. He encounters humans as a self-emptying God, a paradox to human attempts to understand him through philosophies and systems. His self-emptying is so radical that followers in the mystic and prophetic religions of Asia can recognize it in Buddha's silence and in the systems that deny his existence but are committed to human welfare. A kenotic Christology challenges all systems and structures, religious and secular, that prevent humans from unfolding themselves and becoming authentic humans. It preserves, promotes, and integrates everything that is true, beautiful, and good in Asia's cultures and religions as they are the fruits of his Spirit active in them. He lets his disciples gather all the fragments so that nothing may be lost. Thus, a normative Christology for Asia, like other Christologies of Christian tradition, emerges from the Asian context and challenges the disciples to bear witness to their Christic experience by a life committed to the kenotic Christ and to suffer the consequences of that commitment that they may have life and have it in abundance.

3

The Mystery of Christ in Our History

From the beginning until today, Christological discourses are not free from certain polarization in explaining the reality of Christ. The mystery of Christ defies all articulations and definitions. However, since this mystery is a part of our history it is legitimate to seek some meaningful explanations about the mystery of Christ so that we come to realize our vocation in and through the mystery of Christ. All the logical explanations and dogmatic statements using the categories of thought available to the Fathers and the early councils could not adequately explain the mystery of Christ in history. All they could arrive at was a definition about the mystery that defies all definitions. Their conclusions were couched in a philosophical language that might have appealed to the human intellect but not to the human heart. If the vital circle of sharing any original religious experience leads others to the same experience through symbols, doctrines, and dogmas, it must be said that unfortunately many of the Christological dogmas cannot lead one to a Christ experience. The traditional Christology can at best be a "half-way house."[1] The minimum usefulness of the dogmas

---

[1] Francis D'Sa, "Fullness of Man or the 'Fullness of the Human'?," foreword in Raimon Panikkar, *The Fullness of Man: A Christophany* (Delhi: ISPCK, 2006), xvii. The reflections in this chapter owe much to the insights of Raimon Panikkar and Francis D'Sa on the meaning of the mystery of Christ.

The Mystery of Christ in Our History 45

is that it can prevent the dilution or perversion of the content of the faith experience of the early church. The faith experience of the early community in Jesus of Nazareth as the full, decisive, and final self-communication of God in history narrated in the NT must find meaningful ways of sharing this truth at all times. If this revelation is of the utmost importance to humans for their unfolding as humans, it is imperative that it must be shared in a language and thought patterns meaningful to people in different cultures and worldviews.

The fundamental Christian faith affirmation that the absolute mystery of God, who is beyond time and space, entered our history and lived a human life, which is space- and time-bound, baffles the human mind. No human reason can ever fathom or understand how it is possible. Human reason can accept only what is logical and reasonable. The mystery of God becoming human is absolutely impossible for human reason to see. How can infinite become finite, absolute become relative, eternal become temporal, or God become human? The Christian faith affirmation is that it has taken place once and for all in history in the person of Jesus of Nazareth. The contention of the church is that if the truth of this event is accepted, then we can explain the union of divinity—and humanity can be explained by using Greek philosophical categories. In fact, even the most celebrated Christological formula of Chalcedon has only safeguarded the truth of incarnation against heresies by showing what this union of human and divine is not rather than what it is. Perhaps one of the Indian insights into the mystery of the relationship between the absolute and the relative, infinite and finite, or God and world as in the advaitic understanding of reality can give us a better explanation and experience of the mystery of Christ and a better understanding of the unity of divine and human in Jesus Christ than is offered in the Christological formulas. The present reflections on the mystery of Christ in history take into account the Indian worldview of advaitic intuition to understand the mystery of Christ in history.

The Search for Understanding the Mystery of Christ

The primacy of human reason alone without an integral understanding of the reality of God becoming is evident in the search for understanding the mystery of Jesus of Nazareth. Influenced by the Greek thought emphasizing the epistemological principle of contradiction, the post–New Testament reflections on Christ oscillated between affirming either the divinity or the humanity of Christ. The Gnostics and the Docetists affirmed Christ's divinity and rejected his humanity. He could be either God or human, but he could not be both human and divine at the same time. This was their contention. How can the mystery of God be a part of our history? To be in history is to be part of this material world, which was inherently evil according to the Gnostics and the Docetists. God as Spirit cannot be a part of this evil material world, so Christ appears to be human and not really human.

The extreme Alexandrian theology in Apollinaris contended that two different beings cannot become one being. God and humans are two separate beings, and they cannot become one being. So Apollinaris proposed a solution that Christ's human nature is without a human soul, and Logos takes the place of the human soul in order to make Jesus Christ one being. Nestorianism reiterates the same problem of Apollinaris and finds a solution in separating the divinity and humanity in Christ and affirming their union as a moral union. The Council of Chalcedon in 451 CE finds a solution to the problem by affirming that Jesus Christ is one person in two natures—namely, divine and human—without division or separation, without change or confusion. Each nature is in its integrity but united at the level of hypostasis or personhood. Using the Greek categories of thought, Chalcedon skillfully preserved the content of faith in the reality of the mystery of Christ.

However, one can raise the question whether the solution arrived at Chalcedon presupposing Greek philosophical thought

The Mystery of Christ in Our History 47

is meaningful to those people who do not share a Greek worldview or its philosophical presuppositions.

If the Christian proclamation that this human, Jesus of Nazareth, is God, it needs to be meaningfully explained, showing how God can be God and human at the same time. It must be an explanation that transcends the dichotomizing Western explanation of the mystery of Christ, which obscures the mystery and in its ultimate analysis is apparently illogical and untenable. The Chalcedon Formula simply states that the divinity and humanity in Christ are without division or separation, without change or confusion, against the heresies of Alexandrians and Antiochenes, but it does not answer the fundamental question how God can become human.

Karl Rahner has shown in his theology of incarnation following the transcendental Thomism of Joseph Maréchal that humans are created as essentially self-transcending realities—and God is a self-communicating reality mutually attracting—and in Jesus Christ this movement of God and humans meet. Therefore, Jesus Christ is fully human and fully divine. However, his Christological reflections presuppose a philosophical tradition that is meaningful to the Western tradition, and it makes sense to those who follow his theological anthropology.

Can there be a meaningful explanation of the mystery of Christ in our history in the Indian context? If the mystery of Christ can be explained using Indian categories of thought and worldview, it would be not only meaningful to those who share the Indian worldview but it also would enrich the Christian understanding of the mystery of Christ in general. It can overcome the exclusivist claim that the church has held for centuries that the Christian mysteries can be understood and explained only in Greek categories of thought.

Our attempt to explain the mystery of Christ in our history must also transcend the popular Indian explanation of the incarnation of God in the Vaishnava tradition as *avatara*, which is docetic. In the *avatara* theology, God can never truly become

48 *Christ without Borders*

human as it would make God go through the cycle of birth and rebirth. So God—Vishnu—can only appear to be in any form, including human. If the Indian insight into the meaning of the totality of reality through the advaitic intuition is pressed into service to explain the mystery of Christ in history, it would be meaningful to those who share the advaitic worldview but also ever challenging for humans to become Christs, making this world a better place to live in.

An Advaitic Intuition into the Mystery of Christ

The Christian affirmation that Jesus Christ is both divine and human can fall back to a fideistic affirmation that it is possible for God to empty himself of his absoluteness and can become relative in history because everything is possible for God. Or it can rely on the Christological formula of Chalcedon, which presupposes the knowledge and acceptance of Greek categories of thought. It demands from a believer from outside the Mediterranean worldview to open his or her mind to understand, at least, the possibility of affirming the mystery of incarnation using human reason. It can somehow show that the reality of Jesus Christ, God and human at the same time, is possible when we think in terms of person, two natures and the unity of natures both divine and human at the level of hypostasis or personhood. The Chalcedon Formula cannot lead one to encounter the reality of Christ as the ultimate dimension of one's own life. It would not lead one to be another Christ in one's unique identity and be a unique Christophany[2] in this world. But the advaitic intuition into the reality of Christ opens up the possibility of recognizing breadth and length, the height and depth (Eph 3:18) of the mystery of Christ.

The advaitic intuition enables us to see the interrelatedness of everything that exists and its relationship with the source or

---

[2] Panikkar, *The Fullness of Man.*

origin of every existence. *Advaita* is often mistakenly translated by both Indians and Westerners as "monism." It is often explained as a philosophy that considers the entire reality as one. Advaitic intuition resists the temptation to reduce everything to pure unity as in monism or mere duality. It is the nonduality of the absolute and relative, God and the world. God and the world are not two. But they are not pure unity either. They are neither one nor two. God and the world are in a radical relationship. One is not without the other even when one is the source and the fundamental basis of the other. God and the world are different but not separate. They are distinct but not divided. They are "a-dvaita." Not two!

The advaitic intuition liberates us from the tyranny of monism and the confusion of pluralism. It overcomes our frustrations over dichotomies. Everything is interrelated: God, human, and the world. The reality is cosmotheandric, as Raimon Panikkar would affirm. The always-plaguing questions of our mind about how the absolute can become relative, how the eternal and limitless can become time- and space-bound, and how God can become human would find answers if we were able to rely on our advaitic intuition into reality.

If God is the absolute other, incarnation is not possible. But the fundamental Christian faith experience affirms that in Jesus Christ, God has become truly human. It is possible for God to become human, to become a part of this material reality and be a part of our history because the relative and the temporal are related to God in a mysterious way. Though distinct, God and humans are not separate such that God could not become human and reveal the radical relationship between God and humans. "God's love for the world to send his son," as John would witness, expresses the reality of this relationship in a different way but essentially means the same.

Going beyond the epistemological principle of contradiction, the Indian emphasis on the principle of identity in understanding reality can give us a better insight into the meaning of the mystery of Christ in our history. The epistemological principle of identity lets us discover the relationship among the apparently contradictory

50 *Christ without Borders*

realities. While recognizing the distinction among realities, it affirms the inseparability of all that exists with its source or the source of all existence. The principle of identity is seen in Tertullian's explanation of the Trinitarian relationship. According to Tertullian, in the Trinity there is distinction without division, difference without separation. The Father is not the Son or the Spirit, yet there is only one God. The principle of identity is implied in the Chalcedonian faith affirmation concerning the relationship between the divine nature and human nature in Christ. While overcoming the heresies of monophysitism that ignore the distinction between the two natures in Christ—and Nestorianism, which separates human and divine natures—the Chalcedonian Christological Formula affirms the union of natures without separation or division. The epistemological principle of identity, which is not alien to Western thinking, is implied in these faith affirmations. If the principle of identity gives a rational basis for an understanding of the interrelationship of reality, the advaitic intuition opens up the possibility of experiencing a vision of the entire reality that is transforming and challenging.

The mystery of Christ revealed in the reality of Jesus of Nazareth in our history is the manifestation of the totality of reality. It overcomes all human sins of separation and fragmentation, challenging all the philosophies that separate human from God, the absolute from the relative, the eternal from the temporal. In Jesus of Nazareth, the unity of God and human with their world is total and full. Humanity realizes its full meaning as it is revealed as not separate from divinity though distinct; the Divinity is revealed as distinct from humans and their world but not separate. Jesus Christ is both divine and human at the same time, without division, without separation, without confusion, and without change. In him, the unity of divinity and humanity is such that it is the totality of reality: God, human, and the world.

The event of God becoming human in Jesus Christ is an affirmation that God, human, and the world are interrelated.

God cannot be the absolute Other without any mysterious interrelationship with the world. The ultimate Other is in the heart of the world. The otherness of God is not an otherness of separation. It is an otherness of distinction.

Athanasius, the great champion of the divinity of Christ against Arius, affirmed that the Logos was already in the world before incarnation as its source of life and dynamism. If everything is created in, through, and for Christ, and if Christ is "the alpha and the omega (Col 1:15–17; Rev. 1:8), the beginning and the end, or the meaning, of everything, then there is nothing outside the reality of Christ. Panikkar developed this vision of Christ in his Christophany, writing,

> The mystery of Christ is the mystery of the whole reality—divine, human, cosmic, without confusion yet without separation. Christ would not be Christ were he not divine, were he indeed not God. The divine cannot be splintered into parts. Were he not human, were he not the whole of humanity, Christ would not be Christ. Yet this humanity, distended in time, is not yet nor ever will be finished as long as time is time, and time has no end because the end is itself already temporal.... Were not Christ corporeal, were he indeed not the whole of corporeality, Christ would not be Christ.[3]

The Christ of Christian faith experience is the *totus Christus* revealed in space and time and yet not separate from the one who encounters this Christ in the history of his or her life. Panikkar has convincingly shown that a mere identification of Jesus would make him only one of the founders of the religion, a "remarkable Jewish teacher, who had the fortune or misfortune of being put to death rather young."[4] The identity of Jesus Christ is encountered as the

---

[3] Panikkar, *The Fullness of Man*, 140.

[4] Panikkar, *The Unknown Christ of Hinduism* (Bangalore: ATC, 1982), 27.

mystery in which one is involved, and is the bond of everything divine, human, and cosmic, without separation, division, or confusion but distinct from one another.

For Panikkar, this Jesus Christ is not an a-personal principle. "The Christ that 'sits at the right hand of the Father,'" he writes, "is the first-born of the universe, born of Mary: he is Bread as well as the hungry, naked, or imprisoned."[5] This Christ forms our history, yet this mystery is beyond history.

When Jesus Christ is encountered as the reality and symbol of everything human, divine, and material, each human being is given an insight into the mystery of his or her own being, what he or she is and what he or she is called to become. Then everything and everyone is recognized as a *Christophany,* a manifestation of the reality of Christ. The experience of the totality of Christ as the One in whom God, human and the world, the absolute and the relative, the infinite and finite, historical and transhistorical, material and spiritual unite without losing the distinction and difference of each yet inextricably united to one another. Such an understanding of the Christic identity challenges the one who is committed to Christ to be responsible for one's own unfolding as a person in radical relationship to others, struggle with others to create situations where humans can authentically become humans, to be responsible for the entire creation, to be open to celebrate plurality and embrace everything that "God has cleansed" (Acts 10:15). Therefore, it is imperative for us to recapture the NT witness to the whole Christ, the insights of the patristic theology of Trinity and Christology and the *advaitic* intuition to articulate the universal significance of Jesus Christ, challenging all to encounter in this mystery his or her identity.

---

[5] Panikkar, *The Unknown Christ of Hinduism,* 27–28.

4

Christographies and Christologies

The fundamental question about the identity of Jesus Christ is raised again and again in the history of humankind, which was divided by Jesus himself. The known history of the world is recorded as happened before Christ and after Christ. Some people who have a problem with the name Christ have changed the terms BC (before Christ) and AD (*Anno Domini* [year of the Lord]) into BCE (before the common era) and CE (common era). Even such changes cannot hide the reality of Jesus Christ because a question can be raised about the basis of this nomenclature, and the answer would be Jesus Christ. For a believer, Jesus Christ is not only the answer to the questions about history, but he is also the answer to all fundamental questions about the existence of everything, particularly human life.

What is the fundamental question that humans raise about themselves and the world? It is a question about the origin and destiny of human beings and the world. Scientific discoveries may be able to give some answers about the origin of humans, and verifiable scientific evidence proves it true. But empirical science is unable to provide an answer to the question of *why*. The insight into the destiny of human beings and the innate insatiable thirst of humans for something or someone beyond themselves and beyond the limitations of space and time, in fact, would throw light on the question about the source or the origin of their existence. The early

54 *Christ without Borders*

Christian community experienced Jesus Christ as the beginning and the end of their life, the Alpha and the Omega, and indeed, the Lord and God of their life.

The Christologies of the Insiders and the Christographies of the Outsiders

The confession of a community of people—who were strict monotheists—that Jesus is Lord and God was nothing but revolutionary. It would not have been possible for them had they not experienced Jesus Christ as transforming their life in such a way that they could not but proclaim him as Lord, the beginning and the end of their lives. A number of the believers in the early Christian community who encountered Jesus of Nazareth as he lived on earth thought of him as "a man who was a prophet mighty in deed and word before God and all the people" (Lk 24:19). They knew how their "chief priests and rulers delivered him up to be condemned to death and crucified him," and they hoped that he was the one to redeem Israel" (Lk 24:20–21). They had also experienced him as "alive" (Lk 24:23). They certainly knew that he was Jesus of Nazareth, but they could not identify his new mode of existence which transformed their lives in such a way that they began to understand themselves in a new way and struggled to articulate the mystery of Jesus who is alive after he was crucified, buried, and was experienced as alive again.

All Christologies begin from the encounter of this all-embracing Reality that transformed the lives of a number of people who were affected by the encounter in such a way that they could not but affirm it both as Jesus of Nazareth and the Lord and God of their lives. They searched their entire Scripture, beginning in the Torah, going through the prophets, and attending to the histories that fill the book of the Scripture. They recognized this transforming Reality as the prophesied Messiah. In the process they had to change their concepts about the expected political Messiah who would bring liberation from foreign rule to an understanding of the Messiah or Christ who would establish God's reign and bring liberation from all bondages: physical, psychological, social, and spiritual, Then they could answer the question "Who do people say I am?" and "Who do *you* say that I am?" (Mk 8:27–28). These questions, though presented as raised during the historical life of Jesus, in all probability were articulated and answered after the resurrection experience of Jesus. Certainly, the evangelists have a pedagogical reason to present it as happening during the earthly life of Jesus to make the hearers of the gospel understand that Jesus was already Messiah and Lord, even before his resurrection.

Answers to the question about the identity of Jesus were given both by outsiders and insiders, by those who have observed Jesus's life and his activities and made certain judgments about his identity, and those insiders who encountered Jesus as the risen Lord and were transformed by that encounter. The Christology of the outsiders is without any commitment to the person of Jesus and his good news of wholeness and liberation, and the Christology of the insiders is by those who are transformed by the encounter with Jesus and are committed to the person of Jesus and his mission. Thus, two types of Christology have emerged since the time of the New Testament.

Already in the New Testament we have a variety of Christologies, even though Jesus Christ is One. Those who encountered Jesus as Messiah, Lord, and God tried to articulate their faith experience in the context of their lives as well as respond to the contextual needs of their addressees. Those who were outsiders, whether Jews or Greeks, developed Christologies of their imagination based on their worldview and philosophies without encountering and committing themselves to him. When a Jewish-Christian sect called the Ebionites recognized Jesus only as another human being born as the natural son of Joseph and Mary with extraordinary powers, the Gnostics and the Docetists went to the other extreme and denied his true humanity. According to the dualistic philosophy of the Gnostics, whatever is of matter is evil and whatever is of spirit is good. God cannot become truly human because matter is evil, so Jesus Christ could not be really human. The Docetists, having the same philosophy, affirmed that Jesus Christ appears to be human and not really human. Surprisingly, this heretical Christology has influenced the thinking of many Christian believers even today.

The Fathers of the Church, like Ignatius of Antioch and Irenaeus, fought against such heretical teachings and affirmed that everything God created is good and the human body is not evil, so God assumed humanity and became human. Later, when Arius, an Alexandrian presbyter, taught that Jesus Christ was not truly God but only a creature by misinterpreting the NT witness about him, the Council of Nicaea affirmed that Jesus Christ is "God from God, light from light, true God from true God begotten not made, consubstantial with the Father." The issue of Jesus Christ's oneness of being with God was expressed using the Greek categories of thought like *ousia* or essence/substance, but it was an articulation that was faithful to the original Christian confession that Jesus is Lord and God. The expression consubstantial or *homoousios* with God the Father reconciled the belief in the divinity of Christ with the Christian belief in one God or the oneness of God.

The next stage of Christological reflections began with the insiders explaining the unity of divinity and humanity in the one person of Jesus of Nazareth and ended up going to extreme positions by devaluing the human nature of Jesus or separating it from his divine nature. The Monophysites claimed that Jesus had only one nature (*monophysis*) and that his divine nature subsumed the human nature after incarnation, and the Nestorians separated the human and divine natures in Christ, though Nestorius did not take such an extreme position. The Christological controversy about

Christographies and Christologies 57

the union of the divine and human natures in Christ was resolved by the Council of Chalcedon in 451 CE affirming that Jesus Christ is one person, that he is the second person of the Trinity who has two natures, both divine and human. They are united in such a way that this union at the level of the one personhood is "without confusion, without change, without separation and without division." This union of the two natures did not take away their distinction that the peculiar property of each nature is preserved. Though the Fathers of the Council of Chalcedon used philosophical categories in confessing the mystery of Jesus Christ, they affirmed that they were confessing about the only begotten Son of God, the Logos, whom the prophets had foretold and believed and proclaimed as the creed of the church. Council Fathers were articulating the core Christian faith in the reality of Jesus Christ as God became human. Any other Christology that would not recognize this basic affirmation, whatever way this may be expressed, would not be the Jesus Christ encountered, believed, and proclaimed by the foundational Christian community. In fact, the questions raised about the existence and the identity of Jesus in modern times ignored the fundamental Christian confession about the person of Jesus that transformed the lives not only of those who formed the community of the church in the first centuries of the Christian era radically and comprehensively but also in the subsequent centuries, even in those times, the historical existence and the identity of Jesus were called into question.

The church knew from the beginning that the mystery of Jesus Christ defies all formulations and articulations. The classical Christology of Chalcedon is a Christology "from above" or a "descending Christology," or an "incarnational Christology," or what we could term a "theophanic Christology" because its basic axiom is the revelation of the "only begotten" Son of God as human. These faith affirmations about Jesus Christ were questioned by the liberal Protestant theologians of the eighteenth and nineteenth centuries who were inspired by the ideology of Enlightenment. Their interest was not a Christology but a search for the historical figure of Jesus of Nazareth beneath the New Testament witness about him and the church's confession of faith about him. Their attempts cannot be called Christologies but rather investigations into the historical reality of Jesus for questionable purposes. They were moved probably by the spirit of Enlightenment rationalism that asserted that something can be true only if it could be scientifically verifiable.

Futile "Quests" for the Historical Jesus and the Christographies

The quests for the historical Jesus were research projects to find the Jesus of history and his authentic teachings beyond and beneath the NT witness about him and his mission. The first of the quests was the old quest from 1778 to 1906, and then an interim period or no quest from 1906 to 1953, and then in the new quest from 1980 to the present day we have the third quest.

The quest for the historical Jesus began with Hermann Samuel Reimarus (1694–1768), who raised the problem of the relation between the Jesus of history and the Christ of faith in his so-called *Wolfenbüttel Fragments* published by G. E. Lessing (1729–1781). For Reimarus, Jesus was a Jewish reformer, a revolutionary who became increasingly fanatical and politicized—and he failed. It was the idea of his disciples to proclaim him as Messiah and to announce that he rose from the dead and waited for him to bring the world to an end immediately. Reimarus thought that he had found the real historical Jesus, and this discovery would sound the death knell for Christianity.

The quest for the real Jesus of history introduced by Reimarus was brought into sharper focus by David F. Strauss (1808–1874), who stated that the goal of this quest is to recover the "real Jesus" by isolating the "Jesus of history" from the "Christ of faith."

Christographies and Christologies 59

According to him, the Jesus of history lies buried under the layers of myths created by the church. "The historical Jesus was thus turned into the divine Messiah by the pious, but erroneous devotion of the church."[1] Adolf von Harnack (1851–1930) questioned the Hellenization of the original Christian faith and its alienation through Hellenistic metaphysics. Albrecht Ritschl (1822–1889) sought a historical interpretation of Christological dogmas. The liberal Protestant Christology further sought to give rationalistic foundations for the Christian belief in Jesus Christ. This was found in the works of Immanuel Kant (1724–1804), G. W. F. Hegel (1770–1831), and Friedrich Schleiermacher (1768–1834). Kant's philosophical reduction of religion into a practical implication of morality could include faith in Jesus Christ, but it was not necessary, because everyone possessed the archetype of moral living. Hegel's philosophy gave a rational foundation to the Christian faith in the Trinity and incarnation as the unfolding of the "Absolute Idea." For Schleiermacher, the religious experience or the God-consciousness of every human being finds its perfection in Jesus Christ.

In the quest for finding the Jesus of history, most of the liberal theologians attempted to write a biography or life of Jesus based on each one's judgment about what is historical, discarding most of the biblical witness and the church's traditions as fictional. They created their own version of the historical Jesus, contradicting one another in their "lives of Jesus." After almost a hundred years, the old quest came to an end for various reasons. In his book *The Quest for the Historical Jesus*, Albert Schweitzer convincingly showed that each theologian who tried to show the historical Jesus was a creation of his own ideas and not the real Jesus of history. According to him, a socialist makes Jesus a social reformer, a rationalist makes him a revealer of true virtues, and an idealist makes Jesus an embodiment

---

[1] Raymond E. Brown, *An Introduction to the New Testament,* Anchor Bible Reference Library, David Noel Freedman, ed. (New York: Doubleday, 1997), 338.

60 *Christ without Borders*

of true humanity—but the real Jesus escapes and returns to his own age. The old quest was rejected by the representatives of form criticism as they showed that the Gospels used for reconstructing the life of Jesus were also the products of the faith proclamation of the church used for preaching, catechesis, and liturgy and not Jesus as actually lived and acted. Rudolf Bultmann (1884–1976) and Karl Barth (1886–1968) contended that it is impossible to reconstruct the actual life of Jesus. Thus, the effort to produce new lives of the real Jesus of history was abandoned because the faith of the church cannot be based on confusions created by the so-called historians of Jesus.

In spite of the failure of the old quest to reach the Jesus of history, the new quest began with the students of Bultmann led by Ernst Käsemann with his paper on "The Problem of Historical Jesus." Accepting the findings of form criticism and also the affirmation that the NT witness of Jesus is kerygmatic, Käsemann points out that one can separate the authentic traditions about Jesus and the later interpretations of the church about him. Unlike the old quest, which was championed exclusively by Protestants, the new quest also had the collaboration of some of the Catholic scholars. Using various criteria, they could arrive at some authentic sayings and deeds of Jesus with different degrees of certainty and describe some events of this life and death and the origin of Easter faith.[2] However, the findings of the new quest remain ambiguous with regard to the Jesus of history. They were influenced by the historiographical and rationalistic presuppositions that cannot be applied to the Christ event, which is a unique historical and transhistorical event. Further, they followed the positivist school of historiography, which demands that the historian must separate historical facts from their interpretations. But this is impossible as there are no pure facts, and every fact that is known is already

---

[2] Roch A. Kereszty, *Jesus Christ: Fundamentals of Christology,* J. Stephen Maddux, ed. (New York: Alba House, 1995), 6.

Christographies and Christologies 61

interpreted. The new quest also produced the "Jesus of history"; for example, Günther Bornkamm presents Jesus as the sovereign freedom, and Edward Schillebeeckx presents Jesus primarily as the eschatological prophet. All these fragmentary pictures of Jesus cannot adequately present the witness of the New Testament about Jesus Christ. Perhaps a permutation of the new quest is best seen in the Jesus Seminar, begun in 1985 under the leadership of Robert Funk and supported by J. D. Crossan and fifty biblical scholars to analyze the NT texts to determine who Jesus really was and what he really said and did. After a so-called serious investigation and scholarly discussion, the scholars were asked to vote for what they considered the authentic sayings of Jesus using colored beads.[3] The Jesus Seminar scholars published their findings in three reports: *The Five Gospels* (1993), *The Acts of Jesus* (1998), and *The Gospel of Jesus* (1999).[4]

The Christography prepared by the scholars of the seminar presents the figure of Jesus not much different from any "outsider." For those members of the Jesus Seminar, the historical Jesus was a wandering Hellenistic Jewish sage and faith healer who—through his parables and sayings—preached the good news of liberation

---

[3] Red beads indicated that the voter believed Jesus did say the passage quoted, or something very much like the passage (three points). Pink beads indicated that the voter believed Jesus probably said something like the passage (two points). Gray beads indicated that the voter believed Jesus did not say the passage, but it contains Jesus's ideas (one point). Black beads indicated the voter believed Jesus did not say the passage; it comes from later admirers or a different tradition (zero points).

[4] Robert W. Funk, Roy W. Hoover, and the Jesus Seminar, *The Five Gospels: What Did Jesus Really Say? The Search for the Authentic Words of Jesus* (Farmington, MN: Polebridge Press [Macmillan], 1993); Robert W. Funk and the Jesus Seminar, *The Acts of Jesus: The Search for the Authentic Deeds of Jesus* (San Francisco: HarperSanFrancisco, 1998); Robert W. Funk and the Jesus Seminar, *The Gospel of Jesus: According to the Jesus Seminar* (Farmington, MN: Polebridge Press [Macmillan], 1999).

62   *Christ without Borders*

from oppression and injustice experienced by ordinary people of his time. He was a radical and iconoclast who challenged the dogmas of Jewish religion and broke the social conventions both in his behavior and in his teachings. He preached of "heaven's imperial rule," which was translated as "kingdom of God." This imperial rule of heaven was already present among the people but unseen by them. This itinerant preacher and healer presented God as a loving father. He criticized the insiders and socialized with the outsiders. He did not perform any nature miracles. According to the Jesus Seminar members, Jesus was born of two human parents, did not die for sinners, and did not rise from the dead. Some disciples claimed to have visionary experiences of Jesus after his death, but they were not physical encounters. A number of well-known biblical scholars and theologians—including Richard Hays, Ben Witherington, Greg Boyd, N. T. Wright, William Lane Craig, Luke Timothy Johnson, Craig A. Evans, Paul Barnett, Michael F. Bird, Craig Blomberg, Markus Bockmuehl, Raymond Brown, James D. G. Dunn, Howard Clark Kee, John P. Meier, Graham Stanton, Darrell Bock, Edwin Yamauchi, Gerald O'Collins—are highly critical about the presuppositions, methodology, and conclusions of the Jesus Seminar group. One could say that they have created another Christography based on their skepticism about the authenticity of the Christ event narrated by the New Testament witnesses.

The historical research using all the possible methods of inquiry could establish with certainty that Jesus of Nazareth lived at a particular time and a particular place in history. It cannot show how his life was significant for all of humanity and the world. It can only affirm the reality of Jesus's existence but not who he is, because his life extends beyond space and time. The early church experienced and confessed that Jesus is Lord and God, though he lived as a human, and in him and through him humans are transformed and given the power to transform the world. The NT witness about Jesus is that there is continuity between the

Christographies and Christologies 63

historical life of Jesus and his transhistorical existence. He lived once in history and continues to live in history in another mode of his being. He is encountered more deeply and intensively through faith in him than he was encountered by others during his earthly existence—so there is no dichotomy between the Jesus of history and the Christ of faith because he is both: Jesus of faith. There is no more quest for the Jesus of history, and the only valid quest is to find him as the meaning of one's own existence and the meaning of the world. Therefore, the Christological reflections continue for the sake of understanding the mystery of Jesus Christ.

Many of the present-day reflections about the person of Jesus Christ are not Christologies in the strict sense of the term. I would consider them as Christographies. They are only narrations or descriptions about the person of Jesus Christ from the perspective of those who consider him as one who belongs to the special group of people who had great influence on the lives of their contemporaries and on the generations who came after them because of their way of life and teachings. They place Jesus among the founders of religions or religious movements, moral or ethical teachers, sages, prophets or philosophers, social reformers, religious or sociopolitical revolutionaries, and so on. All these and many more labels may fit him, but they would not define him. Certainly, such labels would fit other historically important personalities. The mystery of the person of Jesus Christ goes beyond all categories of thought and description. Jesus is someone *more* than all other historical personalities who influenced the lives of their contemporaries and other generations. What is *more* in him makes the difference. All Christologies are based on what makes him distinct from other great personalities of the world. All Christographies are descriptions about him similar to others who had a positive influence on the lives of other humans. But authentic Christology is the systematic articulation about the *who* and the *what* of Jesus Christ by those who had a transforming encounter with

64 *Christ without Borders*

him and recognized him as the beginning and the end of their life or the meaning of their life.

The so-called Christologies of the present times are not real Christologies but Christographies. There are many. They differ according to the context they emerge from and also according to the specific problems for which they find Jesus as an answer because of his way of life and teachings. Those who propose such Christographies may or may not believe in him as the Lord and God of their lives. Therefore, some Christographies are based on authentic Christology, or they presuppose faith in Jesus Christ as the Logos who became human, but there are other Christographies that do not presuppose the authentic Christian affirmation about the person and nature of Jesus Christ.

Contemporary Christographies

We have made a distinction between Christologies and Christographies. The Christographies try to present Jesus as a significant person of history who transformed history as none had done before or after him. Therefore, those who have recognized Jesus as the one whose quality of life is unparalleled in history would not only search to find out whether he really existed in history but also whether the teachings attributed to him really originate from him. They would also investigate the truth content of the narrations about his life and mission in the New Testament. In the second half of the twentieth century also, such attempts were made as they were done in the two previous centuries we have seen above with different quests for the historical Jesus. Can anyone really find out who Jesus truly was (*in se*) and what his birth, life, ministry, death and resurrection or the totality of the Christ event has done for us (*propter nos*)? The testimony of the early Christians who were of Jewish, Hellenistic Jewish and Gentile origin articulated their transforming experience of Jesus Christ, and subsequent generations accepted it as a credible witness. Their belief in the testimony about Jesus Christ was validated by their own encounter with the same Christ. The testimony of the disciples and the first Christian community about Jesus Christ is articulated in a religious language. No language, however developed it may be, would be able to articulate any ordinary human experience adequately. It is still more difficult to express any religious or spiritual experience. Therefore, the language that articulates any religious experience is descriptive, evocative, symbolic, metaphorical, and mythical. The so-called quests are thus futile attempts when they analyze the texts that narrate the experience of the reality of Jesus in all possible means of literary forms and styles available to them.

Contemporary Christographies try to present a particular image of Jesus Christ that may have some reference in the NT or in the context of the life of the historical Jesus and try to explain the life and mission of Jesus to show that a particular image of Jesus is the real one. They present Jesus as a revolutionist, a charismatic and holy Jew, an eschatological prophet, a social reformer, a Cynic teacher, and so on.

Jesus: A Charismatic and Holy Jew

Geza Vermes (1924–2013) is credited to have begun the third quest with his publications on the historical Jesus.[5] Though born into a Hungarian Jewish family, he was baptized, became a Catholic priest, and later left the priesthood. He subsequently became a professor of Jewish studies at Oxford. In 1973 he published his most debated book, *Jesus the Jew*, then ten years

---

[5] Géza Vermes, *Jesus the Jew: A Historian's Reading of the Gospels* (London: Collins, 1973); *Jesus in His Jewish Context* (Minneapolis: Fortress, 2003); *Jesus and the World of Judaism* (Philadelphia: Fortress, 1983); *The Religion of Jesus the Jew* (London: SCM, 1993).

later *Jesus in the World of Judaism*, and—completing the trilogy in 1993—*The Religion of Jesus the Jew*. All these books affirm that Jesus can be understood only as a Jew and in the Jewish settings. Nobody denies that Jesus was a Jew. It is a truth, according to the NT testimony about him. Vermes asserts that Jesus was a totally eschatologically inspired person, very charismatic, who fit very well into the world in which he lived. Many may not have any problem with that assertion either. But he further denies the divine sonship of Jesus. According to Vermes, Jesus was someone who was concerned about the fate of the Jews at a particular point in Jewish history. For Vermes, Jesus was a Jewish holy man like Honi the rainmaker and Jesus's contemporary Hanina Ben Dosa. The place of Jesus is among such holy people of Judaism. He can be distinguished from other holy men of Judaism only by his preaching of "faith-trust," repentance, and preaching of the kingdom of God. Vermes would not admit that Jesus is truly Christ or the Messiah, or that he is the Son of God as believed and proclaimed by Christians. He holds the view that the New Testament teachings on the person and the mission of Jesus are added to Jesus's story by later Christian writers.

Well-known biblical scholars like John P. Meier and Joseph Fitzmyer and many others dismiss Vermes's view that Jesus was made into Lord and God but affirm that the divinity of Jesus was the faith affirmation of the early Christian community.

Jesus the Apocalyptic Prophet

Many of the present-day Christographies of the West give importance to the Jewish origins of Jesus and try to fit him into the mold of the Jewish tradition of prophets and the Jewish worldview on the origin and destiny of the world. One of such Christographies is the presentation of Jesus as an apocalyptic prophet. Already Albert Schweitzer and Johannes Weiss had dealt with this theme.

In our times, E. P. Sanders, Bart Ehrman, Paula Frederiksen, Gerd Lüdeman, and John P. Meier hold the view that Jesus was an apocalyptic prophet. According to Sanders, like the prophets of the Old Testament, Jesus also proclaimed the destruction and the restoration of Israel, and he was a follower of John the Baptist, who called the people of Israel to repentance and conversion. Jesus continued the tradition of John the Baptist. He believed that he was the agent to renew Israel. For this purpose, he called the twelve disciples representing the twelve tribes of Israel, and he believed that the coming of the kingdom of God was imminent. Meier, a renowned Catholic biblical scholar who has published five volumes on *A Marginal Jew: Rethinking the Historical Jesus,* holds the view that the historical Jesus was an Elijah-like miracle-working eschatological prophet. Certainly, his scholarly works focus only on the historical Jesus and not on Christian faith in Jesus Christ.

Jesus the Prophet of Social Change

There are Christographies that present Jesus as a prophet of social change or a social reformer. Scholars like Richard Horsley and Gerd Theissen view that Jesus was conscious of the sociopolitical situation of his times and proclaimed the inauguration of God's reign, which also involves the liberation and renewal of the entire Jewish society. According to Horsley,

> The focal concern of the kingdom of God in Jesus's preaching and practice, however, is the liberation and welfare of the people. Jesus's understanding of the "kingdom of God" is similar in its broader perspective to the confident hopes expressed in then-contemporary Jewish apocalyptic literature. That is, he had utter confidence that God was restoring the life of the society, and that this would mean judgment for those who oppressed the people and vindication for those who

68 *Christ without Borders*

> faithfully adhered to God's will and responded to the kingdom. That is, God was imminently and presently effecting a historical transformation. In modern parlance that would be labelled a "revolution."[6]

However, Jesus did not advocate violence or support the Zealots or any revolutionary group that used violence as a means to liberate themselves from all kinds of oppression. According to Horsley, Jesus's command of loving enemies was restricted to the enemies within the Jewish society and not to outsiders or foreigners. His mission was to exhort people to live in harmony and peace here on earth, and he did not bother much about life beyond this earthly life. Though Horsley's Christography is appealing and is recognized by many scholars, his views on Jesus's teaching about loving the enemies as exclusively restricted to members of the Jewish society and his neglect of the eschatological aspect of Jesus's teaching are not accepted by biblical scholars.

Jesus the Wisdom Sage or Jewish Cynic

We have seen in general the Christographies of the members of the Jesus Seminar. Some of them, like John Dominic Crossan, Robert Funk, Burton Mack, and Stephen J. Patterson, find similarities between the teachings of Jesus about the practice of virtues like love and compassion as well as devaluing power, possessions, positions, and so on, and the teaching of the Cynic philosophers of Greco-Roman world. According to them, the city of Gadara was not very far from Nazareth and was a center of Cynic philosophy. In Galilee, Hellenistic and Jewish thoughts could mutually influence each other. For John Dominic Crossan, Jesus was more like a Cynic sage from the Hellenistic Jewish tradition than either a Christ who

---

[6] Richard A. Horsley, *Jesus and the Spiral of Violence: Popular Jewish Resistance in Roman Palestine* (Minneapolis: Fortress, 1993), 207–208.

Christographies and Christologies 69

would die to save sinners or a messiah who would liberate Jewish people from foreign rule and establish a Jewish kingdom.[7] There are obviously certain similarities between the images of Jesus presented in the New Testament and the wisdom sages or Cynics of Hellenistic tradition, but it is an absurd conclusion that Jesus was only a wisdom sage or a Cynic.

Contemporary Christologies

Christocentric Christologies

Karl Barth (1888–1968), considered to be the greatest Protestant theologian since Calvin, is the foremost representative of Christocentric Christology. His influence on Western theology has been widely recognized. Reacting to liberal Protestantism's effort to show that ultimately Jesus is "only a human being and provided only an example of moral living but did not save us from our fallen human condition,"[8] Karl Barth affirmed the Christological statements of the councils. According to Barth, there is an absolute difference between God and human beings, and humans have no capacity to know or receive God as they are under the power of original sin. The fallen nature of humans can create only idols, which are mere projections of their minds. Barth is known for his Christocentrism. For Barth there is no other key to the understanding of God, humans, and cosmos except Jesus Christ. Even his main work, *Church Dogmatics*, in all its eleven volumes is "one long explanation and unfolding of this one name, Jesus Christ."[9] He reaffirms the Chalcedonian statement about the

---

[7] John Dominic Crossan, *The Historical Jesus: The Life of a Mediterranean Jewish Peasant* (New York: HarperCollins, 1992).

[8] Kereszty, *Jesus Christ*, 252.

[9] Klaas Runia, *The Present-Day Christological Debate* (Leicester: InterVarsity Press, 1984), 16.

70 *Christ without Borders*

person of Jesus Christ as *vere Deus* and *vere homo*, which would mean that the Logos has taken upon himself human nature in addition to his divine nature. But Barth emphasized the divinity of Jesus Christ as the center of Christian faith to such an extent that Christ's humanity seems to lose its significance.

Anthropological Christologies

Under this title, we can include the Christological trends in various shades of Christologies that have one thing in common: the understanding of Jesus Christ in and through anthropological categories. It would include the demythologizing existentialist Christology of Rudolf Bultmann to Piet Schoonenberg's reversal of the theophanic Christology of Chalcedon.

Rudolf Bultmann (1884–1976), like Barth, revolted against liberal theology but did not share in Barth's renewed interest in classical Christology. Influenced by a Heideggerian existential interpretation of reality and the radical form-critical analysis of the New Testament, Bultmann asserted that we cannot speak of God or Christ without reference to our own existence. Therefore, any theological or Christological discourse cannot but be anthropological. Bultmann, with his religio-historical school's approach to the NT, asserts that the statements in the NT about the person of Jesus Christ are expressed in a mythological lingo, and a radical demythologization of these statements would lead us to the Christ proclaimed by the early church. That Jesus Christ is God is more a confessional than dogmatic statement. It is not an assertion about the ontological nature of Christ. According to Bultmann, any objectifying assertion about God's being is absolutely false. The confession that Jesus is God can be correct only if it expresses the significance of Christ for the believer, *Christus pro me*. God or Christ is to be understood as the event of God's or Christ's acting as a power that affects us in certain moments. Christ's deity is the living experience that cannot be conceptualized. The divine and human dimensions in Christ are not natures, but the miracle of Christ is that the "human word is heard as divine word." Hence Bultmann repudiates both orthodox and liberal attempts to objectify Christ as the one divine person and the historical Jesus, respectively. For Bultmann, the content of the kerygma is the cross and resurrection, or the Christ of faith, and not the historical Jesus.

Bultmann's existentialist Christology is a functional one in the sense that it presents Christ as the one who invites human beings to a fundamental decision for himself. One cannot accept the contention of Bultmann that "Christ is God" is only the experience of the significance of Christ for the believer. Though Bultmann's existential Christology is accused of individualism, it was a new trend in Western Christology. Friedrich Gogarten (1887–1967) and Paul Tillich (1886–1965) developed their own versions of existentialist Christology after Bultmann.

Anthropological Christology finds its best expression in the Christological reflections of Karl Rahner (1904–1984). To Rahner, Christology is transcendent anthropology, and anthropology is deficient Christology.[10] How does Rahner arrive at such a conclusion? Rahner's Christology is built on his anthropology, which has its foundation in what is called "transcendental Thomism." According to transcendental Thomism, every human knower moves continuously from one horizon of knowledge to another, tending toward the infinite horizon. This movement toward the infinite, the absolute, is a constitutive dimension of every human being. According to Rahner, "Human being is spirit, that is, he/she lives life in a perpetual reaching out to the Absolute, in openness to God."[11] These movements toward God would have been absurd if there was no corresponding movement from the

---

[10] Karl Rahner, *Theological Investigations* (London: Darton, Longman & Todd, 1961), 164.

[11] Karl Rahner, *Hearers of the Word* (New York: Herder and Herder, 1969), 66.

side of God toward human beings. In other words, a human being is a self-transcending reality, and God is a self-communicating reality. Jesus Christ is the meeting point of this double movement of God and human being toward each other. In Jesus Christ, humanity has realized the fullness of its possibilities.

Rahner's attempt was to interpret the traditional Chalcedonian Formula, which affirms that Jesus Christ is true God and true human in a way that would make it meaningful to his contemporaries. The doctrine of two natures does not express the full human life of Jesus Christ. It is the human life of Jesus Christ that challenges the entire humanity to realize its potentialities. Rahner's Christology overcomes the dangers of humanistic liberal theology as well as the earlier Barthian negation of the God-given capacity of human beings to enter into relation with God. However, Walter Kasper doubts whether Rahner has taken the historical importance of the Christ event seriously in his effort to give a metaphysical explanation of the same. Further, according to Kasper, Rahner's Christology lacks the dimension of the theocentric dialogical relationship of Jesus to his Father, which was the primary concern of the New Testament.[12] In spite of such drawbacks, Rahner's anthropological Christology greatly influenced contemporary theological thinking, especially in Catholic circles.

Wolfhart Pannenberg (1928–2014), like Rahner, follows an anthropological Christology that must begin from the humanity of Jesus. He objects to the traditional incarnational Christology's approach "from above" because it presupposes the divinity of Jesus and makes it difficult to identify the distinctive features of the historical Jesus. Further, this approach is from the position of God, concentrating on how His Son became human.[13] According to Pannenberg, our approach must be "from below"—from

---

[12] Walter Kasper, *Jesus the Christ* (New York: Paulist Press, 1976).

[13] Wolfhart Pannenberg, *Jesus—God and Man*, 2nd ed. (Philadelphia: Westminster Press, 1977), 34–35.

Christographies and Christologies 73

the historical Jesus who can be discovered behind the apostolic kerygma. Pannenberg attempted to show that from the observation of certain features in the historical Jesus himself one can ascertain that Jesus is the Son of God. Within

> the frame-work of apocalyptic expectation of the end of time, Jesus was certain that in his person and activity God's offer of salvation had irrupted into the present. So he spoke with the authority of God and invited people to avail themselves of this offer of unconditional salvation. But his death on the cross seemed to negate his claims. Yet through the event of resurrection from the dead ... he is one with God and is himself God.[14]

Even before his resurrection he was Son of God, but with the resurrection it became evident.

Pannenberg's approach takes the historical life of Jesus and his resurrection seriously for the development of Christology. Pannenberg insists on taking the humanity of Jesus seriously, although in the process he jettisons some of the NT data (e.g., narratives about the birth of Jesus in Matthew and Luke and the Logos Christology of John), which would not fit into his program of developing a "Christology from below."

In the Christological approach of Piet Schoonenberg (1911–1999), one finds a serious challenge to the traditional Chalcedonian Christology. In his controversial work *The Christ*, Schoonenberg questions the Chalcedonian solution of uniting the divine nature and human nature in one person of the Logos.[15] According to him, such a solution of replacing the human subject with the divine subject would not make Jesus a real human being.

---

[14] Pannenberg, *Jesus*, 323.

[15] Piet J. A. M. Schoonenberg, *The Christ: A Study of the God-Man Relationship in the Whole of Creation and in Jesus Christ* (New York: Herder and Herder, 1971).

74   *Christ without Borders*

The Christologies that consider God and human as rivals would end up finding solutions to the problem of relating "God *and* human" and not "God *in* human." To Schoonenberg the self-evident fact that Jesus is a unity in himself—that is, he is one person—and the fact that Jesus is a real human would be the starting points of Christological reflection. Chalcedon asserts that Jesus is one person and a unity in himself, and the NT confesses that he is a real human and his humanity "comprises all of our existence except sin, thus also a positive reality as well as the spiritual soul of a human being."[16] But his difference from us is his unique relationship with God, which finds expression in Chalcedon that Jesus Christ is the eternal Son of the Father, the second person of the Holy Trinity.

A real human must be a real subject of his personality, so Schoonenberg inverts the doctrines of enhypostasis and anhypostasis. According to him, it is not human nature, which is enhypostatic in the divine person, but the divine nature in the human person. This anthropological approach would overcome the dualism in Christology and affirm that Jesus is a real human being, "the eschatological human" filled with the highest degree of the presence of God. Modifying his position after the intervention of the Vatican authorities, Schoonenberg would add that Jesus is also enhypostatic in the Logos as the ground of the human reality, and the presences are mutual and reciprocal. However, he would assert that the humanity of Jesus is not anhypostatic.

Schoonenberg's approach to Christology is radically new and challenging. He proposes an alternative Christology that is appealing to the modern mind by presenting the real human with the most perfect and the highest presence of God. However, it is doubtful whether Schoonenberg's Jesus Christ would still be the "God from God" and "Light from Light" of the creed.

In the twentieth century, no theologian has made such a thoroughgoing and extensive study of the person of Jesus Christ

---

[16] Piet Schoonenberg, *The Christ* (London: Sheed and Ward, 1972), 72.

Christographies and Christologies 75

as Edward Schillebeeckx (1914–2009) in his many volumes on Christology, including *Christ: The Sacrament of the Encounter with God*, *Jesus: An Experiment in Christology*, *Christ: The Christian Experience in the Modern World*, and *Christ: The Experience of Jesus as Lord*.[17] Schillebeeckx's avowed interest is to make Jesus intelligible and meaningful to his contemporaries. For this he performs an extensive search in the sources of the NT traditions using the methods of critical exegesis to find out the original Jesus behind the "Christ of the church" and behind the layers of the NT traditions. From his studies he reconstructs a picture of Jesus as the eschatological prophet who proclaimed the kingdom of God, healed and exorcised, entered into table-fellowship with the social and religious outcasts, and through the parable of his life presented a liberating experience of God. For Schillebeeckx, Jesus's experience of his *Abba* was the source and secret of his being. His message and manner of life were founded on this unique relationship.

Schillebeeckx's Christology is based on the creedal confessions of the early church. They include the *Maranatha* Christologies that confess Jesus Christ as the eschatological Lord and master of life; the Christologies that present Jesus as the one who performed deeds of power out of compassion for the people; the Wisdom Christologies that identify Jesus as God's Wisdom that reveals God's plan of salvation and brings about salvation; and the Easter Christology that gives importance to the death and resurrection of Jesus. In relating all these Christologies to the historical life of Jesus, Schillebeeckx's notion about the reality of resurrection

---

[17] Edward Schillebeeckx, *Christ: The Sacrament of the Encounter with God* (New York: Sheed and Ward, 1963); Edward Schillebeeckx, *Jesus: An Experiment in Christology* (New York: Seabury Press, 1979); Edward Schillebeeckx, *Christ: The Christian Experience in the Modern World* (London: S.C.M. Press, 1980); Edward Schillebeeckx, *Christ: The Experience of Jesus as Lord* (New York: Seabury Press, 1980);

became very controversial. He emphasized the experience of the disciples about the continued presence of Jesus more than the reality of resurrection. The church believes and confesses the reality of resurrection, which is the source of the disciples' experience that Jesus is alive.

Hans Küng (1928–2021) claims that he wishes to be an apologist for Christian faith, and that is the reason for his interest in interpreting Jesus Christ in a way meaningful and acceptable to all sections of society in the contemporary secularized world. The questions he raises and tries to answer are: Who is Jesus? What did he want? In his most popular books, *On Being Christian*[18] and *Does God Exist?*,[19] he attempts to outline his reflections on Christology.

The picture of Jesus that emerges from the Synoptic Gospels is that of a human who was wholly and entirely a human and a model of what it is to be human and who demanded a final decision for the cause of God and humans. The true man Jesus of Nazareth is the real revelation of the one true God for those who believe in him, and he is God's word and will in human form. He is God's advocate, delegate, and representative whose person and works were vindicated by resurrection. The other statements about the divine sonship, preexistence, creation, mediation, and incarnation are expressed in mythical and semimythical language. They are meant to substantiate the divine origin of the uniqueness, underivability, and unsurpassability of the call, offer, and claim manifested in and through Jesus. Küng's attempt is to liberate the meaning of the person of Jesus Christ from the Jewish and Hellenistic categories of thought and expression. His insistence on a functional Christology starting with the historical Jesus may not end up in affirming that Jesus is true God in the way that the Councils of Nicaea and Chalcedon did. Though Küng's attempts

---

[18] Hans Küng, *On Being a Christian* (London: Collins, 1978).

[19] Hans Küng, *Does God Exist?* (London: Collins, 1980).

were successful in presenting Jesus Christ in a language meaningful to contemporary society, as is evident from the popularity of his writings, it is not clear whether his functional Christology can ignore the support of an ontological Christology.

Theopaschic Christology

In the Christological approach of Jürgen Moltmann and Eberhard Jüngel, Jesus, the crucified, reveals God in a way hitherto unknown. Suffering being a universal experience, a Christological approach that takes the sufferings of humanity into account has a universal appeal. No wonder, then, that this approach to Christology had a tremendous influence on the liberation theologians, especially Jon Sobrino.

The starting point of the Christological approach of Jürgen Moltmann (1926–) is the conviction that the cross of Christ reveals God. In his book *The Crucified God*,[20] he points out that the epistemological principle of the theology of the cross as the dialectical principle that is the deity of God is revealed in the paradox of the cross. Moltmann argues that we have to take the crucifixion of Jesus seriously as the unique event that reveals to us that suffering is a mode of God's being because God is love. The cross is not something that just happened to the human Jesus, but it happened to God himself, and therefore the Christ event on the cross is a God event. It reveals the intra-Trinitarian relationship of the Father, the Son, and the Holy Spirit. The Father suffers the death of the Son in his love for the forsaken human and the liberating force of the cross reaches out to us through the Spirit. The whole history of humanity, both positive and negative, is taken

---

[20] Jürgen Moltmann, *The Crucified God: The Cross of Christ as the Foundation and Criticism of Christian Theology* (New York: Harper and Row, 1974).

up into the "history of God." There is no human suffering or death that would not at the same time be the suffering and death of God himself. Therefore, God's victory over suffering and death is assured, and consequently human salvation is also.

Moltmann's approach to Christology, which I term a "theopaschic Christology," reveals the suffering God in and through the suffering of Jesus and consequently in the sufferings of the whole of humanity. The very concept of a suffering God appeals to suffering people, giving them hope that they are not alone in their suffering. It also gives them courage to oppose the dehumanizing situations in life. Moltmann's Christological approach therefore has sociopolitical consequences. Compared to the anthropological approaches to Christology he seems to stress more the divine revelation in Jesus than the revelation of what human is in relation to God.

Liberation Christologies

Liberation Christological reflections developed in the Latin American countries especially after Vatican II. While remaining faithful to the orthodox doctrines about the person and mission of Jesus Christ, the liberation theologians affirmed that a meaningful Christology must pay attention to orthopraxis more than orthodoxy in order to be relevant for a large majority of the poor and the oppressed in Latin America.

Jon Sobrino (1938–) from El Salvador published the English version of his book on Christology, *Christology at the Crossroads*, in 1978; it was originally written in Spanish and published in 1976. He is critical of traditional Christology with its orthodox doctrines, including that of Chalcedon, which are too abstract and do not have any impact on the lives of the people for whose liberation God has become human. According to Sobrino, Jesus is the true liberator, "so long as we remember that it is through Jesus that we

Christographies and Christologies 79

learn what liberation really is and how it is to be achieved."[21] Like other liberation theologians, Sobrino also gives more importance to orthopraxis or right action than to orthodoxy or right belief.

The starting point of Sobrino's Christology is the historical Jesus and his proclamation of the kingdom of God. Both the understanding of the kingdom of God and God himself developed in the course of Jesus's life. He experienced and proclaimed a God of love and less a God of power. Therefore, the same love of God was the source of Jesus's actions. "Historically, Jesus acted out of love and was *for* all human beings. But he was for them in different ways. Out of love for the poor, he took his stand *with* them; out of love for the rich he took his stand against them. In both cases, however, he was interested in something more than retributive justice. He wanted renewal and re-creation."[22] For Sobrino, the incarnation of God in a sinful world that opposes God is the beginning of the way of the cross. The cross is the outcome of Jesus's historical stand against the systems and structures of injustice and oppression, and it reveals a God who suffers because he is love. The resurrection is the vindication of Jesus's life and the expression of the power of love. Jesus Christ is, therefore, the embodiment of God's liberating love, and following him means to stand for the values of the kingdom and in solidarity with him and with the power of his Spirit to transform the world. So authentic Christology leads to orthopraxy.

Leonardo Boff (1938–) is from Brazil. He uses the title "liberator" for Jesus and titled his book on Christology *Jesus Christ Liberator: A Critical Christology of Our Time,* originally published in Portuguese in 1972. Boff begins his Christological reflections with the life and mission of the historical Jesus as Sobrino

---

[21] Jon Sobrino, *Christology at the Crossroads: A Latin American Approach* (Maryknoll, NY: Orbis Books, 1978), 379.

[22] Sobrino, *Christology at the Crossroads,* 370.

80   *Christ without Borders*

does. According to Boff, "The historical Jesus puts us in direct contact with his liberative program and the practices with which he implements it."[23] The liberation Jesus proclaimed is integral. It is a program of liberation *from* all types of bondage and the liberation *for* the kingdom of God. Marxist social analysis can assist in discerning the factors that create injustice and oppression, which hinder the way of human fulfillment. These factors include social, economic, political, and ideological structures and systems. The liberation from these enslaving structures alone would not be sufficient for the fullness of liberation or salvation that Jesus proclaimed and effected through his life, death, and resurrection, but it includes also the liberation from the oppressive and sinful structures. Boff says, "The salvation proclaimed by Christianity is an all-embracing one. It is not restricted to economic, political, social, and ideological emancipation, but neither can it be realized without them."[24] Boff admits that there is no direct proclamation about the program of socioeconomic and political emancipation in the teachings of Jesus, but his stand against "principalities and powers" and his eventual death by condemnation by those in power indicate that Jesus proclaimed a liberation that is integral or holistic.

Sebastian Kappen, SJ (1924–1993), committed to the person and the mission of Jesus, argued that the authentic Jesus tradition must enter into dialogue with the genuinely original forces of self-transcendence within the religious and cultural traditions of India for an integral liberation of everyone and the cosmos. He develops his Christological reflections in his book *Jesus and Freedom*.[25]

The picture of Jesus that we have from the Gospels is as the one who rejected all forms of political and economic power that

---

[23] Leonardo Boff, *Jesus Christ Liberator: A Critical Christology for Our Time* (Maryknoll, NY: Orbis Books, 1978), 279.

[24] Boff, *Jesus Christ Liberator*, 275.

[25] Sebastian Kappen, *Jesus and Freedom* (Maryknoll, NY: Orbis Books, 1977).

Christographies and Christologies   81

would dehumanize humans. He began a movement of liberation with the powerless poor and the marginalized of Palestine. It is the historical Jesus who can perform the prophetic function that can liberate India from its antihuman structures and systems. But Jesus as proclaimed in India was made to fit into this cosmic religiosity. Therefore, Kappen's plea is to set free the prophet in Jesus to walk freely on the Indian road to challenge the systems and structures that perpetuate dehumanization and exploitation and unite people of all religions and ideologies to work for the unfolding of all humans without excluding anyone, including even the oppressors and exploiters. He was the prophet of a counterculture.

Jesus is the supreme revelation of ethical and prophetic religiosity that has humans as its center. In this religiosity, God experience expresses itself in its concern for humans. The ethical and prophetic religiosity of Jesus is very close to the ethical religiosity of Buddha but also radically different from it. It is not the negation of God or the absolute that brings out the best in humans but surrendering oneself to the absolute, who is the fullness of compassion and love. It is in right relationship with God that humans become truly human and recognize the true humanity of the other. For the God whom Jesus encountered as his loving Father, humans are more important than religion and laws and even Jesus, God's own Self. The God whom Jesus encountered is an anthropocentric God.

The prophetic message of Jesus must enter into dialogue with the Indian religious sense of the oneness of the cosmic, the human, and the Divine of God's dream. Kappen expresses this embodiment of the Divine in Jesus without using the traditional Christological titles like Christ, Messiah, Son of God, Son of Man, and so on. Kappen seems to believe that these titles would alienate Jesus from the realm of history by giving him a mythical self that can be manipulated. So Kappen prefers to express the meaning of the person of Jesus as "the Inspired One," "hitherto unparalleled and unique manifestation of the Divine," the One in whom the human spirit and the Divine Spirit so united to form one flame," "the eternally Other," "the symbol and reality of total negativity," and "the way to wholeness." These descriptions of Jesus, according to Kappen, would reveal the continued presence of Jesus as the Divine in history as the wayfarer and challenge to realize the ultimate hope.

Dalit Christology

A Dalit Christology[26] is being developed in India by those who are oppressed and "broken" (*dalit*) by India's discriminatory and inhuman caste system that condemns millions of Dalits to a life of poverty, misery, and social discrimination. According to James Massey, three elements play an important role in Dalit theology: "the aspiration of Dalits for fuller liberation, the recognition that God is on the side of the Dalits and the conviction that Christ is the model for the struggle, a struggle which continues even today through the Holy Spirit."[27] Among the Dalits about 2.5 million Dalit Christians see Jesus as their liberator, identifying himself with their pains and struggles. According to Monodeep Daniel,

> We see the experience of rejection in Christ. So, the Dalit experience of alienation, of rejection, we see in Christ. For instance, for us, to see the death of Christ and relate it to us as an idea of substitution is very difficult for us. I mean we don't need anybody to die for us. We all die every day. How does the death of Christ substitute our killings every day? It does not relate to us. But solidarity does. Solidarity is salvation for us.[28]

[26] M. R. Arulraja, *Jesus the Dalit* (Secunderabad, India: Jeevan Institute of Printing, 1996).

[27] S. Yesu Suresh Raj and R. Mani, "Jesus Is a Dalit," *International Journal of Research (IJR)* 1, no. 8 (September 2014): 539.

[28] Yesu Suresh Raj and Mani, "Jesus Is a Dalit," 539.

The Dalits recognize that Jesus suffers *with* and not specifically *for* them. James Massey explains further:

> Now, Jesus, who was born in a desperately poor family, spent the whole of his life working for the liberation of the poor and the oppressed. That is why for me, as a Christian, it is a natural expression of my faith commitment to be involved in the movement for Dalit liberation, because Jesus, the person in whom I have put my faith, became for me what I am today—Dalit, oppressed and despised, in order that I and millions of others like me could be liberated. But if Jesus is my source of inspiration, people from other faiths may have their own sources from which they draw their strength, and that is fine by me.[29]

Jesus is believed and encountered as a Dalit who is both the source and example for the Dalits in their liberation struggle to live as dignified humans.

Feminist Christology

The articulation of Christologies from the perspective of women is a critique on traditional Christologies, which are seen to be articulated from the perspective of men who have a patriarchal mindset. The traditional Christologies are accused of interpreting both the biblical revelation and the Christological doctrines in such a way that it supports the domination of men and subjugation of women in the church, which is called to be community of equal discipleship without any gender discrimination.

The main critique is against emphasizing the maleness of Jesus in Christological reflections rather than concentrating on the reality

---

[29] Yoginder Sikand and James Massey, "Dalit Liberation Theology: Interview with James Massey," *Matters India: India's Complete Socioeconomic & Religious News* blog, March 3, 2015.

84 *Christ without Borders*

of God becoming human with its consequences for both men and women and for the entire creation. Feminist biblical scholars like Elisabeth Schüssler Fiorenza (1938–), with her challenging book *In Memory of Her: A Feminist Theological Reconstruction of Christian Origins*, inspired many women theologians to interpret the meaning of Jesus Christ that is liberative and life-promoting for women who suffer various types of oppression and discrimination for the only reason of being women.[30]

Anne Carr (1934–2008), in her book *Transforming Grace: Christian Tradition and Women's Experience*, argues that the classical Chalcedonian Formula speaks only about the divinity and humanity of Christ and not about his maleness. According to her, many women who pray to Christ and pray with Christ experience that the Christ event has been life-giving and liberating for women. But the traditional Christology with its symbols and explanations about Jesus Christ stresses the maleness of Christ and not his humanity, and thus excludes women. As the Church Fathers affirmed, "What was not assumed was not redeemed"; Jesus Christ is the source of redemption for men and women because of their equality as human persons.

The main reason for emphasizing the maleness of Jesus rather than his humanity in the Christological reflections in the past, according to Carr, is the unfortunate influence of the anthropology of Thomas Aquinas. Thomas presumed that the male is the "more noble" sex of the human species and that women are somehow defective as human beings; therefore, God could incarnate only as a male. The male represents the fullness of God's image, and so Jesus's maleness is not just a historical and contingent fact. Headship of society or the church belongs to the male members.[31] This idea of "headship" itself functioned in an oppressive way, though

---

[30] Elisabeth Schüssler Fiorenza, *In Memory of Her: A Feminist Theological Reconstruction of Christian Origins* (New York: Crossroad, 1994).

[31] *Summa Theologiae*, I.q92.a.1 and 2; III.sppl.q39, a.1.

Jesus's headship was exercised by being a sacrificial victim, with self-surrender on the cross and by a servant leadership, according to Carr. The Gospels present Jesus as the one who exhibited remarkable freedom and openness to women and preached an inclusive discipleship. His disciples and friends included Mary Magdalene and others. The first witnesses to his resurrection were women. The New Testament stories provide sufficient indication that women are to be treated as human persons, and as such their equality as persons, must be recognized and affirmed. A Christology from the perspective of women allows women to interpret a meaning of Jesus Christ that is liberative and inclusive.

Elizabeth Johnson (1941–) presents a feminist Christology rooted in the life, ministry, death, and resurrection of Jesus as well as the Wisdom tradition of the Scriptures. The main ideas of her feminist Christology are articulated in her books *Consider Jesus: Waves of Renewal in Christology* (1990) and *She Who Is: The Mystery of God in Feminist Theological Discourse* (1992). According to Johnson, the problem for feminist Christology is the distorted manner in which the maleness of Jesus is interpreted in the traditional Christological discourse and its implication for ecclesial praxis. The official androcentric theology emphasizes the patriarchal image of God; therefore, if Jesus is God, he must be male or there must be some affinity between divinity and maleness. Further, the maleness of Jesus is used to stress the androcentric image of humanity and, consequently, to affirm the superiority of men over women. For Elizabeth Johnson, a feminist Christology can be developed from the attitude and actions of Jesus in relation to women. Jesus's preaching of the kingdom included the proclamation of justice for and peace to all people. He showed preferential option for the marginalized, which included women. Jesus called women to be his disciples, and they stood by him even when his male disciples deserted him at the moments of his agony. He was crucified for the values of the kingdom, which proclaimed especially the equality of all God's children, all men and women who are called to a life of

86 *Christ without Borders*

self-emptying love and compassion. After his resurrection, Jesus was identified as *Sophia*, or Wisdom, "revelatory of the liberating graciousness of God images as female."[32] Therefore, "Women, as friends of Jesus-Sophia, share equally with men in [Christ's] saving mission throughout time and can fully represent Christ."[33] Elizabeth Johnson attempts to reclaim the rightful place of women in society and in the church through her feminist Christology.

Other feminist theologians like Rosemary Radford Ruether and Mary Daly are critical of the traditional Christologies that are developed by emphasizing a patriarchal image of God and the maleness of Jesus based on the androcentric Scholastic and medieval thinking that justified male domination by untenable theological reasoning. Their critique offers new challenges to the development of an inclusive and liberating Christology in our times.

Cosmic Christology

An approach to Christology from the perspective of Jesus's relation to the whole cosmos is primarily Pauline. The cosmic Christ of the Pauline letters to the Ephesians and the Colossians did not develop further, probably due to the fear of pantheism. But the challenges of the scientific theory of evolution to the Christian doctrine of creation and the serious concern for ecological well-being in recent times created a renewed interest in considering Jesus as the cosmic Christ.

It was Pierre Teilhard de Chardin (1881–1955) who initiated the process of reconciling science and religion in a refreshingly new way and contributed greatly to the development of cosmic Christology. According to Teilhard, the process of evolution from elementary particles to complex organisms and finally to

---

[32] Elizabeth Johnson, *She Who Is: The Mystery of God in Feminist Theological Discourse* (New York: Crossroad, 1992), 167.

[33] Johnson, *She Who Is*, 167.

consciousness has its origin and end in Christ. Teilhard asserts that the prodigious expanse of time preceding the birth of Christ was not empty of Christ. He is the alpha and omega point of the process of evolution. The human race as well as the material universe will be finally incorporated into the body of Christ.

Teilhard's Christological approach, rooted in the Pauline cosmic Christology, opens up new possibilities for searching for a meaningful relationship with the material universe as it is also the body of Christ. Pope Francis, in his encyclical *Laudato Si'*, recaptures the Pauline Christological insights about Christ's relationship with the entire creation. Both by the incarnation of the Logos and by Christ's resurrection, the entire creation is positively affected through the humanity of Jesus Christ.[34] It challenges the merely materialistic and consumerist approach to nature, which creates ecological disasters. Further, it can give new insights into ecospirituality.

We have seen that in our times there are many Christographies and Christologies. If Christographies approach Jesus of Nazareth only as a significant human being who existed in history and had a great influence on the history of the word, the Christologies are the articulations of faith in Jesus Christ, who is encountered both as human and divine and as the one who transformed humans and their world through his being and actions. In almost all the modern approaches to Christology, a paradigm shift from the Alexandrine model of Christology stressing the divinity of Christ to the Antiochene model is evident. The stress is on the humanity of the historical Jesus. No modern Christology can avoid the need for asserting the historical reality of Jesus and his real humanity. It is also necessary to have the services of a relevant philosophy to make an intellectually well-founded statement about the person of Jesus Christ.

---

[34] Pope Francis, *Encyclical Letter* Laudato Si' *of the Holy Father Francis: On Care for Our Common Home* (Vatican City: Liberia Editrice Vaticana, 2015), no. 99.

The most important challenge to Christology today, whether in the West or in the East, is to rediscover the meaning of the person of Jesus Christ and the salvation offered by him in the context of the claims of other saviors and mediators of religions and in the context of secularization. Further, the challenge is to see the complementarities of the various approaches to Christology to unfold the mystery of the person of Jesus Christ, who reveals not only who God is, who humans are, and what the world is but also what their unique relationship to one another is.

5

The Challenge to Discover Christ within Cultures

What has Christ to do with cultures? A participant in a seminar on inculturation raised this question. Though the query evoked a mixed reaction among the rest of the participants, the questioner was earnest. Obviously, some thought it was a naïve matter. The questioner explained that whatever he believed about Christ had nothing to do with culture. Jesus Christ was above all cultures. God chose to be born in history, so it had to be in one culture and among a particular group of people with their own traditions, social structures, ethnicity, religious belief systems, attitudes, behavior, lifestyle, food habits, and a way of social relationships and interactions. Of course, Jesus was born in a culture as all of us are. There is nothing more or nothing less to it. Each culture is unique, and we need not bother about such trivial matters. If anything at all is needed, it is liberating Jesus from the trapping of the Jewish culture so that he can remain universal as the Son of God. In fact, the dogmas and doctrines about him have done so. We need not inculturate him in any culture and relativize him. These were the main points of the explanation given by the one who thought that it was a futile exercise to discuss Christ's relation to cultures. However, what the questioner himself failed to recognize was that even the term "Christ" itself is a religio-cultural construct.

We can make an attempt to view Jesus Christ as a part of human culture, whatever its diversity of expressions, distinct from the reality of culture but not separate from it. Culture makes the inner world and worldview of a person in which she or he lives and finds her or his identity in the family and in society, with a language that helps the relationship with others through a system of symbols. Our contention is that Jesus Christ is not exclusively above, against, or of the cultures. He is not a paradox in relation to cultures or a transformer of cultures in the strict sense. He is *within* the cultures. No one can separate authentic human culture from him. With him culture is already transformed. Therefore, the mission of those who believe in him is to discover the transformation he brought about in the culture by his becoming a part of it and to actualize it so that both humans and their world will become what they are called to become and find their destiny.

Christ's Relation to Cultures

In his book *Christ and Culture*, H. Richard Niebuhr attempted to explain the relationship between Christ and culture from the perspective of a Lutheran theologian. In his approach he sees Christ in a double relationship. In his vertical relationship, Christ is in relation with his Father and his whole life is oriented toward him. Christ is primarily theocentric. At the same time, in his horizontal relationship, he is also anthropocentric. In this horizontal dimension of his relationship, culture plays a role. There is not much difference between culture and "the world" mentioned in the New Testament, so what would be his relationship with cultures? Niebuhr suggests five ways of looking at the relationship between Christ and culture that are found in history. They are not mutually exclusive. In a way they are complementary.

Christ against Culture

In its radical form the followers of this understanding of the relationship between Christ and culture would argue that Christians should make a choice between Christ or culture. Both are incompatible. The culture stands for everything that is anti-Christ and anti-Christian. Therefore, there should not be any compromise with the culture in which one lives. Those who subscribe to this view would find a basis for their argument in some passages in the NT. In the First Letter of John, the followers of Christ are exhorted to shun this world of lies and lust, murder and theft, and all kinds of evil (2:8–9, 11, 15, 17; 3:8–11; 5:4–5, 19). This negative attitude toward everything in culture denies the possibility of anything good in culture. It is possible that those who see Christ as against culture have a disincarnated Christ in their faith system, and they find that commitment to him means that it is necessary to disengage oneself from culture. Such an understanding in the final analysis is self-contradictory because culture is the way one is and thinks. One cannot dissociate even the most sublime faith in God from culture. What one can hold is to negate the values and attitudes that seem to be a part of the culture and would not be seen as compatible with one's belief in God revealed through Jesus Christ in a particular culture.

Christ *against* culture is the paradigm of radical following by Desert Fathers, ascetics, and radical monastic orders. Even here, an extreme denial of genuine culture is not envisaged. The allurements of the world and world as a principle opposed to God would be the world that is ungodly and not the world that manifests the presence of God. So too a culture that does not have any relation to the transcendence and has no relation to those values that are beyond the transitory and ephemeral would be the culture that is often seen as opposed to faith in Christ. Tertullian was the first one to develop a negative idea about culture in his books *Apology* and *On Idolatry*. In Protestantism, there are sectarian groups like

92   *Christ without Borders*

Mennonites and Quakers who developed a terribly negative attitude toward culture. They see that faith in Christ is incompatible with recognizing culture as a value.

The *countercultural movements* are often seen as falling into this paradigm of relationship between Christ and culture. But in fact, countercultural attitudes and movements do not fall into this category. It is not against culture as such but against a perversion of culture that creates oppressive structures and systems, dehumanizes humans, and alienates humans from their authentic selves. Counterculture is also culture, albeit a culture opposed to the perversion of culture.

In the missionary enterprises of colonial times, the Asian religions and cultures were seen as opposed to Christian culture and values. Therefore, they were seen as opposed to Christ. The Christ-*against*-culture model was the force behind the legendary missionary zeal of thousands of missionaries from the West. Here again Christ was seen as one who is against particular cultures that were considered steeped in idolatry, superstition, and ungodliness and under the power of Satan and not culture per se. Therefore, Christ *against* culture is an ambivalent model of relationship between Christ and cultures. On the one hand, it cannot be against culture as such while it uses everything positive in the culture to articulate its own position, and on the other hand, it cannot deny the fact that God has become human in a culture and transformed it to be something different from what it was. At best it can be the affirmation of the dominion of Christ over everything and a rejection of everything in culture that is not Christic.

The Christ of Culture

This model of relationship between Christ and culture is seen as the opposite of Christ-against-culture. Christ is understood as the fulfillment of culture, so there is no conflict between Christ and culture. Culture can be interpreted through Christ,

The Challenge to Discover Christ within Cultures   93

and Christ can be interpreted through culture. This approach is often seen as accommodationist as the attempt here is to reconcile Christianity with divergent cultures and the best in all cultures. In the early church, the Judaizers, the Gnostics, and the Hellenists attempted to interpret Christ from their particular cultures and religious and philosophical perspectives.[1] Niebuhr sees in this model of relationship between Christ and culture an error equal to and opposite of the first position. In this understanding of concentration on the world, Christ's relationship with the world is emphasized at the cost of Christ's transcendental or vertical relationship. Without an emphasis on grace or afterlife, religion degenerates into legalistic "self-reliant humanism" and idolatrous worship of humans and denigration of God.[2] This is considered by Lutheran theology as an accommodation of the world by which both the horizontal relationship of humans with the world as well as the vertical relationship with God are distorted.

There are many who oppose this model of relationship between Christ and culture. They find that it would compromise with the Lordship of Christ when he is so much part of the culture. If Christ is of culture, then how would one explain the presence of sin, oppression, injustice, discrimination, and all kinds of evil in all cultures? Therefore, this model would not be the right relation of Christ to culture. However, those who would hold the Christ-of-culture view find it the best way to express the right relationship of humans among themselves as well as the kingdom of God realized in the right relationship among humans as the children of God in this world. In the context of Asia, the Christ of religions cannot be a relevant model of relationship between Christ

---

[1] See Robert Benne, *The Paradoxical Vision: A Public Theology for the Twenty-First Century* (Minneapolis: Fortress, 1995), 26–44.

[2] H. Richard Niebuhr, *Christ and Culture* (New York: First Harper Torch Book, 1956), 113.

94 *Christ without Borders*

and culture, according to Aloysius Pieris.[3] Christ of the culture is based on the fact that God became human and entered into human culture and became very much a part of it.

Christ above Culture

This model of relationship between Christ and culture is also based on his incarnation. Jesus Christ is both human and divine. As a human, he is *of* the culture, but as God he is *above* culture. That Christ was God overtakes the human dimension of Christ, and both cannot be equated. The emphasis is on the divine dimension of Christ. Therefore, though Christ is very much a part of the culture, he is infinitely above culture. Justin Martyr and Clement of Alexandria could be considered the patristic representatives of this model. In the Middle Ages, Thomas Aquinas and the Catholic theological tradition in general held this view of Christ's relation to culture.[4] This approach seems to synthesize the various opposing approaches. It is based on the incarnation of God in a particular culture. However, if this culture is elevated to a position of Christian culture and if it is made universal, it can lead to a cultural hegemony that can stand against or even suppress other cultures. In fact, there are many tragic instances of such an approach to diverse cultures in history.

One of the other dangers of this approach is that it does not take the grace-filled world that was created and re-created by the incarnation of the Word seriously, although it claims to do so. It is the consequence of a faith affirmation in Christ bordering on Docetism. Throughout the history of Christological development,

---

[3] Aloysius Pieris, "Towards an Asian Theology of Liberation: Some Religio-Cultural Guidelines," in *Asia's Struggle for Full Humanity,* Virginia Fabella, ed. (Maryknoll, NY: Orbis Books, 1980), 75–95.

[4] Richard P. McBrien, *Catholicism* (San Francisco: HarperSanFrancisco, 1994), 409.

what the church wanted to overcome was the heresy of Docetism that Christ is not human but only appears to be so. As an offshoot of Gnosticism, with its dualistic philosophy that matter is evil and spirit is good, true incarnation was thought to be impossible. For Docetists, while Jesus Christ is truly divine, he cannot be truly human.

Ignatius of Antioch and Irenaeus fought such heresy, and in the Council of Chalcedon (451 CE) affirmed the church's faith that Jesus Christ is truly God and truly human. However, even today it is difficult for many Christians to believe that Jesus was truly human like anyone of them. It is easy to believe that he is God. In this context, Christ *above* culture would appear to many as Christ has nothing to do with any culture. Such an image of Christ disengaged from any culture makes him universal, and people of any culture could relate to him as the transcendent God. So the fears expressed by those who are not in favor of this approach— that the traditional synthesis achieved by this model does not take into consideration all that is evil and sinful in cultures—become unfounded. Christ can be thought of as truly above all cultures. Though it seems to be a synthesis, in effect, in this model Christ has nothing to do with the cultures.

Christ and Culture

Beginning with Paul there is a certain dualistic understanding of the relationship between Christ and culture. In fact, in this model it is not a relationship between Christ and culture but how a believer relates herself or himself with Christ and culture. The relationship with Christ is permanent, everlasting, and grace-filled, while with the world it is temporal, transitory, and filled with God's wrath and severity. This relationship is expressed by Paul as our relation to the "earthly tent" and "a building from God, a house not made with hands, eternally in the heavens" (2 Cor 5:1–2). Augustine would develop this theme further, contrasting the earthly city with the heavenly city or the city of God. In Luther's view there are two kingdoms: the kingdom of God and the kingdom of the world. The first one is of grace and mercy, and the second one is of God's wrath and severity. The Christian existence is between these two kingdoms until the end when there would be only one kingdom that is the kingdom of God.

The dualistic understanding of Christ and culture has its consequences for Christian commitment to transform this world. It recognizes the evils in the culture. Sin pervades culture. Injustice, dehumanization, discrimination, oppression, exploitation, greed, and violence rule cultures and societies. New cultures are created that would further all kinds of negative values that would destroy the lives of humans and nature. Still, a Christian can live a life without any commitment to this world and take a position of isolating oneself from this world and believe that with the grace of God she or he can remain uncontaminated by this world. Laws, regulations, duties, and so on can be understood as necessary evils one must bear for a short time. As everything in this world is transitory, one need not make any commitment to this world or its destiny.

The dualistic model of relationship between Christ and culture reduces the meaning of God's creation as something good enough that God freely chose it to be a part of God himself through incarnation or hominization. A dualistic attitude to Christ and culture reduces Christ as the one who is above, separate, and isolated from culture and negates the value of culture as something good and as an inalienable dimension of being human. Any dualism between absolute and relative, infinite and finite, God and world, or Christ and culture negates the possibility of God becoming human and thus denies this basic Christian belief.

Christ Transforming Culture

This model of relationship between Christ and culture claims to be based on the participation of the Logos in creation as well as in the incarnation. God created everything through his Word, and it

The Challenge to Discover Christ within Cultures 97

is the same Word: the Son who became human and redeemed the world. Therefore, the Logos transformed the world (John 3:16–18). It is said that in the sacramental vision of John, the ordinary things are transformed into symbols that would be instruments of God's presence in this world, as in the case of the sacrament of the Eucharist and baptism.[5]

In this model it is admitted that the Word became a part of the world, but his function to transform the world would be as if it were from outside of the world. He does not seem to enter into the reality of the world, into its cultures and history. Certainly, in this model, Christ transforms and reorients cultures through his sanctifying and redeeming presence. According to Augustine, though originally everything that God created was good, it was vitiated, corrupted, lost, and dead by sin. Therefore, Christ heals and renews what was perverted by sin. Since God is at work in creation and history, culture and institutions of culture have a positive value, but it needs to be constantly converted to the kingdom of God.

All these models of Christ's relation to culture emphasize one or another aspect of this relationship. If they are seen as mutually exclusive, it would not do justice to the biblical understanding of God's involvement in our history. Though culture is built on nature, if that nature is viewed completely in a negative light, any culture that evolves from the nature of humans will also be something completely perverted and evil. Christ cannot relate to that culture. A terribly negative anthropology would give only a superficial recognition of even what is good and positive in any culture. But if we take the biblical witness seriously, we can see that culture is an extension of the life of humans as humans in the givenness of a particular place with its accumulation of human experiences preserved, transmitted, and lived in history. It is the "world" of humans in which they live, move, and have their being in their

---

[5] McBrien, *Catholicism*, 411.

98 *Christ without Borders*

historical existence. It is through the cultural paradigms they relate with one another and even with the ultimate reality whom they call God or by any name, knowing fully well that this ultimate is beyond name and form. So as humans cannot be separated from the culture in which they are born and have grown, the Word became human also cannot be separated from culture.

Christ within Cultures

If culture is the sum total of everything that gives meaning to a person's existence in history or if it is broadly described as a *way of life*, as Michael Amaladoss expresses it, human beings cannot be separated from it.[6] Through culture, people find their fundamental identification in relation to a family, society, language, ethnic group, or religion. Though one may be able to make abstractions about human nature, a human person can be thought of only in a network of relationships. It is in a conscious and free relationship with other human persons—and with the reality of the world and the ultimate source of everything—that one finds one's identity as a human person. In a way, it is culture that mediates and qualifies relationships. Authentic culture is everything that gives meaning to one's existence as a human person. For a great majority of humans, religion provides a meaning system in which people can discover their beginning and end, or origin and ultimate destiny. No wonder, then, that sociologists and anthropologists include religion in their definition of culture. If culture is such an all-encompassing dimension of humans to be human, then it must be assumed by the Word that everything authentic and true in it must become Christic.

If what we mean by culture is everything that makes human life unfold itself as humans intended by God, Christ can never

---

[6] Michael Amaladoss, *Making Harmony: Living in a Pluralist World* (Delhi: ISPCK, 2003), 63. See also Amaladoss, *Beyond Inculturation: Can the Many Be One?* (Delhi: ISPCK, 1998).

be against, above, or paradoxical to culture. Christ is then really *of* culture or *within* the reality of culture. What is authentic in the culture is Christic. It is Christ who is the beginning and end, the alpha and the omega of authentic culture.

Humans are the ones who develop culture with the evolution of their self-understanding as humans or pervert it to a dehumanizing culture depending on how they use or misuse their freedom. Humans transform culture either for better or for worse. Authentic culture continues to evolve in history at different places and different times according to the self-understanding of humans as humans. Multiculturalism, migration, and shared knowledge open ways of new self-understanding and development of humans, and consequently cultures will also develop progressively.

Christ is *within* cultures because it is in and through him that culture will progress not for its own sake but to make humans evolve into the "full stature of Christ," as Paul puts it. Humans become "mature, attaining to the whole measure of the fullness of Christ" (Eph 4:13). From the perspective of Christian faith, to become human like Christ is the goal of human existence. In authentic culture, humans can reach this destiny, so Christ is not only an exemplar for the development of culture. Christ's power, working through his Spirit, gives dynamism to the evolution of culture as well as the standard by which to judge the authenticity of culture.

In this sense, Christ is really of culture, but not in the way that Niebuhr and others with a selective understanding of culture perceive it. Christ's presence in the culture is seen as related only to a specific culture. This selective application of Christ's presence in the culture of one's choice—limiting Christ to that particular culture—is to make an idol of Christ. This was the problem of Judaizers or Gnostics. It would also be a problem if Christ is reduced exclusively to be a Brahmin Christ, a Dalit Christ, or a tribal Christ.

Christ *within* the culture means that it is Christ who is the inner dimension of everything that is humanizing in every culture but not of anything that is divisive, discriminatory, and exploitative—

100 *Christ without Borders*

and, in fact, dehumanizing in any culture. The specificity and uniqueness of any culture, not its opposition to the other culture, has the capacity to promote the development of humans, opening new vistas for the enhancement of human capacity to become increasingly human and its possibility or relating with other cultures.

Christ and Culture:
Nondualistic Relationship

If we take the incarnation and resurrection of Christ seriously, we must admit that, in God's entrance into history and God's involvement in the movement of the world to its final destiny, Christ has assumed everything that is human except that which negates the unfolding of humans as humans. According to Origen, whatever is to be redeemed must be assumed. God assumes human nature and culture. God's relation to human history and culture would have been different from what it was before the incarnation. However, God was not far from everything human, according to the Church Fathers. For Irenaeus, God created everything with his two hands—namely, Logos and Pneuma, the Word and the Spirit. God has created everything for perfection, and therefore there is an inner dynamism in humans and the entire creation to reach its God-intended perfection. The incarnation itself is for the purpose of leading creation to its perfection, which will finally be "recapitulated" by Christ and returned to the Father. Athanasius would develop the theology of Logos present in the creation as distinct from creation but not separated from it. "In one sense indeed, He was not far from it before; no part of creation had ever been without Him who, while ever abiding in union with the Father, yet fills all things that are. But now He entered the world in a new way, stooping to our level in His love and Self-revealing to us."[7]

---

[7] Athanasius, "The Divine Dilemma and Its Solution in the Incarnation," in *On the Incarnation of the Word* 8.

Further, Athanasius says, "You know how it is when some great king enters a large city and dwells in one of its houses; because of his dwelling in that single house, the whole city is honored, and enemies and robbers cease to molest it. Even so is it with the King of all; He has come into our country and dwelt in one body amidst the many, and in consequence the designs of the enemy against humankind have been foiled and the corruption of death, which formerly held them in its power, has simply ceased to be."[8]

By incarnation, God's relation to the world is revealed as nondualistic. The Word, though distinct from the world, is not separate from the world. As human, the Word assumed everything that makes a human a human. Therefore, the assumption of culture also cannot be separated from the reality of being human. Certainly, the cultural dimension of his humanity was expressed in a definite and historical Jewish culture. Culture cannot be separated from its expression. By being a part of the Jewish culture, Christ is related to every culture. Being in a "single house," as Athanasius would affirm, Christ affects every house. By being in one culture Christ is present in every culture. He is the heart of every culture that provides the "world" for every human to relate with everyone and everything in such a way that she or he evolves into an authentic human being.

Negation of Culture and Christ

A question can be raised about the presence of evil and sin, ungodliness and inhuman values in every culture. What about the culture of greed, war, and violence? How can Christ be related to these so-called cultures of inhumanity and cruelty? How can one justify the perverse presence of discrimination in the name of caste, class, gender, ethnicity, and so on? Is it not the absence

---

[8] Athanasius, "The Divine Dilemma and Its Solution in the Incarnation," 9.

of Christ that one finds in such human attitudes and behavior? Is it not a naïve understanding of culture to see Christ within the cultures when we look at only what is true, good, and beautiful in cultures and ignore their cruel aspects?

It must be admitted that all cultures contain systems and structures of injustice, oppression, and inhumanity. Some humans in cultures develop attitudes and create systems and structures in order to amass wealth, power, and position at the cost of other humans. They would go to any extent of dehumanizing themselves to achieve their evil ends. No culture is free from such persons, who become a law unto themselves by alienating themselves from God, who is the ultimate source of everything; from their own true selves; and from other humans and nature. Everybody and everything become a means for them to exploit to reach their goals. Blinded by their own greed and selfishness, they would not be able to see the road of destruction they are treading and the suffering they cause to God, other humans, and the world. Therefore, the perverse behavior of humans misusing their freedom cannot be considered culture. In every culture, we find such humans who misuse their freedom and negate culture and Christ. The term "culture" cannot be used for any expression of humans' inhumanity to humans through personal agenda, systems, or structures that destroy humans or thwart the innate dynamism of humans to evolve to fullness of humanity.

Discovering Christ within Cultures

The Logos theology of John and the theology of the cosmic Christ in Paul affirm that the reality of Christ encompasses everything that is human and cosmic. If everything is created in him, through him, and for him, and everything is glorified through his resurrection, Christ's presence in all cultures through his Spirit needs to be constantly discovered by the believer. Therefore, one must reverently delve deep into one's own culture as well as enter into the depths of cultures other than one's own. If God has become human in order to reveal what humans are and what they can become, according to God's plan for humans, then the humanizing forces of cultures must be discovered and promoted. This is possible only through genuine dialogue among people of diverse cultures sharing their riches so that the further evolution of humans is made possible through integration of them in their lives.

If anything authentically human is Christic, discovering the humanizing elements in every culture is, in fact, discovering that dimension of Christ hidden from those who had no previous experience of that particular culture. Thus, authentic culture becomes a means of revelation not only of God's diverse presence but also the possibilities of humans to unfold themselves. The riches of every culture thus reveal the goodness of God that gifted such a variety of gifts through humans for humans to become what they are called to become. Christ has already transformed culture. It is the mission of the disciple to discover the transformation that Christ has brought about through his presence in the culture and proclaim it so that it becomes a challenge for humans to accept it for their transformation as better human beings.

It is only through a contemplative attitude toward cultures that one will be able to discover the presence of Christ within cultures. As humans and their culture are in a nondualistic relationship, Christ too is in a nondualistic relationship with cultures. What is authentic in all cultures is a manifestation of his person because nothing is humanizing outside the reality of Christ. Precisely because of his presence in the culture, everything that is dehumanizing and everything that is a perversion of authentic culture must be prophetically denounced. Those structures and systems that dehumanize humans or individual attitudes, behavior, or misuse of power and positions that hinder authentic human relationships need to be opposed with the strength of human spirit for the sake of Christ and culture. In truth, authentic culture would express the presence of Christ and bring people to live in harmony, peace, and communion. Thus, culture becomes the temple of God. It needs true freedom, openness, and an attitude of reverence to discover him in culture and a plurality of its expressions.

A narrow vision of Christ and culture would find both Christ and culture as opposed to each other or Christ above cultures. Culture is permeated by the presence of Christ, as everything is created in him and through him and for him. So the relationship between Christ and culture is neither dualistic nor paradoxical. It is nondualistic in the sense that Christ cannot be separated from culture even though it cannot be identified with him. Everything authentic in culture is Christic. Whatever is negative and dehumanizing, whether systems or structures of injustice, oppression, and dehumanization, whether it is social, religious, or political, is not authentically cultural. They cannot be considered as elements of culture but as misuse of freedom by humans who alienate themselves from their ultimate source of life, themselves, others, and their world. This has to be prophetically denounced. Christ is *within* the culture, and through the dynamic power of his Spirit he makes culture as a means to cultivate human spirit to move to higher levels of being human and thus become the glory of God. God's plan for humans—begun at creation through his Word and further deepened by incarnation and transformed through resurrection—becomes expressed in varied ways through all authentic elements of culture. Therefore, authentic culture becomes a sacrament of Christic presence and means of communion among humans.

6

The Different Christologies of Asia

In the multiverse of Asia, Jesus has many faces. Each culture or nation of Asia develops its own Christology. Though Jesus Christ is one, Asian Christologies are many. The church articulated "who Jesus Christ is" in dialogue with Judaism and the Greco-Roman world. Such a finished Christology with its ready-made Christ image did not make much impact on the peoples of Asia for the last twenty centuries because Asian people have different cultures and worldviews that cannot understand the "language" of Christian proclamation. Moreover, the religions of Asia claim to have their own mediators and saviors who seemed to have shown them the ways of salvation. They might find "Christ an exotic figure more or less appealing, or a suspicious construct associated with the conquering and invading foreigners."[1]

"What do you have to do with us, Jesus of Nazareth?"

Does Jesus Christ offer anything new to the poor of Asia that the religions of Asia cannot give? Is he just another apocalyptic visionary or a true prophetic missionary? How does Jesus Christ,

---

[1] Raimon Panikkar, "A Christophany for Our Times," the Thirty-Fifth Annual Robert Cardinal Bellarmine Lecture, *Theology Digest* 39, no. 1 (1992): 4.

106   *Christ without Borders*

as the self-emptying of God, respond to the situation of suffering in the Asian context, whatever the cause of suffering? Is Jesus Christ just another God competing for supremacy with a myriad of gods and goddesses of the Asian continent? Is he not the God of the colonizers? Can Jesus address the quest for ultimate liberation and the questions of poverty? "Is he an Oriental Pantocrator? A Western divine prophet? The private God of the Christians? The Universal Savior? A Man for others?"[2] The mystery of Christ cannot be limited to any titles or any particular function of Christ. However, the figure of Christ that is encountered, lived, and interpreted in any cultural, religious, social, political, and economic context makes him the liberative force against all types of alienation.

The fundamental Christian kerygma is that Jesus Christ is Lord and Savior. But the question is how to proclaim this kerygma meaningfully in the Asian context. Jesus in Asia has many faces. His presence is "known" or "unknown" in the religious traditions of Asia as well as among the poor as the liberator of the poor and the oppressed in their socioeconomic, political situation of dehumanization and marginalization.

A variety of the Asian faces of Jesus emerged from the struggle of the Christian believers in articulating their faith experience in dialogue with the religious and cultural traditions of Asia in order to proclaim him in a meaningful way to their listeners. They were convinced of the fact that Jesus Christ would not make much impact on the lives of the people of Asia, and his good news of liberation and wholeness would be lost on them if they were presented with the traditional image of Jesus Christ articulated in another culture and historical context that have very little in common with the Asian context. Moreover, the experience of colonialism had blurred their vision of Christ as some of them identified Jesus Christ with the

---

[2] Panikkar, "A Christophany for Our Times," 4.

The Different Christologies of Asia   107

God of the colonizers. In spite of such negative responses to Jesus he had such a powerful impact on some educated people of other religions in Asia that they interpreted Jesus Christ and his message using the categories and images drawn from their religious, cultural, and philosophical traditions.

Chinese and the Other East Asian Faces of Christ

In describing the various faces of Jesus in Asia we can begin with the various Christologies that have emerged in the Chinese context—not only because of the vastness of the country of China, with a population of more than 1.2 billion people, but also because the earliest attempts at interpreting Jesus Christ in Asia began in China. Before the arrival of Jesuits in 1582 CE, the East Syrian missionaries (the Nestorian missionary movement) had reached China already in 635 and the Franciscan John of Montecorvino in 1294. Their proclamation of Christ was to some extent successful, as they could establish Christian communities in China. But both the East Syrian church and Roman Catholicism in China disappeared with the founding of the Ming dynasty in 1368, which systematically "purified" the Chinese culture by removing all foreign elements. Two centuries later the Jesuits had to begin again trying to interpret Christ in a way meaningful to the Chinese people.

Jesus, the Bodhisattva

In dialogue with Buddhism, the Nestorian missionary Alopen, one of the first missionaries to arrive in 635, interpreted the soteriological function of Jesus Christ in terms of the selfless service of the Bodhisattvas to humanity. A bodhisattva is a person who has reached the stage of attaining nirvana but postpones it in order to serve human beings. Alopen made use of the story of Avalokitesvara, a male Bodhisattva who puts on a female form to serve the people, to explain the life and mission

108   *Christ without Borders*

of Jesus. The Chinese called Avalokitesvara in his female form Guan Yin, the goddess of mercy. Alopen explained that God becoming human in Jesus Christ in order to save humans was similar to the self-sacrificing action of Bodhisattva Avalokitesvara. "Four Chinese Christian treatises—the first entitled *Jesus-Messiah Sutra* and the other three grouped under the title *Discourses on Monotheism*—appear to have been written in the seventh century, possibly by Alopen," Bevans and Schroeder note.[3] Jesus is the Bodhisattva par excellence. In Sri Lanka, similar Christologies are emerging today in dialogue with Buddhism.

Jesus, the Greatest Teacher

In the sixteenth century, Matteo Ricci and his Jesuit companions found it extremely difficult to communicate the traditional understanding of the person and mission of Jesus to the Chinese people because their worldview was totally influenced by Confucianism for more than two millennia. Christ's incarnation, death, and resurrection would not make any sense in this worldview. The idea of crucifixion was abhorrent to any follower of Confucianism. At first, for pedagogical reasons, Ricci and companions did not introduce the passion and death of Jesus. They tried to present Jesus as the Greatest Teacher in the tradition of Confucius.

In his attempt to prepare the minds of the people to understand the mystery of Christ, Ricci interpreted the Confucian understanding of the Supreme "Lord of Heaven" from a Christian perspective. In his book *The True Meaning of the Lord of Heaven* (*Tianzhu shiyi*), Ricci explained that the Lord of heaven acted with great compassion and descended into this world to save it and experienced everything. In the second year after Emperor Ai of the Han dynasty adopted the

---

[3] Stephen B. Bevans and Roger P. Schroeder, *Constants in Context: A Theology of Mission for Today* (Maryknoll, NY: Orbis Books, 2004), 105.

title Youan-shou, on the third day following the winter solstice, the Lord of Heaven selected a virgin to be His mother and became incarnate and was born. "His name was Jesus, the meaning of which is 'one who saves the world.' He established his teachings and taught ... in the West. He then reascended into Heaven. These were the concrete actions of the Lord of Heaven."[4]

In his *Introduction to the Incarnation of the Lord of Heaven*,[5] the first Chinese text completely devoted to Christology,[6] Giulio Aleni explained the meaning of incarnation and its relation to the passion, death, and resurrection of Jesus. It was impossible for the Chinese to understand why God had to suffer. But Aleni tried to make them understand the meaning of Jesus's suffering and death in terms of the voluntary self-offering of Cheng Tang, the first emperor of the Shang dynasty who allowed himself to be sacrificed to propitiate the Lord of heaven in order to save his people from famine. For Aleni, the emperor Cheng Tang prefigured Jesus Christ, the greatest teacher who offered himself to the Lord of heaven to save human beings. However, Aleni's explanation about the incarnation, passion, and death of Jesus as the son of the Lord of heaven remained unconvincing for the Chinese people because the Lord of heaven could never become human or live or die in human history. It was possible for them to accept Jesus as a great teacher like Confucius.

---

[4] Jonathan Tan Yun-Ka, "Jesus, the Crucified and Risen Sage," in *Asian Faces of Christ: OTC Theological Colloquium, Archdiocesan Pastoral Centre, Sampran, Thailand, May 11–15, 2004* (Bangalore: ATC, 2005), 84. For a critical translation, see Matteo Ricci, *The True Meaning of the Lord of Heaven (Tien-chu Shih-i)*, Douglas Lancashire and Peter Hu Kuo-chen, trans., Edward J. Malatesta, ed. (St. Louis: Institute of Jesuit Sources, 1985), para. 580.

[5] *Biblioteca Apostolica Vaticana* (BAV), Borgia Cinese 324(5)b.

[6] Aristotle Dy, "Towards a Chinese Christology: Inculturation and Christology in the Chinese Context," *Landas* 15, no. 2 (2001): 56.

110 *Christ without Borders*

Jesus, the Crucified and Risen Sage

In the Confucian world of East Asia—namely, China, Taiwan, Hong Kong, Korea, Japan, and Vietnam—according to Jonathan Tan Yun-ka, a Christology that presents Jesus as the ideal sage, crucified and risen, is meaningful.[7] Different from the Western-Greek approach in seeking truth, the Sinic-Confucian approach is seeking the Way. In this context a "Confucian Christology" is relevant as it attempts to discover the "Way" (*Dao*) of Jesus, the sage (*sheng*). The sage, according to Confucius, is "an example both of *something,* as an embodiment of the Way of Heaven, and an example to *someone,* as a model for emulation."[8] The sage is the fullness of human perfection. The six attributes of a sage according to Mencius are true, good, beautiful, holy, great, and divine.[9] All the attributes of a perfect sage are found in Jesus in their fullness. However, Jesus is more than a perfect sage. Jonathan Tan Yun-ka affirms that the death and resurrection of Jesus the sage make him unique. According to him, the peoples of East Asia would answer Jesus's question "Who do you say that I am?" in the following or similar words:

> You are the sage, the son of the Lord of Heaven who embodies perfect humanity and divinity, discerning and proclaiming to us the nearness of the Way of the Lord of Heaven, showing us by your life, suffering and death on the cross what this Way of the Lord of Heaven

---

[7] Tan Yun-Ka, "Jesus, the Crucified and Risen Sage," 49–87.

[8] Rodney Leon Taylor, *The Religious Dimensions of Confucianism* (Albany: State University of New York Press, 1990), 41, cited by Jonathan Tan Yun-ka, "Jesus, the Crucified and Risen Sage," 73.

[9] M. Fang, "Jesus, the Crucified and Risen Sage: Towards a Confucian Christology—Response," in *Asian Faces of Christ: OTC Theological Colloquium, Archdiocesan Pastoral Centre, Sampran, Thailand, May 11–15, 2004* (Bangalore: ATC, 2005), 108.

entails, and inviting us to imitate you and your preferential option for the poor and the marginalized by joining you in embracing and walking along this Way from its beginning to the end.[10]

Jesus, the Yin and Yang

In the context of Taoism, which has a tremendous influence on the life and culture of the people of the East Asian countries, Jung Young Lee, a Korean theologian, interprets the person and message of Jesus using the symbolism of yin and yang. Originally, yin symbolized shadow and yang brightness. Eventually, yin came to mean female, receptive, passive, or cold, and yang to mean male, creative, active, or warm. In the final analysis, everything that exists can be understood as an interplay between yin and yang. Underlying epistemological principle behind the symbolism is the principle of identity or noncontradiction. Therefore, the emphasis is on the *both/and* category of thinking which characterizes Eastern thinking, and not on *either/or*, which characterizes Western thinking. According to Lee, "Jesus as the Christ, as both God and man, cannot really be understood in terms either/or. How can man also be God? In the West we have to speak in terms of paradox or mystery in order to justify the reality of Christ. However, in *yin-yang* terms, he can be thought of as both God and man at the same time. In him God is not separated from man nor man from God. They are in complementary relationship. He is God because of man: he is man because of God."[11] For Lee all theological issues like

---

[10] Tan Yun-Ka, "Jesus, the Crucified and Risen Sage," 87.

[11] Jung Young Lee, "The Yin-Yang Way of Thinking: A Possible Method for Ecumenical Theology," in

Mission Trends No. 3, G. H. Anderson and T. F. Stransky, eds. (Grand Rapids: Eerdmans, 1976), 37. See also Antonie Wessels, *Images of Jesus: How Jesus Is Perceived and Portrayed in Non-European Cultures,* J. Vriend, trans. (Grand Rapids: Eerdmans, 1990), 156–157.

112 *Christ without Borders*

incarnation, death and resurrection, creation and redemption, sin and salvation, being and becoming, etc., can be better understood and explained through the symbolism of *yin and yang.*

Jesus of the Indian Subcontinent

Though Jesus Christ was known in the southwest of India from the first century or the third century onward, he did not have much impact on the subcontinent in the following centuries. It was in the sixteenth century, due to the missionary movement of Francis Xavier and the inculturation attempts of Robert De Nobili and the other Jesuits in the Mogul court of Akbar, that Jesus Christ and his teachings came to be known to a wider section of Indian society. During the Hindu renaissance of the nineteenth and twentieth centuries, Jesus and his teachings were taken seriously by some Hindu reformers for the transformation of Indian society.

Jesus, the Guru

The father of Hindu Reformation, Ram Mohun Roy (1772–1833), found in the moral teachings of Jesus the powerful message to liberate Hinduism from its superstitions, polytheism, and certain dehumanizing practices. According to him, the moral teaching of Christ is indeed the way to freedom and happiness.[12] Roy's recognition and application of the moral teachings of Christ for the reformation of Hindu society influenced the view of other Hindu reformers about Jesus and his message.

Jesus, the Divine Humanity

Among the Hindu views on Christ, one that comes much closer to the Christian faith affirmation about Jesus Christ is the view

---

[12] Ram Mohun Roy, *The Precepts of Jesus: The Guide to Peace and Happiness* (Calcutta: Unitarian Society, 1820).

of Keshub Chunder Sen (1838–1884). Though he never became a baptized member of any Christian church, Sen's views on Jesus Christ influenced many Hindus as well as Indian Christian thinkers. Sen believed that the correct presentation of Christ to India was his life mission for the regeneration of India. For Sen, the Indian myths of evolutionary incarnations are the portrayal of a process of the evolution in perfection, with Christ at the apex of organic evolution.

Jesus, the Unique Incarnation

In the progressive development of Hindu views on Christ, Pratap Chander Mozoomdar (1840–1950) comes still closer to the Christian confession of faith in Jesus Christ than Sen. In his writing *The Oriental Christ,* he tried to show the soteriological value of Christ being both Son of God and Son of Man. For Mozoomdar, Jesus Christ is a unique incarnation because he completes all other partial and limited incarnations.[13] Jesus Christ was present in all that was great and good in humanity, and he perfectly embodies the true and universal relation between God and man.

Jesus Christ, the Cit or Consciousness

Brhamabandhav Upadhyaya (1861–1907) was an Indian Christian who made a serious attempt at interpreting Jesus Christ using Indian categories and thought patterns. He says, "The Hindu mind is extremely subtle and penetrative, but is opposed to the Greco-Scholastic method of thinking." For Upadhyaya the philosophy of nondualism (*Advaita*) of Sankara is better suited to explain the Christian doctrines. "We must fall back on the vedantic method of formulating Catholic religion to our countrymen. In fact,

---

[13] P. C. Mozoomdar, *The Spirit of God* (Boston: G. H. Ellis, 1894), 239f., cited in M. M. Thomas, *The Acknowledged Christ of the Indian Renaissance* (London: SCM Press, 1969), 89.

114 *Christ without Borders*

the Vedanta must be made to do the same service to the Catholic faith in India as was done by Greek philosophy in Europe."[14]

Upadhyaya made use of the Vedantic understanding of the attribute-less absolute or *Nirguna Brahman*, who is also described in the Vedanta as *Saccidananda* to explain the inner Trinitarian relationship of communion. The communion "within" the Trinity can be explained when Consciousness (*Cit*) is understood as the self-knowledge of God, which is "eternally generated" because God (*Sat*) is eternally in his self-cognition. Bliss (*Ananda*) eternally proceeds from this colloquy of *Sat* and *Cit*. Jesus Christ is God's own Known Self, or God's own Self begotten in thought or the "Acknowledging Self-Image." Thus, he is the *Cit* or Logos of the Father. Jesus Christ is the incarnation of the *Cit* or consciousness of God. In a Christological hymn that he wrote in Sanskrit, the "Hymn of Incarnation,"[15] Upadhyaya presents Jesus Christ as a "transcendent Image of *Brahman* and *Nara-Hari* (God-Man)."

Jesus, the Avatara or Incarnation

A prominent Indian Christian theologian, A. J. Appasamy, considers that the "qualified nondualism" of Ramanuja is better suited to the Christian interpretation of Christ in India.[16] According to the philosophy of Ramanuja, God is a personal and loving being, and the doctrine of *Avatara* holds that the supreme personal God

---

[14] Brahmachari Animananda, *The Blade: Life and Work of Brahmabandhav Upadhyaya* (Calcutta: Roy & Son, 1946), 68.

[15] Robin Boyd, *An Introduction to Indian Christian Theology* (Delhi: ISPCK, 2004), 77.

[16] Aiyadurai J. Appasamy, *Christianity as Bhakti Marga: A Study in the Mysticism of the Johannine Writings* (London: Christian Literature Society for India, 1927), 20–21; *The Theology of Hindu Bhakti* (Madras: Christian Literature Society, 1970), 44ff.

The Different Christologies of Asia   115

Vishnu "descends" in an embodied form from time to time for the sake of liberating the world. The term *avatara* means to appear, to become embodied, to incarnate, or etymologically it means to cross over, come down, or descend. The number of *avataras* vary, but the standard number of *avataras* of Vishnu is ten, and the prominent ones are Rama and Krishna. Other Protestant theologians, including Vengal Chakkarai and P. Chenchiah, hold the view that the doctrine of *Avatara* can be correctly interpreted to explain the Christian mystery of incarnation. The Catholic theologians are of different opinions with regard to the use of the term *avatara* to mean incarnation as understood in Christian theology. However, in most of the regional languages of India, the Christian theological and devotional literature use this term for the incarnation of the Word. Jesus is the once-and-for-all *avatara* of God, different from all other *avataras* who descend from time to time not only to remove wickedness from the world but also the wicked.

Jesus, the Symbol of Cosmotheandric Christ

One of the greatest contributions of Raimon Panikkar (1918–2010) to humanity is his insight into the mystery of Christ, which is at the same time an insight into the mystery of humans and their world. According to Panikkar, Christ is to be seen not only in the limited Abrahamic or Semitic tradition but also in the cosmic tradition of mankind and in all authentic religious traditions. The whole Christ is historical and transhistorical, preexistent, and historically existed at a particular place, time, and culture. He is the living one who can be encountered in the sacraments, in all human beings, and especially in the deprived and the depraved. He is the most perfect expression of the complete harmony between everything that is divine, human, and cosmic or the cosmotheandric reality. Panikkar's insight should not be construed as his attempt to separate Jesus of Nazareth

116   *Christ without Borders*

from Christhood, as some of his critics accuse him of doing. In Panikkar's Christology, Christ is not an a-personal principle.[17] Christ is the second person of the Trinity, the preexistent Christ who reveals himself in Jesus of Nazareth.

Jesus, the Liberator of the Oppressed

Some of the Asian liberation theologians, like Sebastian Kappen (India), Choan Seng Song (Taiwan), Aloysius Pieris (Sri Lanka), George Soares Prabhu (India), Samuel Rayan (India), and others affirm that the liberative thrust of the Christian message must challenge the existing socioeconomic and sociocultural and religious systems that have a preferential option for the rich and powerful and oppress the poor. Kim Chi Ha, the Korean Christian writer, portrays in his play *The Gold-Crowned Jesus* the struggle of the real Jesus to reveal that he is in the midst of the suffering of the poor. A leper looks at the cement statue of Jesus with a gold crown and asks him penetrating questions about the situation of pain and misery, which destroys millions of humans, especially in Asia.[18] C. S. Song says, "The real Jesus and the people in suffering.... Jesus cannot be Jesus apart from such people. Jesus is not real unless he is with them in their daily struggle."[19] Only the real Jesus of the poor can identify himself with the suffering humanity of Asia in their struggles and tragic experience of failures in the face of repressive social, political, and economic systems and powers. So the suffering people reveal the real Jesus, and Jesus the human can reveal the fullness of God as compassionate (suffering with) love,

---

[17] Raimon Panikkar, *The Unknown Christ of Hinduism* (London: Darton, Longman & Todd, 1964), 27–28.

[18] C. S. Song, *Jesus, the Crucified People* (Minneapolis: Fortress, 1996), 121–122.

[19] Song, *Jesus, the Crucified People,* 11.

The Different Christologies of Asia   117

as he did when he lived among the poor and outcast during his time in Palestine.

In the Philippines, where Christianity became the majority religion, a variety of images of Jesus range from pious images like the Santo Niño to the very challenging "theology of struggle" that presents Jesus as the liberator of the poor who struggle daily to live a life worthy of their vocation as human beings. Various titles of Jesus—like *Datung Maraya*, which in Visaya means "the one who gives prosperity"; or *Ngir Omekuul*, meaning anchor or harbor in Palau; or *Abay*, which in Cebuan means traveling companion—reveal the closeness and solidarity of Jesus with those who struggle for a better human life. On the island of Mindanao, Jesus is *Manluluwas-Kauban*, "he who cares, who gives aid to the hungry, who travels with his people, who protects the persecuted, who pardons sinners, in a word, the liberator."[20]

Jesus, the Dalit

The Dalits of the Indian subcontinent are the victims of centuries-old religious, cultural, and social and economic discrimination. Religion condemned them to be untouchables because they were born as outcasts in a social system that is legitimized by the sacred Hindu religious texts. "In a society in which purity-pollution becomes a central principle of social organization, a religiosity centered on sacredness is an effort to exclude the 'impure'; it serves as an ideological device for the subordination of the subalterns like the Dalits."[21] The Indian Constitution has abolished the

---

[20] Theological-Historical Commission for the Great Jubilee of the Year 2000, *Jesus Christ, the Word of the Father: The Savior of the World* (New York, Crossroad, 1997), 49.

[21] Felix Wilfred, *The Sling of Utopia: Struggles for a Different Society* (Delhi: ISPCK, 2005), 155.

untouchability, but the Dalits continue to suffer discrimination in all aspects of their lives. In the context of their struggle to unfold themselves as humans, the Dalits encounter Jesus as the one who suffers with them, struggles with them, and empowers them to attain the fullness of life. According to A. Maria Arul Raja,[22] "Dalits do not discover the meaning of Jesus as mere substance or being but primarily as the co-sufferer leading them to the new heights of realizing the human-divine continuum. This realization enables Dalits to get awakened to transform their suffering as a historical opportunity in a creative manner in their journey toward integral emancipation." Jesus, the Dalit, challenges the systems of discrimination and dehumanization and suffers the consequence of standing for creating a new humanity where all humans are equal brothers and sisters; his prophetic message transforms both the victims and the victimizers.

Jesus, the Minjung

The oppressed people, or *Minjung*, of Korea recognize their powerlessness before the oppressors yet have the will to recover their dignity as humans. The power of the powerless, like the paradox of the cross, is well expressed in the concept of *minjung*, which also connotes liberation and salvation. No wonder then, the oppressed people or *Minjung* found Jesus Christ as Lord and God who can identify with them and yet can liberate them. According to Korean theologian Byung Mu Ahn, Jesus identifies with the *Minjung* and is God's solidarity with the suffering people.[23] Jesus is, indeed, the *Minjung*.

---

[22] A. Maria Arul Raja, "Witnessing to Christ in the Dalit Context," *Jeevadhara* 35, no. 207 (May 2005): 219.

[23] Byung Mu Ahn, "Jesus and People (Minjung)," in *Asian Faces of Jesus*, ed. R. S. Sugirtharajah (Maryknoll, NY: Orbis Books, 1993), 163–172.

The Different Christologies of Asia   119

According to David Kwang-sun Suh, Jesus might have been a great *mudang* who performed miracles, cured the sick, and cast out evil spirits. Jesus might have been the greatest counselor *mudang* for the poor and the deprived. But in the shamanistic mindset, the idea of Jesus as the son of God is beyond comprehension. Jesus, the mudang can take away the *han* or that feeling of pain, frustration, resentment, and indignation, and at the same time submission and resignation and give new life and dignity to the *Minjung*. In the paradox of the power of powerlessness Jesus the liberator continues to have a tremendous influence on the *Minjung* of Korea for the transformation of their lives.

Jesus of Asian Women

Going beyond the traditional images of Jesus, some Asian women have discovered new images of Jesus emerging from their own cultural contexts. "They have expressed Jesus' presence in their culture, in traditional religions, and in secular political movements. They dare to use political-religious symbols of their movements to describe the meaning of Jesus for them. Their Christological images emerge from their struggle for full humanity. Some of these images represent Jesus as liberator and political martyr, while others show him as a mother, a woman, a shaman."[24] The most striking aspect of the Christology of Asian women is that the various images discovered by Asian women appeal to all the oppressed women of Asia belonging to various cultures and religions and empower them to struggle for a fuller human life and their right to be equal partners in building a new society of God's dream and where all are sisters and brothers.

---

[24] Shalini Mulackal, "Feminist Christology in Asia," *Theology Digest* 48, no. 2 (2001): 109.

Jesus Christ can be recognized and proclaimed as the mediator and the unifier of all authentic religious traditions by his hidden presence in them and through the work of his Spirit in them. The revelation of the kenotic Christ without his historical incarnation can be manipulated by vested interests to support any systems of oppression and injustice, whether religious, cultural, social, economic, or political. The challenging *newness* of the revelation in Jesus Christ is that God seeks the integral liberation of human beings not from beyond the cosmic and historical context but from the center of the cosmos and from the heart of human history. God suffers when humans suffer because, in his radical kenosis, he shares everything that humans live and breathe except the alienation that humans choose for themselves. This is the paradox of divine revelation in Christ that Paul speaks about in 1 Corinthians 1:23, "a stumbling block to Jews and foolishness to Gentiles." Asia can only respond to a God who reveals himself from within its own contexts. Therefore, there will be many different faces of Jesus in Asia.

7

Jesus of the Poor and the Christ of Religion

Asia is the continent of the poor and the religions. The absolute poverty of a large number of people in the Asian countries makes human existence intolerable. The religions of Asia generally offer philosophical or religious explanations for the situation of misery or misfortune and the way in which one can experience liberation from this situation. But they do not consider it their task to provide answers to the questions of socioeconomic and political oppression and discrimination. They seem to concern themselves with the questions of life and life-after. The quest for meaning and eternal liberation is not limited to any race, caste, or class. It is fundamental to all humans, no matter where they are, in the East or in the West. So the basic concern of liberation from this world of misery overrides the interest in the transformation of this world. The prophetic dimension of the religions and their capacity to create a new world give way to an apocalyptic vision that lulls the spirit in the face of misery. The poor are fed on the hopes for a better life hereafter, and religions become the mediators of such hopes. So the situation of misery remains unchanged.

Does Jesus Christ offer anything new to the poor of Asia that the religions of Asia cannot give? Is he just another apocalyptic visionary or a true prophetic missionary? Can Jesus address the questions of poverty and the quest for ultimate liberation? Jesus

122 *Christ without Borders*

Christ is Lord and Savior. This is the fundamental Christian kerygma. But the question is how to proclaim this kerygma meaningfully in our context. Proclaim him as Jesus whom the poor can encounter or as the Christ, the Logos, whose presence is "known" or "unknown" in the religions of Asia?

In the following pages an attempt is made to show that Jesus Christ can be encountered as the source of integral human liberation in Asia provided that the poor can recognize him as one of their own kind sharing their poverty and misery and yet as the one who can empower them to struggle for a fuller human life and who can satisfy their quest for the ultimate meaning of life.

What Are the People Saying about Jesus?

Jesus of Nazareth asked a simple question to his disciples: "Who do the people say that I am?" (Mk 8:26). The response was a report about the public opinion about him. The hoi polloi, the poor, recognize him as the one who stands in the great tradition of the prophets. They would even consider him as the reappearance of Elijah or Jeremiah—but indeed, a prophet who disturbs the comfortable and comforts the disturbed. This prophet spoke with authority hitherto unknown to his predecessors. In his presence the people could be themselves. They could relate to him spontaneously. The way Jesus related to them empowered them to experience themselves and God in a new way. So they cried out after observing the way Jesus brought a dead man back to life: "A great prophet has arisen among us and God has visited his people" (Lk 7:16). God's visitation is also God's vindication. He will vindicate the poor and the wretched of the land. Therefore, this prophet is God's own presence. Call it Jesusology or Christology. This is the people's Jesus. This may be a poor Christology, but it is the Christology of the poor. It is the articulation of the significance of Jesus from "below," from the encounter of the people with Jesus of Nazareth. Such an approach to the understanding of the person of Jesus found its way to the early kerygma: "This Jesus whom you have crucified, God has made both Lord and Christ" (Acts 2:36). For fear of the heresy of adoptionism the church abandoned such a Christology from below—that is, a Christological reflection beginning from the humanity of Jesus Christ.

What Is God Saying about Jesus?

A Christology from below must be completed by a Christology from above. Otherwise Jesus would be just another prophet with a message and not an identification of the messenger and the message as encountered by the believers. Therefore, a second question follows the first one: "Who do you say that I am?" The answer: "You are the Christ, the Son of the living God" (Mt 16:16). Though this answer is given by a disciple, he is not the source of this answer. It was given from above. It was also expressed in the theophanies at the baptism of Jesus, "Thou art my beloved Son" (Mk 1:11), and at Mount Tabor, "This is my Son, my chosen" (Lk 9:35). It is a voice from the clouds, a voice from above. Its origin is not from the human heart. Since the answer is given from above, it opens up the possibility of infinite ways of articulations and proclamations and even manipulation.

The human mind can speculate about this mystery. It did speculate and made abstractions about the Son, his person, and his nature. As he is the Son, he is the preexistent Logos. "He is begotten not made, one in being with the Father," so confessed the Fathers at the Council of Nicaea (325 CE). Further, the Council of Chalcedon (451 CE) confessed in a static formula that he was "truly God and truly man." It was the articulation of a Christology from above, and most of the Christologies from above continue to provide elaborate systems of interpreting the meaning of Christ starting from his divinity.

124 *Christ without Borders*

In the development of Christological reflection, a Christology from below was avoided for fear of adoptionism, but a Christology from above can lead to "an unconscious Docetism of the churches."[1] Christ, the divine, God from God with two natures, as Chalcedon teaches, seemingly "represents Christ to us merely as an object of knowledge."[2] The being of Christ becomes an object of speculation leading to an ontological Christology. Christ as God, the second person of the Trinity, receives worship in the Christian religious practice. In the Asian religious landscape, Christ is the God of the Christians, like the gods of other religions.

Is Jesus Christ just another god competing with the myriad of gods and goddesses of the Asian continent for supremacy? Can we discover what God has said about Jesus from the history of his people, from their struggles, from their hopes and frustrations? What God has said about his Son must be heard in unheard-of ways and must be seen in hitherto-unseen ways that we do not force God to reveal through the familiar framework of our minds. It is simply letting God be God. The religion of his time could not recognize in Jesus the revelation of God because he had failed to fit into their understanding of God. So the Christology from above cannot be truly from above. It is the voice of God breaking the silence from below, in the voice of the voiceless and sigh of the oppressed.

Would the Real Jesus Speak Up?

How easy it would have been if Jesus were to tell clearly who he was, who he is, and who he will be! To the inquiry of John the Baptist conveyed to Jesus by two disciples of John, "Are you he who is to come, or shall we look for another?" (Lk 7:20). Jesus answered,

---

[1] John Macquarrie, *Jesus Christ in Modern Thought* (London: SCM Press, 1990), 343.

[2] Gerald O'Collins, *What Are They Saying about Jesus?* (New York: Paulist Press, 1977), 11.

Jesus of the Poor and the Christ of Religion   125

"Go and tell John what you have seen and heard: the blind receive their sight, the lame walk, lepers are cleansed, and the deaf hear, the dead are raised up, the poor have good news preached to them. And blessed is he who takes no offense at me" (Lk 7:22–23). His identity is in his relationship with those who struggle to live a fuller human life. His being is to be recognized in relationship and not through titles given by anyone. They call him Rabbi and Prophet and even consider him the Messiah. But he was not comfortable with any of these titles as they were loaded with false or illusory expectations of the people. He did not proclaim himself. He proclaimed the good news of the reign of God breaking into the present, demanding response by conversion. His words and deeds revealed that he was the unique agent of a radically new revelation that God suffers when humans suffer because God is love. Therefore, God offers his unconditional love and forgiveness for a new way of being human. Jesus reveals God's essence as love, a love that is not abstract or a-historical but encountered in history, amid the experience of the dehumanizing lack of love manifested in the oppression of the lowly and the powerless. The real Jesus presents the reality of God then and now. According to Jon Sobrino,

> The reality of God is love, and God is the partisan of human beings. Love for human beings, then, is the privileged way for gaining access to God. This is pointed up clearly in the Gospels, particularly in those passages where it seems that love for human beings would clash with God's rights. As Jesus sees it, God does not choose to claim any right for himself out of real and effective love for human beings.[3]

If Jesus revealed such a God in history, he could not have done this without entering into an effective and transforming relationship of

---

[3] Jon Sobrino, *Christology at the Crossroad* (Maryknoll, NY: Orbis Books, 1978), 166.

126   *Christ without Borders*

love with those whom society and religion condemned as outcasts
and sinners. The real Jesus is, then, the Jesus who stands for a
God for whom humans are more important than the Sabbath,
cult, and ritual purity. He reveals a God from below and not from
above—a God who identifies himself with the poorest of the
poor, the dehumanized and the marginalized, the economically
poor, the physically and mentally sick or handicapped, the socially
outcast, women, children, tax collectors, and prostitutes. Jesus had
table-fellowship with those whom religion considered ungodly and
accursed by God. If the early community encountered this man
Jesus who was crucified as "Lord and God" at resurrection it shares
such a new and radical revelation of God. It is not the revelation
of a God of the religion, not the God of the philosophers but the
God who struggles with the poor and the oppressed and all who
strive for a fuller human life.

The Suffering Jesus of the Poor

Is the real Jesus to be sought only in doctrines and dogmas? We
may get only a distorted image of him if we seek him there in the
doctrines, though they claim to provide a correct image of him. Is
he to be sought only in the solemn and elaborate liturgies or in the
ecstatic outbursts of the spiritually inebriated in the emotionally
charged atmosphere of huge prayer meetings supported by those
imported electronic sound systems? Some claim that they get an
inexplicable spiritual experience in such cultic celebrations that
compensate for their experience of misery and hopelessness in
their daily life. They feel helpless in their situation of oppression
and injustice. Religion provides a Christ who helps them to escape
from the tyranny of misery. But he is "the Gold-Crowned Jesus"[4]

---

[4] Kim Chi Ha, *The Gold-Crowned Jesus and Other Writings*, Chong Sun
Kim and Shelly Killen, eds. (Maryknoll, NY: Orbis Books, 1978).

who seems to understand the misery of the people but does not seem to be affected by it. He is beyond the history of the people. It makes no difference whether God had once entered human history or not, if this history does not continue to be a part of his divine life. He could have been worshiped in one name or another as other religions do, even though they do not believe in his entry into history for its transformation. The "gold-crowned Jesus" is the Christ of religion. He is just another god. He is not the real suffering Jesus of the poor.

The Christ of religion lets the theologians speculate about his person and nature and conduct discourses about his preexistence and transhistorical existence. He lets himself be captured by artists and sculptors to give visual satisfaction to those wretched men, women, and children who are despised, humiliated, and treated as the scum of society because they are poor and powerless. But this Christ seems to be silent in the midst of such tragic experiences of real people in their real history of life. Kim Chi Ha, the Korean Christian writer, portrays in his play *The Gold-Crowned Jesus* the struggle of the real Jesus to reveal that he is in the midst of the suffering of the poor. A leper looks at the cement statue of Jesus with a gold crown and asks him penetrating questions about the situation of pain and misery that destroys millions of humans, especially in Asia. The gold-crowned statue of Jesus is silent. Though the leper wanted a dialogue, it proceeds as a monologue. Finally, he makes the discovery that it is not the real Jesus. The real Jesus cannot remain passive and silent in the midst of such intolerable suffering caused by humans' inhumanity to humans. The leper shares his discovery with his fellow beggar, who refuses to believe it at first and wants to know if the gold-crowned cement Jesus is not the real Jesus, who then is the real Jesus. The leper knows only that the cement Jesus is not the real Jesus. Suddenly, to his astonishment and utter confusion, the cement Jesus with the gold crown breaks his silence and speaks to him:

128 *Christ without Borders*

> I have been closed up in this stone for a long, long time . . .
> entombed in this dark, lonely, suffocating prison. I have
> longed to talk with you, the kind and poor people like
> yourself, and share your sufferings. I can't begin to tell
> you how long I have waited for this day . . . this day when
> I would be freed from my prison, this day of liberation
> when I would live and burn again as a flame inside you,
> inside the very depths of your misery. But now you have
> finally come. And because you have come close to me I
> can speak now. You are my rescuer.[5]

In the words of the cement Jesus, the author recaptures the Jesus
of the poor revealed in the New Testament. The real Jesus is the
one who identifies himself with the poor and empowers them to
insurrection and finally to resurrection. This is the real Jesus who
suffers with all those who are denied the opportunities to unfold
themselves as humans. In this real Jesus, one discovers the suffering
and compassionate God. Reflecting on the dialogue between the
leper and Jesus, C. S. Song says, "The real Jesus and the people in
suffering. The real Jesus and men and women striving for freedom
and justice. The real Jesus and human persons longing for life, for
eternal life. Jesus cannot be Jesus apart from such people. Jesus is
not real unless he is with them in their daily struggle."[6] According
to Song, the meaning of the real Jesus is revealed in what Jesus
said to the leper. "Here is, then, a clue to the question of the real
Jesus. Here is the secret of the historical Jesus. And here is an entry
into the mystery of the 'messiah' who enables people to have faith
in the God of love and compassion in the world of greed and
selfishness."[7] Only the real Jesus of the poor can identify himself

---

[5] Kim, *The Gold-Crowned Jesus and Other Writings*, 121–123; C. S. Song, *Jesus, the Crucified People* (Minneapolis: Fortress, 1996), 11.

[6] Song, *Jesus, the Crucified People*, 11.

[7] Song, *Jesus, the Crucified People*, 11.

with the suffering humanity of Asia in their struggles and tragic experience of failures in the face of repressive social, political, and economic systems and powers. So the suffering people reveal the real Jesus, and Jesus the human can reveal the fullness of God as compassionate (suffering with) love as he did when he lived among the poor and the outcasts during his time in Palestine.

The poor who reveal the real Jesus include all those who are deprived of the basic necessities of life—food, shelter, clothing, and at least a minimum recognition of them as human persons with dignity. These poor, the hungry and thirsty, the naked, the sick, the homeless, and the unjustly imprisoned are the true vicars of Jesus (Mt 25:34–40). To encounter them is to encounter the one who identifies with them. Does not such a suffering Jesus of the poor inspire them to accept oppression and injustice with passivity and resignation? The history of the rapid spread of Christianity in the Roman Mediterranean world, it is argued, was the result of a revolt of the oppressed, both slaves and women who claimed equality as members of the Body of Christ. Julie M. Hopkins says, "It would appear then that the earliest Christian proclamation of a suffering prophet of God and the scandal of the cross prompted social and even revolutionary impulses. The identification through analogy of persecuted early Christians with their suffering Jesus did not lead to masochism, dependency, or powerlessness.... Meditation upon a suffering Jesus-messiah prompted solidarity in the face of suffering, resistance to unnecessary suffering and strategies to survive through hope in a new liberated future."[8]

The Asian face of Jesus needs to be discovered in the poor as the poor of Jesus's time discovered in him the compassionate love of God. Ashok Mehta, a former union minister of India, challenged Christians to prove their commitment to Jesus Christ by

---

[8] Julie M. Hopkins, *Towards a Feminist Christology: Jesus of Nazareth, European Women, and the Christological Crisis* (Grand Rapids: Eerdmans, 1994), 53.

130 *Christ without Borders*

their concerted action for the liberation of the poor. He says, "If it is the claim of the Christians that even to this day they feel the agony of Christ on the cross whenever humanity suffers as it were, it has to be proved in action and not by any statement."[9] The real Jesus speaks up in the suffering of the poor, the oppressed Dalits, the bonded-laborers, the deprived children, and the discriminated women. The whole way of life and message and the consequence of Jesus's option for the poor during his life reveal his identification with all the oppressed and outcast people. His history continues in the history of his suffering people. Hence, the Christology of the poor is not an ontological or functional Christology, not asking the questions about his being, who he is in himself, or his functions, what he has done for them. It is a relational Christology in which they see their face in him and his face in them and thus find meaning in their suffering and empowerment in their struggles and ultimate meaning of their life as he is experienced as the beginning, middle, and end of their lives.

The Christ of Religion

In the Asian context of the plurality of religions, where do we begin a reflection on the significance of Jesus Christ? If one's concern is to enter into dialogue with other religions at the level of doctrines and dogmas or from the articulations of God experience, one may be tempted to begin with a Christology from above because the Christian experience of God is in Jesus Christ. In fact the pioneering attempts of the Indian Christian theologians, whether Catholics or Protestants, were to follow the tradition of the Fathers of the Church in interpreting the meaning of Jesus Christ. Confronted with the plurality of religions and the

---

[9] Kurt Dockhorn, "Christ in Hinduism as Seen in the Recent Indian Theology," *Religion and Society* 21 (December 1974): 40.

philosophies of the Greco-Roman world and the questions raised about the Christian faith in a crucified man as God by the educated of their times, the Christian apologists presented Jesus Christ as the Logos incarnate. Logos was a familiar concept for the Greeks and the Romans as the reason for everything that exists or as the meaning of the universe and human existence, the link between the absolute and the relative. Based on the "descending Christology" of Paul and John, the Fathers could elaborate on the meaning of the Logos as the one who became human in Jesus Christ. The Councils of Nicaea and Constantinople I adopted this theological affirmation into creedal formulas. Since then, the Christological reflections began with a Christology from above and articulated Christologies using Hellenistic categories of thought.

The Indian Christian reflection in the context of Hinduism tried to interpret Christ within Indian religio-philosophical categories of thought. The main inspiration of the Indian Christian theologians seems to be the Logos Christology of the Fathers. B. Upadhyaya argued that if the Fathers could use the Hellenistic categories of thought to interpret the meaning of Christ, Indian Christians could make use of Indian categories of thought to interpret the meaning of Christ in the Indian context. In this line of reflection, Jesus Christ was seen as *Cit* (consciousness) of the absolute, *Isvara*, and *Avatara*. It was clearly a Christology from above in Indian categories. Christ was also seen as "the unknown Christ" (R. Panikkar), "the acknowledged Christ" (M. M. Thomas), or "the unbound Christ" (S. J. Samartha) of Hinduism. Discovering Christ in the ancient religions of Asia gives a glimpse into the marvelous mystery of God, who has "spoken to our fathers in many and varied ways" (Heb 1:1). However when we begin with a Christology from above, we end up with a Christ of religion. It is a legitimate approach because it has a foundation in the Christology of Paul and John. But the history of Christianity up to the Second Vatican Council and the emergence of Latin American liberation

132   *Christ without Borders*

theologies give ample evidence of the pitfalls of making Jesus Christ a God of religion. He becomes an object of worship and doctrine alienated from the suffering of the people, from their "history as people, culture as men, women and children and religion as human persons."[10] Excessive importance given to the Christ of religion neglecting the historical Jesus and the historical presence of Jesus in the suffering and struggles of the poor for fuller life undermined the very essence of Christian faith. The historical Jesus and the suffering people are the clues or the hermeneutic principles that help us to draw closer to the understanding totality of the mystery of Jesus Christ that alone can empower us for radical Christian praxis.

The significance of Jesus Christ cannot be deduced from an analysis of the concept of God. It must begin from a transforming encounter with him. So it must be a relational Christology, not an ontological Christology or a Christology from above. It cannot also be a functional Christology. In the context of the poor and outcasts of India, the Dalits' Jesus comes much closer to the historical Jesus than the Brahmin's Christ.

The poor of Jesus's time encountered him as a prophet in whose presence they experienced the unconditional love and forgiveness of God. They called him prophet "mighty in word and deed" because they had no other terms to identify him. Who he was in himself or what he did for them were not as important as what he meant to them. He identified himself with their sufferings, and the kingdom he preached was the realization of their hopes. In his presence the poor, the outcast, the sick, the marginalized, women, and children experienced wholeness through a new and radical relationship he offered to them. The fullness of such a relationship was experienced after his resurrection. At the resurrection he was encountered as the absolute meaning of

---

[10] Song, *Jesus, the Crucified People*, 11.

their lives. No one can be the absolute meaning of human life except God. It is in this awareness that they recognized Jesus, the human, as God's own revelation of his Son. So they confessed and proclaimed him as "Lord and God." St. Augustine says in one of his sermons, "Through the man Christ you move to the God Christ" (Sermon 261.7). In Jesus, the human, God revealed that God continues to love and suffer when human beings struggle and suffer to become what they are called to become. Therefore, the proclamation of this Jesus Christ is a dangerous enterprise as it involves a radical commitment to the liberation of the suffering poor and the suffering Jesus and facing the consequences of such an option.

8

Rejection and Reception of Christ in India

In challenging yet fascinating ways, God's Word finds expression in the world. We don't need to reach the heights of contemplation to encounter the Word in the everyday realities of life. Everyone is endowed with an "ordinary mysticism" to recognize that somehow everything in the creation is "wordified." John, in his Prologue, witnesses to this fact when he says that the Word was in the world, and the world knew him not; he came to his own, and his own received him not; but to all those who believed in him, he gave the power to become children of God (John 1:10–12). Already in his Prologue, John introduces the theme of the rejection and the reception of the Word before he narrates the historical unfolding of it in Jesus Christ, the Word. For John, even though the life and mission of Jesus Christ take place in Palestine, he is beyond space and time.

When we discuss how the Hindus see Jesus, we consider the views expressed by some prominent persons who claim themselves to belong to one or another form of Hinduism and who have influenced their co-religionists' view of Jesus Christ. Their views range from extreme rejection of Christ to a complete surrender to him, accepting him as the Lord and Master of life, at times entering into the church and sometimes without doing so.

Though Jesus Christ was known in the southwest of India from the first or third century onward, he did not have much impact on the subcontinent in the following centuries. Not until the sixteenth century—with the missionary movement of Francis Xavier and the inculturation attempts of De Nobili and the other Jesuits in the Mogul Court of Akbar—and Jesus Christ and his teachings come to be known to the wider Indian society. During the Hindu renaissance of the nineteenth and twentieth centuries, some Hindu reformers took seriously Jesus and his teachings for the transformation of Indian society. Also at this time, Christ and Christianity were devalued by some apologists of Hinduism. Before we discuss the positive and inspiring views of Jesus Christ expressed by some eminent Hindus, it is important to see the negative image of Jesus projected by some anti-Christian apologists to complete the whole spectrum of the Hindu view of Christ.

In the following discussion, we chart the evolution of views on Christ from the Hindu point of view. However, it is not a historical evolution of the reflections on Christ but a thematic development as it happened at the beginning of Christological development.

Rejection of Jesus, the Word, by the Anti-Christian Apologists

It is often stated that all Hindus accept Jesus as one of the avatars or the manifestation of the absolute. This seems to be an overstatement. Some Hindus have completely rejected the person of Jesus Christ as a false manifestation to deceive the followers of the *Sanatana Dharma* or the eternal religion. Nilakantha Goreh, a scholar from Varanasi, India, appalled by the tremendous appeal of Christ and Christianity, wrote a treatise in Sanskrit in the first half of the nineteenth century to prove that Christ could not have been a real manifestation of God and Christianity was of a demonic origin. According to Goreh, Jesus Christ was a *mohavatara* (delusory manifestation) and Christianity was a *mohadharma* (delusory religion).[1] Their purpose, according to him, was to wean away the followers of the true religion and to lead them to their own destruction. In fact, in the fifth century CE some myths were created for apologetic reasons that Vishnu, the supreme God, himself produced illusory and delusory forms from his body—as Mahavira, the founder of Jainism, and Buddha, the founder of Buddhism—to deceive the enemies of gods so that the gods could destroy them. Probably, Goreh meant that Jesus Christ too was a delusory manifestation like Mahavira and Buddha. However, a few years later, in 1848, Goreh experienced a conversion, surrendering himself to Jesus, the incarnation of the Eternal Word. He took the name Nehemiah and contributed much to an Indian Christian theology.

In the mid-nineteenth century various Hindu revivalist societies, such as the Society of the Four Vedas, were formed in Madras by prominent Hindus to resist the influence of Christianity. Certain Umapati Mudaliar of the Society of Four Vedas created a story that since heaven was overcrowded with devout Hindus and hell was empty, the king of hell, Yama, sought the help of God Vishnu to recruit some for hell. Vishnu advised Yama to send one of his soldiers to the Virgin Mary, to be born as her son—who would be killed as a criminal but would eventually be considered God by evil men. Their doctrines would deceive people and thus lead them to hell. Such stories—new versions of the archaic myths explaining the presence of good and evil in the world—were put to service for apologetic reasons to show the extreme negative view of Christ. Such negative views of Christ, however, are nothing compared to many other Hindus' admiration and acceptance of him.

The Hindu reformers of the nineteenth century who influenced modern Hinduism drew much inspiration from Jesus

---

[1] R. S. Young, "Adversarial Image of Jesus Christ in 18th–19th Century Buddhist-Hindu Folklore," *Dharmadeepika* 2 (1996): 68.

Rejection and Reception of Christ in India

Christ and Christianity to transform Hinduism. They acknowledge the influence of the person and teachings of Jesus Christ in their lives and their vision of a new Indian society.

Jesus, a Guru for Moral Transformation

As mentioned earlier, Ram Mohun Roy (1772–1833) found a powerful message for the reformation of Hinduism in the moral teachings of Jesus. For Roy, Hinduism could find value in the moral teachings of Christ as the way to freedom and happiness.[2] In a letter he wrote to a friend in 1815, Roy says, "The consequence of my long and uninterrupted search into religious truth has been that I found the doctrine of Christ more conducive to inculcate moral principles and better adapted to the use of rational beings than any other that has come to my knowledge."[3] Though Roy recognized the superiority of the moral teachings of Jesus and accepted the titles of Jesus as Son of God, Messiah, Lamb, Light, and so on, he rejected the content of faith expressed by these titles. Influenced by the strict monotheism of Islam and the a-Trinitarian theology of the Unitarians, he could not accept that Jesus was the incarnate Son of God.

Jesus, the *Satyagrahi*, the Prince of Nonviolence

For Mahatma Gandhi (1869–1948), the social and political reformer of modern Indian society, Jesus Christ is the ideal *satyagrahi* or one who clings to Truth. He says, "Jesus Christ is regarded as Prince of those who practice nonviolence. I maintain that nonviolence in this case must be understood as satyagraha, satyagraha and nothing

---

[2] Ram Mohun Roy, *The Precepts of Jesus: The Guide to Peace and Happiness* (Calcutta: Unitarian Society, 1820).

[3] Hans Staffner, *The Significance of Jesus Christ in Asia* (Anand: Gurjarat Sahitya Prakash, 1985), 6.

138 *Christ without Borders*

else."[4] Gandhi never hesitated to acknowledge the influence on him of the person of Jesus and his Sermon on the Mount. In his book *The Message of Christ,* Gandhi writes, "The gentle figure of Christ, so patient, so kind, so loving, so full of forgiveness that he taught his followers not to retaliate when abused or struck but to turn the other cheek—it was a beautiful example, I thought, of the perfect man."[5] Gandhi recognized Jesus as perfect man with a divine dimension. He affirms the influence of Jesus on all human beings. He says, "I refuse to believe that there now exists or has ever existed a person that has not made use of Christ's example to lessen his sins. ... The lives of all have, in some greater or lesser degree, been changed by his presence, his actions, and the words spoken by his divine voice."[6] For Gandhi, Jesus is not the monopoly of Christianity. Jesus belongs to the entire world, to all races and peoples, though they may differ in religious practices. Gandhi's views on Christ represent the view of many educated Hindus who recognize Jesus as an apostle of peace and one of the divine messengers who achieved the Hindu ideal of self-realization in its fullness.

Jesus, the Perfect Yogi, the Ideal Sannyasin or Ascetic

Those Hindus who follow the advaitic or nondualistic tradition of Hinduism consider Jesus a perfect yogi or an ideal ascetic. In the advaitic tradition there is no duality between the absolute and the relative, between God and the world. They are not one and not two. It is not a rational statement. It is an intuition, an experience. So in the advaitic tradition, the self-realization of a person consists in the ultimate realization of one's identity with the absolute. For Advaitins or so-called neo-Vedantins like Vivekananda and

---

[4] Staffner, *The Significance of Jesus Christ in Asia*, 25.

[5] M. K. Gandhi, *The Message of Christ* (Bombay: Bharatiya Vidya Bhavan, 1963), 3.

[6] Staffner, *The Significance of Jesus Christ in Asia*, 26.

Rejection and Reception of Christ in India　　　139

Radhakrishnan, Jesus is the perfect yogi who attained the fullness of self-realization. Jesus realized the ideal of the Hindu view of life, namely, the experience "I am That" (*aham brahmaasmi*), or the realization of identity between the individual and the absolute. They often quote the Johannine statement of Jesus, "I and the Father are one" (John 10:3), as the articulation of the nondualistic experience of Jesus Christ. Jesus realized this truth about himself progressively. Everyone has the potentiality to become like Christ or to realize the divinity within through self-denial. Vivekananda says, "Christ was a Sannyasin, and his religion is essentially fit for Sannyasins only. His teaching may be summed up as: 'Give up.'"[7]

He further confesses that this way of life is suitable only for a favored few. In this view Jesus is not fully God by his very nature but attains the fullness of divinity by his own effort. He seems to claim a deep insight into the mystery of the person of Jesus Christ. He says, "I pity the Christian who does not reverence the Hindu Christ. I pity the Hindu who does not see the beauty in Jesus Christ's Character."[8]

Radhakrishnan, an eminent Indian thinker, seems to express the same when he says, "Though conscious of his imperfections, Jesus recognized the grace and love of God and willingly submitted himself entirely to him. Thus delivered from all imperfection and taking refuge in Him, he attained a divine status."[9]

Those Hindus who follow the advaitic or the nondualistic tradition would not accept that Jesus is the true Son of God as Christians confess. But they find him as the ideal of human

---

[7] Swami Vivekananda, *The Complete Works of Swami Vivekananda*, vol. 6 (Calcutta: Advaita Ashrama, 1966–1971), 109.

[8] Daniel E. Bassuk cites Vivekananda to show his critique of both Christian and Hindu attitudes toward Christ. Bassuk, *Incarnation in Hinduism and Christianity: The Myth of the God-Man* (London: Springer, 1987), 180.

[9] Manilal C. Parekh, *The Brahma Samaj: A Short History* (Rajkot: Oriental Christ House, 1929), 31.

140 *Christ without Borders*

perfection, which all can attain. If he is Son of God, all can become Sons of God like him if one follows his way of self-denial, discipline, meditation, and commitment to work for the welfare of others. They admire Jesus for achieving the Vedantic ideal of self-realization and acknowledge his tremendous influence on their lives. But he is not true God as the Christians believe, confess, and proclaim.

Jesus, Incarnate Son of God

Keshub Chunder Sen became a significant influence on Hindu views on Christ. Sen attempted to reconcile the Indian concept of incarnation (*avatara*) and the Christian theology of incarnation. However, he tried his best to show that Jesus Christ was not an incarnation like the incarnations of Hinduism. He exhorted Christians, "Tell our people distinctly that Christ is not an incarnation like the myriad deities worshipped in this land."[10] Unlike Ram Mohun Roy, Keshub Chunder Sen was deeply committed to Christ. He confessed, "Unless I can live Jesus to some extent at least, I cannot talk Jesus. Nor could I undertake to preach Jesus to my countrymen till I am fully persuaded that the time has come for such a preaching."[11] Sen believed that the correct presentation of Christ to India was his life mission for the regeneration of India.

For Sen, the Indian myths of evolutionary incarnations are the portrayal of a process of the evolution in perfection. "Indian Avatarism," he said, "is indeed a crude representation of the ascending scale of Divine Creation."[12] Long before Teilhard de

---

[10] David C. Scott, *Keshub Chunder Sen: A Selection* (Madras: Christian Literature Society, 1979), 241.

[11] Parekh, *The Brahma Samaj*, 155.

[12] Keshub Chunder Sen, *Keshub Chunder Sens's Lectures in India*, vol. 2 (London: Cassell and Company, 1901), 14.

Chardin articulated his views on the relationship of Christ to evolution, Sen affirmed that Christ is the apex of organic evolution. In Christ, evolution has reached its maximum perfection. Sen calls this perfection in Christ "Divine Humanity."[13]

Is this Divine Humanity, this Christ, God-became-man or God-in-man? Sen oscillates between these two notions, seeming to term both as incarnations. For Hindus, according to Sen, Christ as God incarnate would mean that the Father has become human. This way of understanding and preaching Christ as the "Father in human shape" is a preaching of idolatry, heresy, and antichrist. As such, Sen preferred the term "God-in-man" rather than "God-became-man" to explain incarnation. Yet he insisted that the preexistent Logos expresses itself in full humanity in Jesus.

Further, he affirmed that in Jesus Christ, the ultimate term of evolution, the Logos is offered to all. "The problem of creation," Sen argued, "was not how to produce one Christ but how to make every man Christ."[14] Sen affirmed that Christ is not the monopoly of Christianity.

> I deny and repudiate the little Christ of popular theology, and stand up for a greater Christ, a fuller Christ, a more eternal Logos of the Fathers, and I challenge the world's assent. This was the Christ who was in Greece and Rome, in Egypt and India. In the bards and poets of the Rig Veda was he. He dwelt in Confucius and in Sakya Muni [Buddha]. This is the true Christ I can see everywhere, in all lands and in all times, in Europe, in Asia, in Africa, in America, in ancient and modern times. He is not the monopoly of any nation or creed.[15]

---

[13] Sen, *Keshub Chunder Sens's Lectures in India,* 2:13.

[14] Sen, *Keshub Chunder Sens's Lectures in India,* 2:15.

[15] Scott, *Keshub Chunder Sen,* 237–238.

142 *Christ without Borders*

Sen did not hesitate to confess Christ as the Divine Son of the Father, the second person of the Trinity, whom he called *Saccidananda* (*Sat* meaning truth, *Cit* meaning intelligence, and *Ananda* meaning bliss). At the same time, he affirmed that Jesus was born of the Virgin Mary and was an Asiatic ascetic or yogi—full of Hindu devotion, communion, and self-surrender. Approaching Christ this way, Sen was certain that Hindus would recognize him as their brother and friend, their Lord and master, and not as a doctrine.

Jesus, the Unique Incarnation

Pratap Chander Mozoomdar approaches the Christian confession of faith in Jesus Christ in an important way for this project. In *The Oriental Christ*, Mozoomdar focused on the soteriological value of Christ through the incarnation. As both Son of God and Son of Man, Jesus Christ's incarnation completes all other partial and limited incarnations. Other incarnations are

> of one age . . . are partial, local, imperfect, bounded by time, nationality and circumstance. Socrates is for the Greeks, Moses for the Hebrews, Confucius for the Chinese, Krishna for the Hindus, and Mohammed for the Musalmans. . . . The need of a man is for a central figure, a universal model, one who includes in himself all these various embodiments of God's self-manifestation. The need of man is for an incarnation in whom all other incarnations will be completed. Such an incarnation was Christ.[16]

The articulation of the experience of Jesus Christ was developing in the early church as the disciples encountered other cultures and peoples beyond the borders of Palestine. They had to transcend

---

[16] P. C. Mozoomdar, *The Spirit of God* (Boston: G. H. Ellis, 1894), 239f., cited in M. M. Thomas, *The Acknowledged Christ of the Indian Renaissance* (London: SCM Press, 1969), 89.

Rejection and Reception of Christ in India 143

the Jewish or the Hebrew worldview when Christianity spread to the Hellenistic world.

The inexhaustible mystery of Christ needs to be interpreted in every culture and language by those who encounter Christ and are transformed by Christ. The various Christologies that emerged and are still emerging in India have their ultimate source in Christ, who transcends all cultures and languages and yet manifests himself through these cultures and languages so that he can be encountered by those who are open to him and committed to him and his values.

9

The Newness of Jesus Christ

The word of God is not bound (2 Tim 2:9). This truth is confirmed by the infinite ways in which God's Word finds expression in the world. Above all, it is true in the unique expression of the Word in Jesus Christ. He transcended everything that bound him, even death. The early theologians of the church interpreted Jesus Christ as the Messiah of Jewish expectations as well as the fulfillment of the hope cherished by the Gentiles of all times. Ignatius of Antioch, for example, proclaimed Jesus Christ as the "ground for hoping that [all of humanity] may be converted and win their way to God." Further, he affirmed that Jesus was "our common name and common hope."[1]

The followers of Jesus Christ believe that he is indeed the common name and common hope meant for the whole of humanity. They encounter him as the Way, the Truth, and the Life. They experience him as the beginning and the end of their lives, and therefore the ultimate meaning of their lives. They confess him as the Lord of history and the universe who lived and died at a particular time in history and yet came alive after his death, leading all to the fullness of life. But something that is bound up with this transforming experience of Jesus Christ is that it must be shared, it must be proclaimed in a meaningful way that the same Jesus Christ can be encountered by people of all cultures and languages. It is

---

[1] Ignatius of Antioch, *Epistle to the Ephesians* 10.1; 1.2.

The Newness of Jesus Christ   145

absolutely imperative for the church that "lives, moves and has its being" in Jesus Christ to proclaim him in a way that other people can really "hear" the word of proclamation.

In a multireligious society of the Roman Empire, the early church found creative ways to theologize and proclaim the universal significance of Jesus Christ. When the Roman Empire accepted Jesus Christ as its Lord and Savior, Christianity became a monoreligious culture without any challenge to its claims about Jesus Christ from outside. It had to face only the internal challenges with regard to the wrong interpretations of the person of Christ, which were countered by the early councils, especially the Council of Chalcedon. The church articulated "who Jesus Christ is" in dialogue with Judaism and the Greco-Roman world. Such a finished Christology with its ready-made Christ image did not have much impact on the peoples of Asia for the last twenty centuries because Asian people have different cultures and worldviews that cannot understand the "language" of Christian proclamation. Moreover, the religions of Asia claim to have their own mediators, saviors who seemed to have already shown them the ways of salvation. The understanding of Christ and Christianity as a threat is growing stronger in India and elsewhere in Asia. This is clearly seen in the anti-Christian propaganda of Hindu fundamentalists in India, which led to the martyrdom of some missionaries recently. In this context, what are the ways to proclaim Jesus Christ in a language meaningful and challenging to the people of other religions so that they can encounter him as the fullness of life and not as such a threat to their authentic cultures and traditions that they reject him?

I would like to emphasize these concerns and show why such an approach to Christology is imperative in the Indian context if we take seriously the "mission command" of Jesus Christ (Mt 28:18–20). Further, in the context of religious pluralism in India, I suggest an approach to proclaiming Jesus Christ that is challenging and not threatening, respectful and not aggressive, relational and not relative.

Toward a Meaningful Indian Christology: Problems

We must proclaim Jesus Christ. We must invite people to experience his life-giving presence in and through His Spirit in the church. But should we go on repeating certain Christological affirmations articulated in a language that is not only not meaningful to our listeners but also has such a negative impact on them that they reject our message? Should we use exclusive and absolutist expressions to proclaim the centrality of Jesus Christ in the universal salvific plan of God that hinder the people of other religions from hearing the good news of salvation? Should we make absolute statements about other religions, their founders, and their religious experiences—sometimes even denigrating them as if we know all about the mysterious ways of God who "shows no partiality" and to whom "in every nation anyone who fears him and does what is right is acceptable" (Acts 10:34–35)?

The history of Christian proclamation in the colonial era had been, to a great extent, aggressive, exclusive, and triumphalist. It contradicted the Apostle Peter's exhortation, "Always be prepared to make a defense to anyone who calls you to account for the hope that is in you, yet do it with gentleness and reverence" (1 Pet 3:15). Earlier, I argued that the colonizers could not discover Christ's presence through His Spirit in the positive values of the religious traditions of their colonial subjects. Doing so would have impeded their claims of military, religious, and cultural superiority.

In the colonial and postcolonial eras in Asia and particularly in India, the Christian claims of being the only true religion possessing the absolute truth—including Christological claims to the uniqueness of Jesus Christ and His church for salvation—faced two notable challenges. They were not understood by the followers of other religions, and these claims conveyed to them the opposite of what such claims intended. For people who hold an inclusive and relational worldview, any absolute and exclusive claims about Jesus Christ and his church would reduce Jesus Christ to a tribal god and the church to a religious sect. Jesus Christ, thus, becomes one among the founders of religions, one of the incarnations, a great guru, a prophet, or one who reached the fullness of self-realization. They would consider him as one among many historical manifestations of the absolute.

How did this confusion happen? Was the proclamation not clear and unambiguous? Indeed it was, but it was only meaningful to those who shared the Mediterranean worldview. For those whose worldview operates on the epistemological principle of identity rather than on the principle of contradiction, for whom transhistorical truths are more real than historical facts, liberation from ignorance is more important than liberation from sin, and symbolic religious expressions are more evocative and experiential than creeds and dogmatic statements. Any exclusive statements fail to fit into the Indian scheme of things. So the struggle of any Indian Christian theologian is to translate the church's faith affirmation about the person and mission of Jesus Christ in a language meaningful to the people such that they can respond to him with their whole heart and mind.

Toward a Meaningful Indian Christology:
Prospects

Presenting a meaningful Christology in the Indian context is not easy. In fact, the plurality and complexity of the situation demand a plurality of Christologies encountering the "great traditions" and the "little traditions," which have their own worldviews as well as both liberative and oppressive elements. An openness to positive elements can enrich the Christian understanding of the mystery of Jesus Christ, and the Christian experience of Jesus Christ as the fullness of life can challenge the dehumanizing elements of these cultures and religions. The possibility of enriching our present understanding of the mystery of Christ presupposes that we forfeit the idea that we

148 *Christ without Borders*

have exhausted the possibility of understanding the mystery of Jesus Christ. We must also give up the idea that present articulations about him are clear for people of all cultures and worldviews.

For those who encounter Jesus Christ in the living tradition of the church and understand the challenges of their inherited Indian worldview, clearly our faith affirmations about the uniqueness of Jesus Christ cannot be understood by those with an Indian worldview to whom it is proclaimed. The attempts of Indian theologians to present the same truths of Christian revelation in various ways that are meaningful to the Indian context may be construed as relativizing the fundamental truths of Christian revelation if such pedagogical methods are not properly understood. The proclamation of Jesus Christ in dialogue with the Indian context of religious pluralism and dehumanizing sociocultural and economic situations convinces proclaimers of the gospel that

> Jesus Christ's trans-historical and living presence through his Spirit in all that is good and beautiful and perfect must be point of departure and his historical presence must be point of arrival in our proclamation. This is imperative as the overemphasis on the historicity of Jesus at the beginning of the proclamation reduces him to one among the historical founders of religion.

and

> Jesus Christ cannot be proclaimed in isolation, separated from the "many and varied ways God has spoken to our fathers" (Heb. 1:1). Other founders of religion and other ways of salvation need not be understood as parallel or complementary to God's revelation through Jesus Christ.

In the quest for meaningfulness, Christian theologians in India recognize another way of expressing our human desire for an integral harmony. The undeniable quest for an integral wholeness or salvation is for both an otherworldly and a this-worldly experience,

The Newness of Jesus Christ 149

individualistic *and* communitarian, oriented toward material welfare *and* spiritual satisfaction. The awareness that all is not right with the world and human societies, the haunting thought of a possibly meaningless death and an uncertain future beyond the grave, heighten the quest for an integral wholeness, liberation, or salvation. As one's religious, cultural, social, and economic context shapes both perception of and desires for liberation, these contextual aspects inform what a particular people considers to be ultimately significant for their lives. People of different cultures and traditions have appropriated the significance of Jesus Christ for their lives in diverse ways.

The apostolic community responded to Jesus's question "Who do you say that I am?" (Mt 16:15) with decisive and existential answers. Theirs were decisive answers because they gave a new meaning to their own life and changed their understanding of God, human beings, and the world. They were existential because their understanding of Jesus's identity was intertwined with their self-understanding about themselves and the ultimate meaning of their lives. The answers concerned their existential search for salvation, wholeness, and a practical orientation to their lives.

The question of identity may be the most basic question that a human person can confront. When Jesus asks it, the question becomes a fresh articulation of the same question of meaning that human beings ask of themselves. This is an ultimate question, and any answer to it is significant for the integrally whole person in their encounter with Jesus.

The seekers of all times and all cultures express in different ways the quest of humans for an ultimate answer to the mystery of life. The various world religions that emerged in Asia have something in common: they all admit that life in this world, in the final analysis, is not satisfactory; there is a longing for liberation and wholeness; and finally, there are different ways to attain liberation. Christianity, being one of the religions born in Asia, admits that God, the Ultimate Reality, has mysterious ways to lead humans to liberation, even those who deny the existence of any Ultimate

Reality. But it also claims that the way of Jesus is not just another way to liberation but *the Way*. Unlike other great teachers and founders of religions who showed the way to the attainment of liberation, he *is* the Way; he is the liberation, as his name suggests (Jesus = *Yehoshua* = "God is savior" or "God saves"). Hence, Christians claim that Jesus Christ is the unique savior or liberator. However, if Christianity is seen as a religion like any other religion and its founder like any other founder of a religion, the claims to superiority, exclusiveness, uniqueness, and so on become untenable.

The disciples encounter Jesus Christ as the revelation of the ultimate reality, the beginning and end of everything that exists, the ultimate meaning of life and not the founder of a religion. Christianity, in its true sense, cannot be a religion but must become a community of transformed people who experience the ultimate meaning of their lives in the abiding presence of the one who is the absolute yet became relative, transhistorical yet became historical, eternal yet became temporal, immortal yet became mortal. The mystery of this paradox surpasses all articulations and all comparisons. It is to be experienced and lived. Deep silence can be the loudest proclamation of this Christic mystery.

An authentic Christology for India should not yield to the temptation to analyze the mystery of Christ that surpasses all understanding, to define the indefinable and to make claims about having a clear and complete knowledge of the mystery as everything about it seems to be neatly categorized and formulated. On account of this, Indian theologians emphasize the need to develop a Christology that is more symbolic and evocative than descriptive and dogmatic. Such an approach to the understanding of the person and message of Jesus Christ and the proclamation of the same attracted many Hindus to encounter Jesus Christ as the Lord and master of their lives. The approaches of the NT writers and the early churches to articulate their Christ experience from their own particular contexts give an insight into the process of developing a normative Christology for Asia.

10

Christ beyond Chalcedon

An Indian Interpretation of the Meaning of Christ

Theologizing, if it is genuine, originates from a vision. In this vision, something of the mystery of existence is disclosed. Therefore, any vision, if it is authentic, has the character of being "given from above." Babani Charan Banerjee, who took the name Brahmabandhab Upadhyaya (1861–1907)—translating his baptismal name, Theophilos—was the one who was given a vision that he became a visionary with a mission to communicate the truths of his Catholic faith in a meaningful way to the people of his beloved country of India. He was both a mystic and a prophet. As a mystic he savored the sweetness of the truth that he experienced as encompassing him, and as a prophet he suffered the consequences of his standing for all of what he believed to be true. His deep knowledge of the culture and the philosophical thought of Hinduism and his experience of Christ—and his deep knowledge of Christian doctrine, theology of the Fathers, and scholastic philosophy—equipped him well to understand and articulate the significance of Christ in the Indian context. The original and courageous attempt of Upadhyaya to interpret the meaning of Jesus Christ in the Indian context is deeply profound and relevant. He entered into a transforming trilogue of Hindu religious and cultural tradition with the truths of Christian faith and with himself as an "insider" and inheritor of these traditions.

152   *Christ without Borders*

Upadhyaya's Theological Method

The theological method of Upadhyaya emerges from his conviction that the universal faith is deposited in the church by the apostles of Jesus Christ, and that Indian thought patterns are capable of communicating this universal faith in a meaningful way to the people of India. Therefore, theological reflections must be to explicate this deposit of faith in Indian categories and thought forms if it is to "grow, blossom and fructify till the end of time."[1] As Thomas Aquinas approached Aristotelian philosophy to explicate the Christian doctrines, "Attempts must be made to win over Hindu philosophy to the service of Christianity as Greek philosophy was won over in the Middle Ages."[2] According to Upadhyaya, "Indian soil is humid and its humidity will make the ever new Christian Revelation put forth new harmonies and newer beauties, revealing more clearly the inviolable integrity of the Universal Faith deposited in the Church by the Apostles of Jesus Christ."[3] He affirms that the religion of Christ is *supernatural* and the truths in Hinduism are of pure reason illuminated in the order of nature by the light of the Holy Spirit. "But though the religion of Christ is beyond the grasp of nature and reason, still its foundation rests upon the truths of nature and reason. Destroy the religion of nature and reason, you destroy the *supernatural* religion of Christ."[4] Hence, for a meaningful proclamation of Christ and Christian doctrine, one needs to study and research to find out the truths of Hinduism. Upadhyaya's Christological reflections take

---

[1] Brahamabandhab Upadhyaya, "*Sophia-Monthly*, July 1887," in *The Writings of Brahamabandhab Upadhyaya*, vol. 1, Julius Lipner and G. Gispert-Sauch, eds. (Bangalore: United Theological College Publishing, 1991), 20. Henceforth, referred to as *Writings I*.

[2] Upadhyaya, *Writings I*, 20.

[3] Upadhyaya, *Writings I*, 19.

[4] Upadhyaya, "*Sophia-Monthly*, January, 1895," in *Writings I*, 6.

seriously the theistic truths contained in Hindu Scriptures and Vedantic categories of thought.

B. Upadhyaya was attempting to restate Christianity in terms of Vedanta.[5] This is necessary for an effective proclamation of Jesus Christ in India and for the renewal and revitalization of the church in India. In short, he argued that the original Christian experience about God, humans, and the world revealed in Jesus Christ must be rearticulated through the lived experience of the Indian context.

In the stated objectives of the journals he had founded we get an insight into the basic approach of Upadhyaya in dealing with the doctrines of Hinduism and Christianity. In the objectives of the journal *Harmony*, he states that while expounding Hindu and Christian doctrines he would attempt "to reconcile and harmonize pure Hinduism with pure Christianity." Another objective of this journal was "to preach Christ as the Eternal Son of God, as the Logos in all prophets and saints before and after His incarnation and as the incarnate perfect righteousness by whose obedience man is made righteous."[6] The journal also had the objective of discussing social questions and social reforms.

Upadhyaya was convinced of the possibility of proclaiming Christ in India by entering into dialogue with the religio-philosophical systems of Hindu religious tradition. But as a theologian committed to his Christian faith he was not prepared to make any compromise with Hindu doctrines that he found incompatible with Christian doctrines. The main points of Upadhyaya's theological method can be summarized as follows:

I. Separation of the content of Christian faith from its ways of expression in Greco-scholastic categories of thought and European cultural context.

---

[5] Upadhyaya, "*Sophia-Monthly*, September 8, 1900," in *Writings I*, 33.

[6] Upadhyaya, "Harmony," in *Writings I*, 2.

154   *Christ without Borders*

II. Expressing the content of Christian faith in the Vedantic categories of thought with proper discernment. This means acceptance of those categories of thought which can express the mysteries of faith more intelligibly than those hitherto employed, re-interpretation of certain Indian philosophical categories in the light of Christian faith and the use of them to express the mysteries of Christian revelation, and an absolute rejection of those categories and thought forms which would dilute the uniqueness of the revelation of God in Jesus Christ.

III. Making a distinction between the natural religious truths of Hinduism and the Supernatural religious truths of Christianity, and attempting to graft the revealed truths of Christianity on to the natural theology provided by Hinduism.[7]

IV. The practical aspect of this theologizing is to proclaim the Christian faith by living it out in the Indian cultural context.

Upadhyaya's Christological Reflections

The Christological reflections of Keshub Chunder Sen and some later Protestant theologians like Vengal Chakkarai (1880–1958) could not escape from the heresy of adoptionism because they tried to develop a Christology from below without paying much attention to the old heresy of adoptionism. The approach to Christology from below cannot but end in some form of adoptionism or Docetism because of basic Indian anthropological conceptions. From the beginning itself, the church fought against such heresies, because she believed that this would endanger not

---

[7] Julius Lipner, "A Modern Indian Christian Response," in *Modern Indian Responses to Religious Pluralism*, Harold G. Coward, ed. (Albany: State University of New York Press, 1987), 308–309.

only the meaning of incarnation but also the basic belief in God's offer of salvation in Jesus Christ. Therefore, Upadhyaya interprets the Vedantic concepts of God, world, and man to avoid such heresies—and employs these categories to explain who Jesus Christ is.

Jesus Christ, the Cit-Logos of Saccidananda

The presupposition of both a natural and a supernatural order in explaining the relation between Hinduism and Christianity is very clear in Upadhyaya's exposition of Jesus Christ as the *Cit* in the Saccidananda description of God or Brahman. He considers the Vedantic concept of God or Brahman as the highest point human reason can arrive at in the natural order, while in the supernatural order the revelation of the Triune God as the Father, Son, and Holy Spirit is the highest point.[8] "We can boldly and safely affirm that the Vedantic conception of the nature of the Supreme Being marks the terminus of the flight of the human reason into the eternal regions. The Catholic belief," he writes, "is exactly the same. God is the only eternal being.... He knows Himself and reposes in Himself with supreme complacency."[9] Upadhyaya tries to interpret the Christian doctrine of the Trinity in terms of the Vedantic conception of Brahman as Saccidananda and develops a Christology in the framework of this Trinitarian understanding.

Keshub Chunder Sen, who used the term "Saccidananda" for the first time in describing the Christian understanding of the Trinity, could not escape from modalistic explanations of

---

[8] Brahamabandhab Upadhyaya, "An Exposition of the Catholic Belief as Compared with the Vedanta," in *Sophia-Weekly* (January 1898), 11; Kaj Baago, *Pioneers of Indigenous Christianity* (Madras: Christian Literature Society, 1969), 40.

[9] Upadhyaya, "An Exposition of the Catholic Belief as Compared with the Vedanta," 11; and Baago, *Pioneers of Indigenous Christianity*, 40.

156 *Christ without Borders*

it due to Unitarian influences. But Upadhyaya is very careful to avoid this mistake. First of all, he considers that the Brahman of whom the Vedantists speak is the same as the *esse per se* of Thomistic natural theology. The highest conception of God in Vedic thinking is Nirguna Brahman, the "attribute-less" absolute. This description of the Godhead finds its real and fuller meaning in the Christian doctrine of the Holy Trinity. However, the personalist understanding of Brahman as absolute with attributes (Saguna Brahman) by the theistic schools is according to the nontheistic schools to be on a lower level than the suprapersonalist understanding of Brahman. But the revelation in Christ is that of the Supreme God who cannot be relegated to the lower level, even if this idea of the absolute contains attributes, which would contribute to the Christian concept of God as person. Moreover, it would then admit that the concept of God in the natural order is higher than the concept of God in the supernatural order. The Brahman of Vedanta, although the highest point of upanishadic thinking, is not the abstract absolute Being of the rationalists.[10] He is an absolutely perfect Being, self-sufficient in himself, but he can be approached not only by the spiritually elite but by everyone. Some argue, however, that the infinite can be approached only by the spiritually advanced, and others must be satisfied with worshiping the finite until they advance to the spiritual level of the enlightened. Upadhyaya asks, "Is the Infinite really unapproachable? If it had been so, Reason would be anomaly. The perception of the Infinite is the dawn of Reason."[11]

The Nirguna Brahman, the attribute-less absolute, is also described in the Vedanta as Saccidananda. Brahamabandhab Upadhyaya interprets this description of the Brahman as the point

---

[10] See Robin Boyd, *An Introduction to Indian Christian Theology* (Delhi: ISPCK, 2004), 69–74.

[11] Brahmachari Animananda, *The Blade: Life and Work of Brahmabandhav Upadhyaya* (Calcutta: Roy & Son, 1946), 101.

Christ beyond Chalcedon 157

of departure for his exposition of Christology from the doctrine of the Trinity, which he explains at first by using these Vedantic categories. As the one who is "unrelated" without, "*Brahman* is Being itself. He alone is identical with His own Being while creatures have no right of being, but have a merely participated and dependent existence."[12] But within himself he may be related as Being (*Sat*), Consciousness (*Cit*), and Bliss (*Ananda*). This communion "within" the Trinity can be explained when *Cit* is understood as the self-knowledge of God, which is "eternally generated" because God (*Sat*) is eternally in his self-cognition and so eternally proceeds, Bliss Ananda, from this colloquy of *Sat* and *Cit*.

Upadhyaya explains:

> The differentiation of the Divine Self as subject and object can be served by no other medium than the Undivided, Infinite Substance which is Pure Knowledge.... It is knowledge and nothing but knowledge which can distinguish the Knowing Self of God from His Known Self. Jesus Christ has told us that there is a response of knowledge in the Godhead. God knows His own Self-begotten in Thought and is known, in return, by that Begotten Self. God reproduces in knowledge a corresponding, acknowledging Self-Image, and from this colloquy of Reason proceeds His Spirit of Love which sweetens the Divine Bosom with boundless delight.[13]

According to Upadhyaya's description of the doctrine of the Trinity, Jesus Christ is "God's own Known Self" or "God's own self begotten in Thought" or the "Acknowledging Self-Image." Thus, He is the *Cit* or Logos of the Father. Through this description,

---

[12] Brahamabandhab Upadhyaya, "The True Doctrine of Maya," *Sophia* (1899), in Baago, *Pioneers of Indigenous Christianity*, 147.

[13] Brahamabandhab Upadhyaya, "Christ's Claim to Attention," *The Twentieth Century* (1901), in *Writings I*, 116–117.

158 *Christ without Borders*

he tries to explain to his countrymen that the God whom the Christians worship is the Supreme Brahman or *Saccidananda*, and Jesus Christ is this Supreme God because he is the incarnation of the *Cit* of God. In a hymn that he wrote in Sanskrit, Upadhyaya addresses the Holy Trinity as *Saccidananda* (being, consciousness, and bliss).[14]

This hymn describes the Father as the "Sun, Supreme Lord, Unborn, the seedless Seed of the tree of becoming, the Cause of all, Creator, Providence and the Lord of the Universe," Jesus Christ is "the infinite and perfect Word, the Supreme Person begotten, sharing the Father's nature, Conscious by essence, Giver of true salvation." The Holy Spirit is the one who proceeds from *Sat* (being) and *Cit* (consciousness), "replete with the breath of perfect bliss, the Purifier, the Swift, the Revealer of the Word, the Life-giver." The ingenuity of Upadhyaya's theological method lies in the fact that he uses Hindu philosophic-religious terminologies with necessary distinctions to express the basic Christian doctrines. He avoids the Greek and Latin expressions, which are not only loaded with their own history of development but also unintelligible in the Indian context. While avoiding the heresies of modalism and tritheism, which any explanation of the mystery of the Trinity can fall into when translated into Indian languages, his approach expresses meaningfully the orthodox Christian belief in the Vedantic categories.

Upadhyaya attempts to show that Jesus Christ, the *Cit*, is also the Supreme Lord, and not a mere aspect or "mode" of the Supreme Brahman, as Keshub Chunder Sen thought him to be, although Sen considered Christ to be the Wisdom of God. Upadhyaya holds that this Divine Wisdom—this *Cit* of the *Saccidananda Brahman*, this *Sophia*—is none other than the Incarnate Logos, Jesus Christ. For he says, "*Sophia*, according to the Catholic

---

[14] Brahamabandhab Upadhyaya, "Our New Canticle," in *Sophia* (1898), *Writings* I, 126.

Christ beyond Chalcedon 159

Faith, is more than an aspect of the Godhead. It is the Word of God, the Son, who became man for our sake and died for us on the Cross."[15] The traditional Catholic understanding of the person and function of Jesus Christ is also very clear in his hymn to the Incarnate Logos,[16] where he explains the mystery of incarnation using again the Indian categories of thought.

The question of how the Divine Wisdom, the eternal *Cit*, can become real man if the world itself is illusory or *maya*, at least according to the advaitic philosophy of Sankara, is answered by Upadhyaya by interpreting the teaching of Sankara on *maya*. He expounds his understanding of *maya* using Thomistic expositions on the nature of necessary and contingent beings. He writes, "*Maya* is what St Thomas calls '*creatio passiva*'—passive creation. It is the quality of all that is not *Brahman* and is defined by the Angelic Doctor as 'habitude of having being from another, and resulting from the operation' of God."[17] In the same line of thinking, Upadhyaya explains that creatures have only dependent and participated existence, in comparison with Brahman, who is identical with his own Being, and is indeed necessary Being.

Creatures are not necessary beings, but rather are contingent. Apart from Brahman, creatures are indeed darkness, falsity, and nothingness (*tenebrae, falsitas et nihil*). He further states,

> *Maya* is a mysterious divine operation; It is neither real or unreal.... It cannot be real in the sense of its being essential to the Divine Nature because *Brahman* is self-sufficient and cannot be said to be under the necessity of being related to finite. Nor is it unreal, for by *maya*

---

[15] Animananda, *The Blade*, 121.

[16] Brahamabandhab Upadhyaya, "The Incarnate Logos," in *The Twentieth Century* (1901), in *Writings I*, 190ff.; Baago, *Pioneers of Indigenous Christianity*, 140–141; Boyd, *An Introduction to Indian Christian Theology*, 77–78.

[17] Upadhyaya, "The True Doctrine of Maya," in *Writings I*, 214.

160 *Christ without Borders*

> comes to exist the finite which possesses being, though
> not essentially—the essence of the finite not being
> identical with its existence. From an unreality nothing can
> proceed. *Maya* is neither real or necessary, nor unreal but
> contingent.[18]

Upadhyaya interprets the advaitic term *maya*—which expresses
the nonbeingness (*asat*) of everything other than the Brahman
and "illusion" in the popular understanding—in such a way that
this term can serve to express the Christian doctrine of creation
and the contingent reality of the world. According to him, *maya*
can also express the absolutely free and creative power of God
(*sakti*), which calls the world into existence, the sin of considering
oneself as absolute without acknowledging the dependence on
God and also "in a sense the prevenient grace which awakens in
our hearts the desire to return to him."[19] This interpretation of
maya expressing the reality of the created world as dependent on
God is very important for Indian Christology. Incarnation of
the eternal *Cit* has no meaning if the created world is nonbeing
or illusory.

Jesus Christ, the Transcendent Image of Brahman and Nara-Hari

In his Christological hymn, B. Upadhyaya uses Indian terminologies
and tries to answer the basic Christological question: Who is
Jesus Christ? And the soteriological question: How does Jesus
Christ bring about salvation for mankind? Although poetry is no
substitute for systematic theological reflection, one could easily
detect a systematic development of the theme of the person and
function of Jesus Christ in this Christological hymn by Upadhyaya.

---

[18] *Writings I*, 215.

[19] Boyd, *An Introduction to Indian Christian Theology*, 76.

He writes,

> The transcendent Image of Brahman
> Blossomed and mirrored in the full-to-overflowing
> Eternal Intelligence—Victory to God, the God-Man.
> Child of Pure Virgin,
> Guide of the Universe, infinite in Being
> Yet beauteous with relations, Victory to God, the God-Man.
> Ornament of the Assembly
> Of saints and sages, Destroyer of fear, Chastiser
> Of the Spirit of Evil, Victory to God, the God-Man.
> Dispeller of weakness
> Of soul and body, pouring out life for others.
> Whose deeds are holy, Victory to God, the God-Man.
> Priest and Offerer
> Of his own soul in agony, whose Life is Sacrifice,
> Destroyer of sin's poison, Victory to God, the God-Man.
> Tender, beloved,
> Soother of the human heart, Ointment of the eyes,
> Vanquisher of fierce death, Victory to God, the God-Man.[20]

Upadhyaya does not seek to compromise the content of the Catholic belief in the Incarnate Logos, who is the second person of the Blessed Trinity and truly human and truly divine, when he uses Indian terminology. His attempt is to provide a deeper understanding of the meaning of these mysteries for his countrymen. The preexistent Christ is the transcendent image of Brahman, the eternal *Cit* of the Godhead. Though he is Cit of the *Nirguna Brahman,* as born of the "pure Virgin" he reveals that he is "beauteous with relations" (*saguna*). Here again, Upadhyaya

---

[20] This version of the hymn "Incarnate Logos" by Brahmabandhav is from Charles Freer Andrews, *The Renaissance in India: Its Missionary Aspect* (London: Church Missionary Society, 1912), appendix 8; also cited in Boyd, *An Introduction to Indian Christian Theology,* 77.

seems to emphasize that it is not the personal aspect of God (*Saguna Brahman*) that was born of the Virgin but the absolute *Cit* of the *Nirguna Brahman*, the Godhead. He prefers to use the term *Nara-Hari* (Man-God). In the refrain referring to the incarnate Logos, Jesus Christ—the one person in whom the two natures, the human and the divine, are in a hypostatic union—*Hari,* though a synonym for God in common Hindu parlance, has Vaishnavite sectarian overtones. Some Christians may not be happy with this use of the term *Hari* (God) in connection with *Nara* (Man) to express the two natures in Jesus Christ because *Hari* is a proper name or Vishnu, the absolute personal God in the Vaishnava religious sect of Hinduism. But in the context of Upadhyaya's reflection on Christology with his selective use of Indian categories and his interpretation of them to express the content of Christian faith, we can conclude with certainty that he uses the term *Hari* as a synonym for God evoking devotion to Jesus Christ, the *Nara-Hari* rather than evoking theological controversies.

Jesus Christ, the God-Man

We have already seen how Upadhyaya used the term *Nara-Hari* (Man-God) in addressing Jesus Christ in his hymn of incarnation. Faithful to the Christological Formula of the Council of Chalcedon, he tries to explain how we can understand the one person of Jesus Christ as having two natures, both divine and human. He uses the Indian philosophic-anthropological categories to explain this mystery of hypostatic union. In his journal *The Twentieth Century,* he writes,

> According to Vedanta, human nature is composed of five sheaths or divisions (kosa). These sheaths are: (1) physical (*annamaya*); (2) vital (*pranamaya*); (3) mental (*manomaya*); (4) intellectual (*vijnanamaya*); (5) spiritual (*anandamaya*). These five sheaths are presided over by a personality (*ahampratyayi*), which knows itself. This self-knowing

Christ beyond Chalcedon 163

individual (*jiva-chaitanya*) is but a reflected spark of the Supreme Reason (*kutastha-caitanya*) who abides in every man as the prime source of life and light.[21]

From this understanding of the nature of man with five sheaths, which is typically Indian,[22] Upadhyaya tries to explain the hypostatic union of divine and human natures in Jesus Christ the God-Man:

> The time-incarnate Divinity is also composed of five sheaths: but it is presided over by the Person of Logos Himself and not by any created personality (*aham*). The five sheaths and the individual agent, enlivened and illumined by Divine Reason ... make up man. But in the God-man the five sheaths are acted upon directly by the Logos-God and not through the medium of any individuality.[23]

Some detect in this explanation of the hypostatic union of the divine and human natures in Jesus Christ a certain closeness to Apollinarianism,[24] which taught that the divinization of the flesh of Christ was so total that the Savior was not a real man but only "appeared as a man." It denied Christ the presence of a human free will and normal human psychological development.[25] But in Upadhyaya's explanation of the hypostatic union using the Indian philosophic-anthropological categories, the human intellectual and volitional faculties in Jesus are not assumed by the Logos-God or eternal *Cit*, and therefore Jesus remains one like us. The difference between him and us is that in him dwells the Logos-God as he is,

---

[21] Upadhyaya, "The Incarnate Logos," 191.

[22] Joseph Mattam, "Interpreting Christ in India Today: The Calcutta School," *Indian Journal of Theology* 23 (1974): 196.

[23] Upadhyaya, "The Incarnate Logos," 191.

[24] Boyd, *An Introduction to Indian Christian Theology*, 80.

[25] J. N. D. Kelly, *Early Christian Doctrines*, 5th ed. (London: A&C Black, 1989), 296.

164   *Christ without Borders*

and we have in us only the general presence of him as the "prime source of life and light." So in his humanity, he is like us, although in his divinity he is essentially different from us, because "Jesus Christ is God by the necessity of His being, but He became man of His own free choice. It was compassion for us, which made Him our Brother, like us in sorrow and suffering but without sin. Jesus Christ is perfectly divine and perfectly human. He is the incarnate Logos."[26] Before judging whether Upadhyaya's explanation is close to Apollinarianism, one must consider that the philosophical and anthropological presuppositions of Apollinaris are different from those of Upadhyaya and that the latter conveys the meaning of hypostatic union without doing violence to the understanding of human nature and divine nature in the one person of Jesus Christ.

Jesus Christ, the Unique Incarnation of God

The Hindu theistic traditions, especially Vaishnavism, believe in the "descent" or *avatara* of God Vishnu in human form from time to time "for the protection of good, for the destruction of the wicked and for the establishment of the law."[27] According to these traditions, there is a multiplicity of *Avataras:* prominent among them are Rama and Krishna. They are the incarnations of Vishnu who himself is believed to be the manifestation of Brahman. In this context of Hindu belief in *Avataras,* Upadhyaya is totally opposed to the idea of considering Jesus Christ as an *avatara* not only because it removes the uniqueness of the incarnation of Brahman in Jesus Christ but also because it undermines the Christian doctrine of atonement. So from the Christological and soteriological point of view, according to Upadhyaya one cannot substitute the doctrine of the unique incarnation of God in Jesus Christ with a Christian doctrine of *avatara*. He is convinced

---

[26] Upadhyaya, "The Incarnate Logos," 191.
[27] *Bhagavad-Gita* IV.7.8.

Christ beyond Chalcedon 165

that there is a fundamental difference between the doctrines of incarnation and *avatara,* which lies in the basic Christian belief that God became man to redeem mankind from sin and there is nothing like this in the doctrine of *avatara.*[28] Krishna as an *avatara* of Vishnu cannot be compared to Christ, the unique incarnation of Brahman, because Krishna and other *Avataras* belong simply to the realm of *maya* or contingent beings. However, the *avatara* doctrine, according to him, can give an insight into the Christian understanding of the God-given capacity of humans to be united with God. He says,

> The erroneous Vedantic doctrine of God realizing Himself in spiritual heroes and *avatars* (incarnations) illumines in a new way, as far as a mystery can said to be illumined, the transcended Christian belief that man is destined to become perfect like God by union with Him who is *real* God and *real* Man, fully realized God-in-Man.[29]

Once the uniqueness of the incarnation of God in Jesus Christ was safeguarded, Upadhyaya did not find any difficulty in defending the so-called *Avataras* of Hindu traditions as historical personalities or moral teachers or both, probably because he believed that their complete rejection would not be in the best interests of the nationalistic movements and of the preservation of the Indian culture, which was under the onslaught of the West during British colonial rule.

Upadhyaya also rejected the doctrine of *Isvara* in describing the personality of Jesus Christ. According to this doctrine, *Isvara* is the personal aspect of absolute God, capable of entering into relationship with the world. Although *Isvara* stands for the *Saguna* (with attributes) aspect of *Nirguna Brahman* (attribute-less absolute

---

[28] Julius Lipner, "A Case Study in 'Hindu Catholicism': Brahmabandhab Upadhyaya (1861–1907)," *Zeitschrift für Missionswissenschaft und Religionswissenschaft* (1988): 49.

[29] Upadhyaya, "*Sophia-Monthly,* July 1887," in *Writings I,* 191.

166 *Christ without Borders*

God). *Isvara* is considered to be of a lower level than that of the absolute God. Upadhyaya therefore opposed describing Jesus Christ in terms of *Isvara,* because it would mean for the Hindus that the God whom the Christians worship is lower than the absolute God. While attempting to explain the meaning of Christ using Vedantic categories of thought, Upadhyaya would not compromise the content of Christian faith with any of them.

An Appraisal of Upadhyaya's Approach

Upadhyaya's attempt to develop an Indian theology has not generally received the attention and appreciation it rightly deserves. The critical evaluations of his methods of theologizing range from real appreciation and approval to extreme rejection. Alfons Väth, who claimed to have attempted a critical study of the person and work of Upadhyaya,[30] asserts that Upadhyaya not only failed in his attempts because "as an Indian and a former Hindu he did not understand clearly the essence of Hinduism like an outsider" but also because he falsely believed that he could introduce Christianity into Hinduism and win over Hinduism. In fact, Hinduism won over Christianity in the person of Upadhyaya, although not completely due to his untimely death.[31]

Väth claims that, as a "critical historian," he attempts to evaluate the life and work of Upadhyaya because the earlier biography of Animananda was not only influenced by the latter's admiration for the master but also was too Indian.[32] Väth seems to be sympathetic to his subject of study, but his attitude seems condescending and not free from many of the prejudices of the

---

[30] Alfons Väth, *Im Kampfe mit der Zauberwelt des Hinduismus: Upadhyaya Brahmabandhav und das Problem der Überwindung des Höheren Hinduismus durch das Christentum* (Berlin: Dümmlers, 1928).

[31] Väth, *Im Kampfe mit der Zauberwelt des Hinduismus,* 197–198.

[32] Väth, *Im Kampfe mit der Zauberwelt des Hinduismus,* 10.

European missionaries of his time, especially with regard to the idea that inculturation is a dangerous affair. On the other hand, Schmidlin recognizes and appreciates Upadhyaya's theological enterprise and compares it with the Thomistic attempts at using Aristotelian categories of thought with necessary interpretation for expounding the Christian doctrine.[33]

Non-Catholic authors recognized and evaluated positively Upadhyaya's efforts to evolve an Indian theology. F. Heiler not only recognizes the original and creative contribution of B. Upadhyaya in developing an Indian theology but also finds fault with the Catholic Church for silencing such a creative Indian Catholic thinker.[34] R. Boyd echoes the general Protestant criticism of Upadhyaya that he was too preoccupied with interpreting and evaluating Indian philosophy with the Thomistic frame of thought with the result that it had curtailed his creative thinking. He says, "All through his expositions one feels that the Angelic Doctor looms too large and the Bible too small. If only he had been free to take the deposit of faith as found in the Bible, or even in the undivided Church of the first four centuries and then to carry out the work of a Clement or an Origen, what a wonderful work had been accomplished."[35]

Today, questions can be raised about the attempts of Upadhyaya in interpreting the significance of Jesus Christ through the Vedantic categories of thought: Was he not Hindu-izing Christianity? Was he right in using terms and expressions of Hindu thought that originate from a different worldview other than Christian to serve his purpose? Was he addressing only the elite of the Brahmanic tradition without taking into account the

---

[33] Josef Schmidlin, "Swami Upadhyaya Brahmabandhav," *Zeitschrift fur Missionswissenschaft und Religionswissenschaft* (1924): 217.

[34] F. Heiler, *Christlicher Glaube und indisches Geistesleben: Rabindranath Tagore, Mahatma Gandhi, Brahmabandhav Upadhyaya, Sadhu Sundar Singh* (Munich: Verlag von Ernst Reinhardt, 1926), 79.

[35] Boyd, *An Introduction to Indian Christian Theology*, 77.

popular Hindu beliefs or explaining the meaning of Jesus Christ to the poor and to the so-called dominated castes or outcasts? By resurrecting the theological ideas of Upadhyaya, are we not succumbing to the temptation of continuing our dialogue with Brahmanic Hinduism, which does not seem to have any result and neglecting our commitment to the subaltern people?

Upadhyaya's Christological reflections are not dissimilar to that of the Fathers and are very close to the interpretation of incarnate Christ as Anthropos-Logos. According to M. M. Thomas, Upadhyaya's Christology does not "distinguish clearly between the eternal Logos and the incarnate Logos, and therefore lacks the basis of the human individuality of Jesus Christ. But his position is not outside the Christological framework of traditional Christianity."[36] The relevance of his Christological approach lies in the fact that it recognizes the value of the philosophical categories of Indian tradition in conveying the meaning of the person and work of Jesus Christ in a way understandable to the Indian people.

B. Upadhyaya's attempt was not simply an academic exercise, but he had the enthusiasm of a learned Hindu convert to Christ who wanted to bring his countrymen to this Christ experience and find in Christ the true salvation. In theory and practice, be opened the way for an Indian theology. The value of his approach can be judged against the further development of Indian theology through theologians like Pierre Johanns, Jules Monchanin, Abhishiktananda (Henri le Saux), Raimon Panikkar, Bede Griffiths, D. S. Amalorpavadass, J. B. Chethimattam, Antony Mookenthottam, and Michael Amaladoss.

The history of the development of Christological reflection shows that the interpretation of the meaning of the Christ event was necessitated by the context of Christian proclamation about Jesus Christ. The NT provides us with dense material about it, and

---

[36] M. M. Thomas, *The Acknowledged Christ of the Indian Renaissance* (Madras: CLS, 1976), 110–111.

the terms used to express it needed to be clarified. The authors of the New Testament were of Jewish origin, and the categories of thought they used were of the Hebrew worldview. If Christ were to be proclaimed meaningfully in the Hellenistic world, these terms were to be restated in Greek categories of thought. It was also necessary to enter into dialogue with the educated class of the Greek world who were attracted to the Christian message. In fact, John and Paul had already begun such a dialogue in their writings. The Fathers of the Church found it legitimate and necessary for the proclamation of the gospel.

Upadhyaya's attempt to interpret the meaning of Jesus Christ is in the same tradition as the Fathers. His approach to interpreting the Christ event does not exclude the other ways of proclaiming the meaning of Christ to the poor and the marginalized. He did not have any hidden agenda of Hinduizing Christianity or Christianizing Hinduism. His writing shows that he had an insight into the possibility of explicating in a deeper and clearer way the marvelous mystery of God revealed in Jesus Christ through Vedantic categories of thought than the Greek and Scholastic categories of thought are capable of doing. He overcomes the exclusivist tendency of the Catholic Church's thinking that Christ and his message can be communicated only through Greek philosophy. He did this not by negating its value but by completing it with Indian philosophical thought. He made the Christian theology more catholic, not sectarian. Therefore, Upadhyaya's attempt to theologize in the Indian context was to catholicize the meaning of Christian doctrine, to expand its horizon and open up the hitherto unknown depths of Christian revelation more than to dialogue with the Hindu partner, whether educated or uneducated. He believed that it was his Christian duty to preserve and explain what is good and true in the Indian tradition both for its own sake and for the sake of the explication of Christian revelation.

In two studies on Upadhyaya by Julius Lipner, there is a shift in the evaluation of his theological enterprises. The first is very

170   *Christ without Borders*

critical, and the second, sympathetic. He writes, "Upadhyaya's contribution to Indian Christianity is major but latent: more in the nature of banners waved and kites flown than a systematic attempt to indigenize the faith."[37] In the second study he writes, "He [Brahmabandhab] ushered in a new mode of thinking. He gave Indian Christians the impetus to reassess their faith in a new light, to search for a religious identity rooted in their native culture. By encouraging Indian Christians to be authentically Indian, his example helps them to be the surer witnesses of their faith."[38] This last evaluation of Upadhyaya seems to be closer to his real contribution to the Indian church and theology as a pioneer in theologizing in the Indian context.

It is true that Upadhyaya attempted to interpret the meaning of Jesus Christ in dialogue with the Vedantic tradition of Brahmanic or Sanskritic Hinduism. But he does not claim that it is the only way to interpret God's revelation in Jesus Christ. But he affirms that in complementarity with the traditional Hellenistic and Scholastic interpretation, it can widen the scope of understanding the mystery of Christ and make theology more catholic. Any exclusive Christology—whether Western or Eastern, Brahmanic or Dalit, white or Black—making claims that it is the only way to interpret the mystery of the Christ event can become dangerously sectarian and oppressive. While developing other important and relevant Christologies in the Indian context, such as Dalit, tribal, feminist, and liberation Christologies, theologizing in the Indian context must carry forward the attempts of Brahmabandhab Upadhyaya in dialoguing with the Vedantic tradition to interpret the meaning of Jesus Christ to deepen the understanding the mystery of Christ beyond the traditional Western interpretation of it and to proclaim Christ meaningfully to those for whom the Vedantic tradition of interpreting reality makes sense.

---

[37] Lipner, "A Modern Indian Christian Response," 308–310.

[38] Lipner, "A Case Study in 'Hindu Catholicism,'" 51.

11

The Suffering Christ of the Subcontinent

The fundamental question "Who is Jesus Christ?" can be answered in two ways. It can be answered by referring to his functions and identification marks that separate him from others. This answer will single him out from everyone else. By identifying him as Jesus of Nazareth, we can speak of his uniqueness. For example, we can show how he is different from other mediators and saviors, how his claims are unique, and how his life and teachings are different from other teachers and prophets. But Jesus's identity is different. It answers the question of "who" Jesus Christ is. It is a deeper question. It refers to the mystery of Christ and to the mystery of the one who raises the question. Both the answers, one referring to his identification and the other referring to his identity, are needed. The first one cannot but be contextual. The second one too, though universal and absolute, cannot escape the limitations of historical, social, cultural, and philosophical terms that are used to articulate it. His identity can only be only encountered, and any articulation of that encounter must lead to that transforming encounter with him. The problem with Christology has always been confusing identification of Jesus Christ with his identity or mixing them up or separating them by absolutizing one or the other.

Any identification of Jesus Christ, however meaningful in one context for centuries, need not necessarily be meaningful in another context. Jesus Christ is proclaimed in such a way that his identity

172 *Christ without Borders*

is encountered. For Christ's sake we may have to give up some of his identifications, which are culturally conditioned, in order that people may encounter his identity and be transformed. It is a difficult task. It is a call to encounter him in one's life situation and identify him in the *logoi* of the context.

Christic Identification and Identity in the Early Church

Christic identification does not actually answer the question of who Jesus is, but it does answer what Jesus is. Jesus is known by what he has done. This was the emphasis of functional Christology, summed up in the Latin phrase *Christus pro me*: Christ for me. This approach is adequately justified in the New Testament, as Jesus's own self-identification according to Luke is based on what he *does*. When John the Baptist sends his disciples to inquire whether Jesus is the expected one who is to come, Jesus answers, "Go and tell John what you have seen and heard: the blind receive their sight, the lame walk, lepers are cleansed, and the deaf hear, the dead are raised up, the poor have good news preached to them" (Lk 7:22). This is the actualization of the mission manifesto of Jesus that Luke had already systematically presented at the beginning of Jesus's Galilean ministry, quoting Isaiah (Lk 4:18ff.).

Is there anything about his identity here? Nothing! For Luke, John the Baptist's inquiry is not just to satisfy his personal curiosity but to know whether Jesus can be identified as the expected one or "he who is to come" by all those who were waiting for the liberation of Israel. If he is not the one who is to come, then *we* have to look for another. But Jesus's answer points to his function as the one who comes, so the identification is done. Is this identification sufficient to establish his identity? If it were to be so, would Jesus have been recognized as Lord and God even before his resurrection? Critical studies on the New Testament witness about the person of Jesus have shown us clearly that the confessional statements about his identity are made after the post–Easter encounter with him.

Implied in the question "Who do you say that I am?" is another question that often escapes our scrutiny and appropriate response. The question Jesus raises is apparently concerned with his identity, but his identity is inextricably intertwined with ours, such that we cannot answer Jesus's question without referring to the implied question "Who do you think you are?" If the first question can be answered only in faith, the second, too, can only be answered in faith and grace. Both can be answered only with assistance from above. Jesus's question is directed at the fundamental question humans ask about themselves: *Who am I?* It is concerned with the mystery of human existence, its origin and destiny, or its source and its goal.

What is the absolute significance or meaning of human existence? Someone or something cannot give absolute meaning and significance to human existence if it is not of infinite or absolute value. It cannot be anything other than the infinite Other, God himself. Humans can discover themselves, the meaning or significance of their lives, only by referring to the source and destiny of their lives. In their discovery of themselves, they discover who God is. In this process, humans can discover, though they may not always, that they belong to the mystery of God. Though distinct from themselves, they are not separate from God. He is not, then, the absolute Other, the God of the philosophers. Rather, God is the God of relationship, for "in him we move, live and have our being" (Acts 17:28).

Jesus's "Who do you say that I am" is answered by discovering him as the absolute meaning or the beginning and end, the alpha and omega of human life. The first disciples made this discovery after encountering him as the one who rose again from the dead. They shared their lives for three years with Jesus of Nazareth,

174   *Christ without Borders*

and, in the beginning, they experienced him as someone different. In him, they experienced a rabbi or a prophet who spoke with authority unknown to his predecessors, who forgave sins and freely and unashamedly entered into table-fellowship with the poor, the marginalized, and so-called sinners. They experienced one who spontaneously called God *Abba*, who prophetically denounced the social and religious structures of oppression and the powers that sustain and manipulate such structures for their own end. This transforming experience of him as the resurrected one made them confess that he was the beginning and end of their lives, the absolute meaning of their lives, the *alpha* and the *omega*. Indeed, he was the Lord and God of their lives, but it took a lot of time for them to articulate this transforming experience of the risen Jesus. The experience was so real and overwhelming that, in it, they discovered his identity as Lord.

The title *Kyrios* is perhaps the last of the Christological titles. The Gospel narratives about this profound confession occur within dramatic interplays of visibility and invisibility, blindness and sight, absence and presence. These narratives give insight into the discovery of who Jesus is. Dogmas and doctrines can only make adequate symbolic statements about Jesus that can evoke certain insights into the fuller mystery of his being. Faith in him, however, refers to his identity in response to encounter with him. Encountering him is a transforming experience that grounds a faith affirmation about him. As these encounters do not exhaust his identity, no faith affirmation can fully articulate his identity. It remains as the mystery in which we are involved. Jesus is to be experienced. All authentic Christologies are faith affirmations about him that can lead one to the faith experience or the experience of his identity, which cannot be separated from the identity of the believer who confesses him as Lord and God.

In the context of these various identifications of Jesus by ordinary people as one of the prophets, Peter makes the confession

The Suffering Christ of the Subcontinent 175

of Jesus's identity in relation to him. In the context of her brother's death in Jesus's absence and her own suffering in grief, Martha made her confessional statement about his Lordship. In the context of shutting himself out by his doubts about Jesus's new identity as the risen One, Thomas was graced to discover Jesus as his Lord and God in the presence of the community from which he had separated himself. All these confessions could not have been the immediate articulations of their faith experience but a gradual unfolding of their recognition of the identity of Jesus of Nazareth as Jesus of faith, the absolute meaning of their lives.

Confronted with the resurrection experience, the apostolic community struggled to express the content of its experience. In the light of the resurrection, it began to understand Jesus in a new light. It was a difficult task. It had no terminology to express this mystery. At the same time, the community found itself deeply involved in the mystery of the risen Jesus. He was the same Jesus with whom the disciples had shared their lives during his ministry, but he was also different. This *difference* made all the difference in their lives.

They had no words to articulate it, so their understanding of the person of Jesus was expressed in some of the confessional formulas of the New Testament. The apostolic communities found it difficult to proclaim Jesus as the Messiah or the Christ immediately after his resurrection because the political expectations related to the Messiah were not fulfilled in Jesus. He was the Messiah or the Christ, but not according to the expectations of the Jewish people. Though each of the evangelists, Paul, and the other authors of what became the New Testament had their own methods of communicating in a systematic way that Jesus was the fulfillment of their expectations, there was no systematic reflection on the person of Jesus Christ. However, the catechetical needs of the community and the challenges it had to face in proclaiming the reality of the risen Jesus determined the New Testament Christologies.

176 *Christ without Borders*

Both the identification and the identity of Jesus are ultimately important for humans to realize their unfolding and final destiny. Therefore, the answer to the question "Who do you say that I am" must be answered at two levels: his identification and his identity. All believers in all times and places can recognize his identity. But his identification cannot be done in universal categories. His identification is intimately related to the context in which Jesus is encountered. The whole history of the development of Christology deals with the articulation of his identification in the context of those who encountered him and experienced his identity. Jesus's identification was made in such an intelligible way that they were graced to encounter him as he is. They were transformed by the gift of the revelation of Jesus's identity in relation to the believers. Therefore, it was not only a revelation of who Jesus was but also a revelation of the identity of the believers themselves and the revelation of what humans and the world are called to become. Every meaningful Christology is, therefore, the articulation of the believers' identification of Jesus in the context of their lives. They identified him as the answer to the fundamental questions they raise about themselves and their world as understood by them. But the Christic identity is absolute. It can never be relativized. It is universal, radically relational, cosmotheandric,[1] and tempiternal, and as such can be encountered historically but history cannot contain it. It includes and transcends history.

Christic Identification in the Indian Context

How is Jesus known and recognized in the Indian context of religious pluralism? How would one distinguish him from other gods, goddesses, and founders of religions? Here, the question is about his identification in the Indian context. In the past,

---

[1] Raimon Panikkar, *The Unknown Christ of Hinduism* (Maryknoll, NY: Orbis Books, 1981), 20.

The Suffering Christ of the Subcontinent   177

Western missionaries dismissed the worship of different gods and goddesses by Hindus as a pernicious superstition, a horrendous worship of devils, a blatant idolatry or the affirmation of an untenable pantheistic belief system. They hoped that it would slowly fade away with the advent of Western education and the eventual secularization of the society. They affirmed that all these mythological divine figures would disappear with the passage of time when the believers realize that a god with an elephant head or a monkey head and thousands of such manifestations could not have existed in reality but only in the fertile imagination of those who created them. But they are all there with a wider acceptance and a stronger appeal even among the educated classes. They are worshiped with festive celebrations, pilgrimages, special prayers, fasting and other religious observances.

People have the innate need to be connected to everything that transcends them, especially with the absolute reality that they acknowledge as the One beyond name and form. Therefore, whatever form through which one establishes this relationship is unimportant, but people realize that the need to be related to this reality is important. Where is Jesus Christ in this religious context of India? Is he like Rama or Krishna, the incarnated appearances or *avatar*s of Vishnu? Or is he like those historical founders of religions like the ascetic Mahavira or the Buddha, the enlightened one with a prophetic mission? Or a prophet who revealed God's will like Muhammad? The Christian answer would be an emphatic "No."

The Christian proclamation asserts that Jesus Christ cannot be compared with any of the gods of the Hindus or with Buddha the enlightened or with Muhammad the prophet. Jesus Christ is the unique Son of God. He is the Lord. He lived and died at a particular time and place. He was the expected Messiah. He saved humans from sin and meaningless death by his own death on the cross and by his resurrection. He is the only mediator and savior. All these faith affirmations and historical facts are absolutely clear to a Christian believer. But all these identifications of Jesus

178 *Christ without Borders*

Christ and faith affirmations would not be meaningful to those who do not share the Judeo-Christian view of God, humans, and the world. Some would respect this view of Christians; sometimes they may even be sympathetic to Christian claims. But some have real theological, epistemological, or ideological problems with the Christian proclamation.

It is a serious theological problem for the Hindu mind when Jesus Christ, who is a particular historical person, is proclaimed to be the only Savior and God. For the Hindu view of reality, it is not a "folly" to proclaim a historical person as Lord and God or Son of God. They would affirm that there were many such persons, and each one of them had a particular and unique message to give. The exclusive claim that Jesus is the only Savior and Lord would not resonate in the Hindu mind. Moreover, the overemphasis on the historical existence of Jesus Christ—as if the historical dimension were to be the only important dimension of reality—is not acceptable to those who hold that the spatiotemporal existence is perhaps the least aspect of the whole of reality. In other words, whatever is real need not necessarily be historical. Such a notion is not alien to the Christian worldview, as certain fundamental faith affirmations are not based on historical facts. Further, the belief in a God who can relate to humans only after the historical appearance of Jesus on earth and only with those who believe in him seems to be partisan, exclusive, and unconcerned about millions and millions of humans who may never come to believe in him.

The epistemological problem consists in attributing universality to something particular and historically limited. Jesus Christ, as presented by the traditional Christian proclamation, cannot claim any universality because he is presented as a tribal god or sectarian god, who excludes all who have other names for the ultimate reality whom he claims to reveal.

The ideological problem connected with understanding the person and mission of Jesus Christ is that he is brought by the colonial powers who oppressed the people, destroyed their national identity, violated their sovereignty, and robbed them of their wealth. The image of Christ as the Lord and God of the ruthless colonizers naturally would not appeal to those who seek not only liberation of their own selves but also from socioeconomic and political oppression.

The believers in Christ insist on his particularity and uniqueness that distinguish him from other saviors and mediators. But in the process they have made him one of the avatars who is to be approached by cult and rituals and other religious observances similar to those followed by people who believe in the gods and the goddesses of the Hindu pantheon. Therefore, Jesus Christ of the Christian proclamation does not challenge the listeners to make a radical decision to encounter him and experience their own liberation and transformation of their society. For them he is the Christian God, one among many.

An identification of Jesus is necessary, but it should not be a repetition of those symbols and images of identification that emerged in a particular cultural context yet would not be meaningful in the Indian context. The creative commitment to Jesus's tradition is to discover in the Indian context symbols and thought patterns that would reveal the real identity of Jesus Christ—such that they can encounter him and discover the mystery of their own being in relation with him and with the world.

A meaningful Christology in the Indian context must be one that articulates the Christic identity in a way that is intelligible, challenging, and decisive for the seekers of Truth to encounter Jesus Christ as the beginning and end of their lives. In this they should find their own identity and meaning of their existence in the world, offering a transforming and joyful insight into the mystery of their own being in relation to other humans, the world, and God.

The New Testament witness gives a deep insight into the fact that the proclamation of Jesus cannot be and should not be limited to his historical identification but an identity that transcends historical limitations, although it does not exclude the historical dimension of Jesus's existence. This mode of existence is not something new to the Christian tradition. Originating from the Christic identity for which I have no other term to express other than an apparently contradictory term, *inclusive transcendence*—the traditional Christian worldview and Christian anthropology speak of a continued existence of humans that transcends historical existence but is determined by it. There are various instances of such a Christic identity as inclusive transcendence in the New Testament—for example, the apostolic encounter with Jesus in his historical existence as well as with his transhistorical mode of being as the risen Lord; Paul's encounter with the resurrected and yet suffering; the cosmic Christology of Paul and the Logos Christology of John; and the reference to the whole reality of Christ, namely, his preexistence, historical existence, and transhistorical continued existence articulated in the Christian confession, "Jesus Christ is the same, yesterday, today and forever" (Heb 13:8).

The Christian experience of God as Trinity—a communion of three divine persons without separation and division, yet at the same time with distinction and difference; the mystery of incarnation by which God became human and thus embraced the whole world; the encounter of God in the sacraments; the Indian religio-philosophical insight into the advaitic relationship between the absolute and relative as "not one but not two"—can lead us to an understanding of the Christic identity as different from the Christic identification.

Panikkar has convincingly shown that a mere identification of Jesus would make him only one of the founders of a religion, a "remarkable Jewish teacher, who had the fortune or misfortune of being put to death rather young."[2] The identity of Jesus Christ is the living Christ and the mystery in which one encounters and is involved in the bond of everything divine, human, and cosmic,

---

[2] Panikkar, *The Unknown Christ of Hinduism*, 27.

without separation, division, or confusion but distinct and different from one another. But this Jesus Christ is not an a-personal principle. "The Christ that 'sits at the right hand of the Father' is the first-born of the universe, born of Mary: he is Bread as well as the hungry, naked, or imprisoned."[3]

Recognizing this identity of Christ is both a grace and a task. When he is encountered as the only mediator of everything human, divine, and material, each human being is given an insight into the mystery of his or her own being, what he or she is and what he or she is called to become. Then everything and everyone is recognized as a Christophany, a manifestation of the reality of Christ. In this insight lies perhaps the deepest meaning of the Eucharist, the greatest Sacrament of Communion, where God, human and the world, the absolute and the relative, the infinite and finite, the historical and transhistorical, the material and spiritual unite without losing the distinction and difference of each but inextricably united to one another. Such an understanding of the Christic identity challenges the one who is committed to Christ to be responsible for one's own unfolding as a person in radical relationship to others, to struggle with others to create situations where humans can authentically become humans, to be responsible for the entire creation, to be open to celebrate plurality and to embrace everything that "God has cleansed" (Acts 10:15).

Therefore, it is imperative for an Indian Christology to recapture the New Testament witness to the whole Christ, the insights of the patristic theology of Trinity and Christology, and the advaitic intuition to articulate the universal significance of Jesus Christ. Doing so can challenge us to encounter the mystery of his identity. This can meaningfully explain his presence in everyone who is searching for the meaning of the mystery of their being and in everything that eagerly waits for liberation.

---

[3] Panikkar, *The Unknown Christ of Hinduism*, 27–28.

Christ, the Suffering God of the Subcontinent

Nowhere does the identity of Christ become so universally felt and his inclusive transcendence become so real and decisive as in the struggle of the suffering millions of the subcontinent for a fuller life unfolding their God-given humanity. Here it is not the imagery of a triumphant Pantocrator, or Christ the king, or a cultic figure of Christ, or any such identification that attracts many to encounter him who seek liberation from their misery and misfortune. The Hindus have much more fascinating, strong, and comely images of gods and goddesses. But a God who suffers, Jesus on the cross, is something that touches the Indian mind, especially for the poor and the deeply marginalized.

The Jesus Christ of the Indian subcontinent cannot be identified with a triumphant Messiah whom nobody is expecting. He is discovered by the poor in their struggle for a fuller humanity, just as the poor of Jesus's time discovered in him the compassionate love of God. The real Jesus speaks up in the suffering of the poor, the oppressed Dalits, tribal peoples, bonded laborers, deprived children, and women who are victims of discrimination. They are not a minority. They are not just statistics. They are millions of humans with their own unique personal histories. They are men and women with flesh and blood going through meaningless suffering because the system created by the oppressors would not let them be what they are and become what they are called to become.

The traditional discrimination against the lower castes, the outcasts, the tribal peoples, women, economically poor classes, and poor and orphaned children has worsened. The advent of globalization and the new market forces have helped the middle class and the rich to enjoy further the benefits of modern science and technology. The poor have become dispensable. They are not needed. Their survival, let alone their unfolding of themselves by their unique participation in sustaining life in this world through work, is not the concern of those who make economic policies and political decisions. The worst aspect of the poverty that the poor experience is that it does not let them live as dignified humans. In the Indian context, with class and caste discrimination, the suffering is doubled for the poor people of lower castes and outcasts, and still worse for women in these groups.

The Advaita or the Nonduality of Suffering

The way Jesus lived his life, his message, and the consequence of his option for the poor during his life reveal his identification with all the oppressed and outcast people. Many such prophets and reformers have appeared in the history of the world. Their cause may continue in the history of their followers and admirers. They may be moved to follow the ideology of those great men and women and dedicate their lives to continuing their ideology. But the God revealed through the cross is a suffering God who suffers when human beings suffer because he is absolute love and compassion. The cross reveals that the suffering of humans and their world, whatever its causes and whatever forms, affects God. Suffering subverts the Eastern affirmation about the impassibility of God. A strong resistance against acknowledging Jesus Christ as human by the Docetists and the Gnostics in the early Christian centuries was their refusal to accept the true meaning of the cross. We can see even in the New Testament the struggle of the early Christian community to come to terms with this radical revelation of God, as there is a tendency to an eventual mystification of the cross.

God, who became human in a situation that would not let God be human, would not also let humans be human. It would condemn him to death for God's sake! But this god is the god of the religions and systems that do give more importance to anything other than humans. The cross reveals a God who suffers, a new *advaitam because the suffering of humans cannot be separated from the suffering of God. They are not one but also not two. They are distinct but not separate.* If suffering is a mode of God's being in relation to humans and the world, then should we not let it continue? No, it would be a blasphemy!

God's suffering is concerned with the unfolding of humans to become what they are called to become. Therefore, systems and structures that prevent this process through oppression, injustice, dehumanization, and violence are to be denounced and transformed. Any authentic struggle with consequent sufferings to create a kingdom situation is always liberative and is participation in God's own cause for humans. Therefore, it is a way of reaffirming the divine image of communion in humans and thus alleviating God's own suffering.

Christic Identity in Human Suffering

The Christic identity encountered in the suffering of humans is hitherto unknown in the history of the world. He continues to live in the history of his suffering people. Hence, the Christology of the poor is not an ontological Christology as traditionally understood, asking questions about his being, or he is in himself, or a functional Christology, discussing his roles and what he has done for them. It is a relational Christology that includes both ontological and functional Christologies and yet transcends them. In this relational Christology, humans see their face in him and his face in them and thus they find meaning in their suffering. In this new and radical revelation that Christ suffers with them, they experience empowerment in their struggles for a fuller humanity, and thus they recognize him as the ultimate meaning of their life, as he is encountered as the beginning, the middle, and the end of their lives.

Proclaiming Christ in the Indian context as a powerful dispenser of divine favors to those who take refuge in him is a temptation. He is presented as if he is competing with other gods and saints of popular religions to assert his supremacy. Christ seems

The Suffering Christ of the Subcontinent   185

to help people forget their situation of pain, and thus they are able to tolerate the tyranny of their misery. But he does not seem to understand people's misery or be affected by it. He is beyond the history of the people. It makes no difference whether God had once entered human history, if this history does not continue to be a part of his divine life. He could have been worshiped in one name or another as other religions do, even though they do not believe in his entry into history for its transformation. He is the Christ of religion. He is just another god. He is not the real suffering Christ of the poor.

Many doctrinal statements can be made about this Christ. Humans can be subjugated in his name. Structures and institutions can be built to perpetuate his name to the advantage of his protagonists. He can be manipulated to justify both totalitarianism and terrorism. But he also can be captured by artists and sculptors to give visual satisfaction to those wretched men, women, and children who are despised, humiliated, and treated as the scum of society because they are poor and powerless. But this Christ seems to be silent in the midst of such tragic experiences of real people in their real history of life.

The real Jesus Christ is the one whose identity cannot be separated from the sufferings of the poor. He empowers them through his Spirit to insurrection for and resurrection of their dignity as humans. This is the real Jesus Christ, who suffers with all those who are denied the opportunities to unfold themselves as humans. In this real Jesus Christ one discovers the suffering and compassionate God.

If commitment to and identification with the suffering prophetic image of Christ can inspire such an unleashing of the liberative potential of the people, how much more can the revelation that God in Christ suffers with the poor, the downtrodden, the marginalized, and the discriminated ones. A one-sided projection of Jesus Christ as a revolutionary prophet or social reformer on the one hand or to proclaim him as a God who is different from other gods—but on the other hand who needs to be approached with cult and worship as is done with other gods and goddess—is to destroy "the power and the wisdom" of the cross.

Christ of the subcontinent continues to suffer as he would anywhere in the world when humans are prevented from unfolding their vocation to become truly humans. His blood continues to mingle with the blood of the Sudras; Dalits; tribal peoples; Naxalites; real or so-called bonded laborers; women who are exploited and raped, discriminated against, discarded, and paraded naked; victims of religious bigotry and fanaticism; children who are forced to work in match factories, stone quarries, and tea stalls; and many other oppressed and marginalized.

This identity of Christ as the God who suffers with the least, last, and the lost—as well as in those who create systems of oppression as they are dehumanizing themselves—is a radically new revelation of God in the cross of Jesus. Therefore, any spiritualization of the cross that takes place without revealing a God who suffers with humans who suffer and that does not demand a radical commitment to the integral transformation of society would empty the cross of its absolute significance. The Christ who suffers resurrects *in* those people and movements that strive for a better human life.

12

Christ of Christian Faith in Dialogue with Islamic Faith

The Christian articulation of the God experience stands or falls depending on how it confesses who Jesus Christ is and the God who is revealed through him. The development of the Christian doctrines on Jesus Christ and the understanding of the oneness of God as Trinity had to go through centuries of debates, discussions, condemnations, and even martyrdom—all because the foundational experience of Jesus Christ by the apostles and the apostolic community as articulated in the New Testament was received by the early Christian community as the word of God, normative for life and faith. Therefore, the church had to preserve the faith against those who claimed to be Christians and yet did not accept the original faith of the apostles.

In the history of the church, we have a long list of those who would pick and choose what they thought to be the correct understanding of Jesus's person and mission. The Ebionites, a Jewish-Christian sect, followed Jewish practices but accepted Jesus as a prophet and even an archangel. They did not believe that Jesus was virginally conceived but born of Joseph and Mary. Gnostic Christians taught that since matter was evil, God could not enter into evil matter and become truly human. Therefore, no true incarnation was possible. For them, Jesus was God but

188   *Christ without Borders*

not human, and so he could not have suffered on the cross. Some of the Gnostics taught that a substitute for Jesus was crucified. Docetists believed that Jesus only appeared to be human but was not really human. He could not have suffered but only appeared to have suffered on the cross. Arius, a priest in the fourth century, claimed that if the Word was there in the beginning, as John said, then the Word had a beginning, and therefore the Word was not God but only a creature. He would further add that the title "Son of God" was only an honorific title. He believed that such an understanding would protect the strict monotheism as well as give a higher place for Jesus, almost as an intermediary creature between God and humans. The Council of Nicaea in 325 had to affirm that Jesus Christ was "light from light, true God from true God, begotten not made, one in being [consubstantial or *homoousios*] with the Father." Using Greek philosophical categories and the symbolic word "begetting," the fathers at the council tried to defend the oneness of God and at the same time the divinity of Christ to affirm that he was not a creature.

The Alexandrine Christology went to the extreme position of Eutyches that Jesus had only one nature, namely, the divine nature (monophysitism). Julianism, which emerged from monophysitism, propounded that, from the moment of incarnation, Jesus's body was incorruptible. Therefore, he could not have died. Antiochene Christology went to the extreme in Nestorianism, which separated divinity and humanity in Jesus—therefore, Mary would seem to be the mother only of the human nature of Christ. On the other extreme of this position, according to fourth-century heresiologist Epiphanius, a group called Collyridianists worshiped Mary as a goddess.

The New Testament witnesses to the encounter of Jesus by the apostles and the early community as the risen Lord and the experience of the transforming power of the Holy Spirit. They knew for certain that Jesus, during his earthly life, called God *Abba*,

Father. Jesus himself was encountered as Lord and God after the resurrection. At Pentecost, the community experienced the Holy Spirit. They were strict monotheists like any other Jews and like the Muslims of later times, and it would not have been easy for them to reconcile this experience of the threeness of God with his oneness. But they could not deny their experience either. So they affirmed the oneness of God at the same time they proclaimed and worshiped this one God as Father, Son, and Holy Spirit. They began to baptize in the name of the Father, Son, and Holy Spirit. Irenaeus (died 202), in his Norms of Faith (*Regulae fidei*), affirms that Christians all over believe in One God who is Father, Son, and Spirit—who is above all, through all, and in all (Eph 4:6). They never speculated about how it is possible to believe that God is One and yet three at the same time. But later in the theological reflections, at first by laypeople, many tried to settle the problem by advancing various theories that either overstressed the unity and bypassed the distinctions or overemphasized the distinctions and bypassed the unity. One such heresy proclaimed that God is one principle but has three powers (dynamic monarchianism). Some others claimed that God is one but has three modes of being God (modalism); Sabellius, who was well known in Arabia, was among them. Both these heresies overstressed the unity of God at the cost of his distinctions as revealed in the plan of salvation. To counteract this one-sided emphasis—which disregarded the experience of the distinction in God encountered by the early community—an attempt was made to show that the Father is the Supreme God, while the Son and Spirit are subordinate to him (subordinationism). This again was an affront to the unity of God. In an extreme case, some believed the Holy Trinity was three separate Gods (tritheism).

The church condemned all these aberrations and taught that God is One in essence or substance or nature, but God is three persons or three hypostases or *prosopon*. In sum, what they were trying to say was that the Father is not the Son or the Spirit, the Son

190   *Christ without Borders*

is not the Father or the Spirit, and the Spirit is not the Son or the Father—yet they are absolute Oneness, absolute Communion, and absolute Love. They are distinct but not separate, different but not divided (Tertullian). God is one reality with threeness in being God. St. Augustine had warned about counting with regard to the Trinity: "If you count, you err." Oneness cannot be counted but only experienced. Therefore, oneness is not human speculation about the mystery of God but God as revealed in the history of human salvation as experienced by the followers of Jesus Christ, articulated in the Bible, and celebrated in the community through its worship. For Christians, this apostolic testimony is the foundation of their faith. St. Paul warned Christians against any other doctrine that denied the fundamental Christian experience that he had received from the Risen Lord himself. "For I did not receive it [the gospel] from man nor was I taught it, but it came through a revelation of Jesus Christ" (Gal 1:12). Therefore, Paul has no hesitation to affirm, "But even if we, or an angel from heaven, should preach to you a gospel contrary to that which we preached to you, let him be accursed" (Gal 1:8). The whole of the New Testament is one gospel that proclaims the death and resurrection of Jesus Christ, who is encountered as Lord and Savior. It is the revelation of a God who in his infinite mercy has sent Jesus Christ, his Word, and has continued to give life through his Spirit.

What do we gather from the development of the doctrine on God and Jesus Christ in history? Along with the apostolic faith, which is held to be normative for all times and places, certain doctrines also grew that were not compatible with the original faith. These false doctrines also gathered groups of believers who held that God is one but has three powers, or there are three Gods; either Jesus is only human or only God; he was created by God and was given the title son of God; Jesus was only an ordinary human being who was adopted by God at his baptism; he appeared to have died and did not die; a substitute died for him; Mary was a goddess, and so on. These heretical beliefs found expression in apocryphal writings. The *Proto-Evangelium of James* speaks about an angel feeding Mary as a child. It further narrates that when she was twelve a guardian was chosen by lot to take care of her, and she was making a curtain for the Temple at the time of annunciation. Some apocryphal writings exaggerated the miraculous powers of Jesus even from the time of his infancy. The miracle of the boy Jesus creating birds from clay that flew at the clap of his hand is found in the *Infancy Story of Thomas*. Both these works were available in their Syriac translations during pre-Islamic times. The apocryphal work the *Arabic Infancy Gospel* mentions Jesus speaking when he was in the cradle. The *Gospel of Pseudo-Matthew* has the story of the miracle of the dates from the palm tree that fed Mary and the stream from which she drank on her flight into Egypt. Both these works are of later origin but drew heavily from Syriac sources. The religion of Mani, called Manicheism, had many followers in the Persian Empire from pre-Islamic times. Mani taught that Jesus was a prophet but denied that he was crucified. He believed that the Paraclete was not fully revealed until he had his first vision. It is suggested that this provided a precedent for the apparent identification of Prophet Muhammad with the Paraclete (Sura 36:13–25). It also appears that Islam had some links with Manicheism. The Holy Qur'an has 114 Suras like that of the apocryphal writing the *Gospel of Thomas*, which has 114 logia that the Manicheans held in high esteem.[1]

The Arabic world in which Islam originated and grew had a complex situation of Jewish-Christian sects, Monophysites, Nestorians, Manicheans, and various Christian heretical groups. There was no unity of faith in Jesus Christ or in the God revealed through him. Various apocryphal writings and popular beliefs further complicated the matter. It was a cafeteria of Christian beliefs from which one could pick and choose what suited him to create any new sect or religion. The pagans and their idolatrous religious practices,

---

[1] Neal Robinson, *Christ in Islam and Christianity* (Albany: State University of New York Press, 1991), 21.

192   *Christ without Borders*

Jews and their anti-Christian propaganda, decadence of moral living, and so on, provided sufficient background for a new religion to be born, simple in faith, logical in its understanding of God's dealing with humans, and attractive in its claims.

Sectarian Christologies' Influence on the Islamic Understanding of Jesus

The Qur'anic references to Jesus and Mary echo much of what we read in the Syriac Christian literature from the time of the Prophet Muhammad. It must be noted that the canonical Gospels were not available in Arabic at the time of Muhammad. But the Arabic world of pre-Islamic times was influenced by the Syriac Christian literature, both orthodox and heretical, and the popular beliefs of various Christian sects and groups. One important influence on Qur'anic claims about Jesus probably comes from Tatian's *Diatesseron*, which combines into one book some sections of Matthew, Mark, and Luke using the framework of John. Tatian's compilation of the Gospels begins with John's prologue, which speaks of the Word, and follows Luke's story of the angelic announcements to Mary and Zachariah and Matthew's narration of Mary conceived by the power of the Holy Spirit. According to Neal Robinson, the Holy Qur'anic reference to "the Gospel" rather than to the Gospels, the designation of Jesus as God's Word that God cast into Mary and the importance given to Zachariah and Mary and the apparent identification of the angel Gabriel with the Holy Spirit, and so on correspond to Tatian's gospel, which was available to the Arabic world at the time of Islam's origin.[2] The Gospel according to Luke mentions that, in Mary's dialogue with the angel (Luke 1:34), she says that she did not "know" man. Tatian's version would make a slight change: Mary affirmed that "no man had known her," giving a male an active role in any marital union. This is reflected in the

---

[2] Robinson, *Christ in Islam and Christianity*, 19.

Holy Qur'an's version of the same incident as Mary insisting that no man had touched her (Sura 3:47; 19:20).

The very name *Isa* used in the Holy Qur'an for Jesus probably was influenced by the Syriac Christian use of *Isho*, as other biblical names that appear in the Holy Qur'an are similar to the same usage of the names in the Syrian Christian literature. The reference to Mary as "Sister of Aron" (Sura 19:28)—although some Christian polemists considered it as a mistake from mixing up the name Miriam, the sister of Aron and Moses—would have been in keeping with the Syrian church's typological exegesis, which interpreted the Old Testament in light of the New Testament[3] rather than as a mistake. This way of typological exegesis also explains the episode of the meal shared (the table spread) by Jesus and his disciples at the request of the disciples found in the Holy Qur'an (Sura 5:112–115), so that their hearts might be at rest and that they would know that Jesus had spoken the truth. This episode is reminiscent of the Last Supper scene in John 14:1 in which Jesus reminded the disciples that their hearts should not be troubled and asked them to believe in God and believe in him. A typological exegesis would also relate the event with Psalm 78:19, "Can God spread a table in the wilderness?" The relation between certain texts concerning Jesus in the Holy Qur'an and the Syrian Christian writings and other sources available during the pre-Islamic period (both orthodox and apocryphal) might be obvious to a critical reader, but a devout Muslim would find it difficult to accept such observations.

Christian Response to the Islamic Understanding of Jesus Christ and a Triune God

The Holy Qur'an gives a lot of importance to Jesus, Son of Mary on its own terms. He is called Messiah, prophet, apostle, servant, and more. The divine intervention in Jesus's birth and Mary's virginal

---

[3] Robinson, *Christ in Islam and Christianity*, 18.

194   *Christ without Borders*

conception of him is told with some details that are not found in the canonical Gospels, but they can be found in various versions in the other sources mentioned above. The annunciation to Mary is twice mentioned in the Qur'an. In one version, the annunciation was made by angels and the other by God's Spirit in the form of a perfect man who claimed that he was a messenger of the Lord (Sura 3:42–47; 19:16–22). Some Islamic commentators take it for granted that Jesus was the "word," *kalimah,* while others would play down its importance to show that it meant only prophecy and there was no allusion to the virginal conception of the word.[4] However, some of them are silent about the mention in the Holy Qur'an that the conception took place by God breathing His Spirit into Mary (Sura 21:91; 66:12). Jesus's public life and teachings do not find much attention in the Qur'an. Jesus as a miracle worker fashioned a bird out of clay and when he breathed into it, it flew away; he healed the blind and the leper and raised the dead; and he would know what people had eaten and what they had stored in their houses (Sura 5:17). Jesus is among the prophets whom God inspired (Sura 4:163). It is affirmed that the Messiah Jesus, Son of Mary was only a messenger of God. He is God's word that he communicated to Mary and is a spirit from God (Sura 4:171). Like Adam, Jesus was also created from the dust (Sura 3:59), and God made him a servant to be an example for the children of Israel. If God wished to destroy him and his mother with everyone else, no one would have hindered God (Sura 5:17). God informed Jesus that he wished to "receive him" (or cause him to die), raise Jesus to himself, and purify him from the unbelievers (Sura 3:54; 5:117). People of the Book who spoke calumny against Mary also claimed that they killed the Messiah, Son of Mary, but they did not kill him or crucify him, although it appeared so to them. God raised him to himself (Sura

---

[4] See Maulvi Muhammad Ali, *The Holy Qur-an: Containing the Arabic Text with English Translation and Commentary,* 2nd ed. (Lahore: Ahmadiyya Anjuman-I Ishaat-I- Islam, 1920), 154, 1094.

Christ of Christian Faith in Dialogue with Islamic Faith   195

3:54f.). It is also affirmed that peace was upon Jesus the day of his birth, the day of his death, and the day of his being raised to life (Sura 19:26–33). These are only some of the statements about Jesus made in the Qur'an.

For those who accept the Qur'an literally as God's word given to the Prophet, as almost all followers of Islam would do, it is absolutely impossible even to consider the truth claims of any of the essential beliefs of the right Christian faith. The Qur'an clearly says that Jesus is wrongly called Son of God, for God is far above taking a son (Sura 4:171; 9:30). Further, the Qur'an affirms that only unbelievers say that God is the Messiah, Son of Mary, or that God is the third of the three (Sura 5:72), which according to the Qur'an Jesus himself denies when confronted by God (Sura 5:116). Though there is a possibility of interpreting the statements of the Qur'an concerning the death and resurrection of Jesus as the Christians would understand and believe, the tendency among the Islamic theologians and commentators is not to give into such a possible interpretation of the Qur'anic texts and deny the fact of the crucifixion and the reality of Jesus's resurrection from the dead.

The Qur'anic revelation about Jesus and God as understood and articulated by the Prophet Muhammad comes almost seven hundred years after the apostolic community's experience of the risen Lord and the experience of the one God as Trinity. Thousands of Christians went to martyrdom under the Roman emperors because they professed their faith in Jesus the Lord and their experience of God as the Triune God. In the New Testament there are a number of references to Jesus as human as well as divine. It also very clearly refers to God as Father, Son, and Holy Spirit. It is true that Jesus never proclaimed that he was God or that he was the second person of the Holy Trinity. If Jesus were to claim that he was God, the very meaning of the incarnation of God's Word and the self-emptying of God would have become superfluous. Paul, in his Letter to the Philippians 2:6–11, quotes the early Christian hymn, "He was in the form of God but did not count equality with God a thing to be grasped but emptied himself and took the form of a slave." Through God's self-emptying, God becomes the other, the human. Before this infinite mystery of love, humans can only kneel with humility. An arrogant human mind can make the derisive statement, "If you are Son of God, come down from the cross" (Mt 27:40). Here is the paradox of the Christian experience of God. God's power is revealed in His powerlessness, God's wisdom in foolishness!

The New Testament articulates the apostles' and apostolic communities' experience of Jesus as Lord and God after the experience of the risen Jesus. Once those who were strict monotheists began to experience God as Father, Son, and Holy Spirit. They looked into the Old Testament and found that God created everything through his Word and the Spirit. Sometimes God communicated through an angel who is his own self-communication, as in the case of the dialogue with Hagar in the desert and with Moses in the burning bush. God also communicated through his Spirit. The evangelists had no hesitation in mentioning all three persons at the baptism of Jesus (Mk 1:9–11; Mt 3:13–17; Lk 3:21–23) and in the mission command at the end of the Gospel according to Matthew (Mt 28:18–19). There are a sufficient number of references in the New Testament to show that Jesus was human as well as divine. One can selectively cite a number of quotations to prove that Jesus was only human and another can cite a number of other quotations to prove that he was divine. For those who do not believe in Jesus as the Lord and Savior of their lives, the whole of the New Testament witness about Jesus's divinity and humanity and the revelation of the Triune God can be explained away as meaningless or false expressions about God and Jesus Christ. Paul reminds us that no one can say that "Jesus is Lord" except by the Holy Spirit (1 Cor 12:3) and that, "If you confess with your lips that Jesus is Lord and believe in your heart that God has raised him from the dead, you will be saved" (Rom 10:9). The Christian belief in the death and resurrection

Christ of Christian Faith in Dialogue with Islamic Faith 197

of Jesus and the encounter of him as Lord and Savior cannot be based on a few references in the New Testament. The whole of the New Testament bears witness to these fundamental truths of the Christian faith.

From the beginning of Islam to the present day, Christians and Muslims both approach each other's Scriptures for polemic or apologetic reasons. Both the Qur'an and the Bible can be approached literally, and one can select passages to discredit each other's claims. Most of the anti-Christian texts by Muslims and the anti-Islamic texts by Christians follow the same method of approaching the Holy Books literally to prove the superiority of one over the other. Both of them follow the epistemological principle of contradiction. If one claim is true, the other must be false. Therefore, all efforts are made to show that the other is false. Both fail to realize that there is no divine language to communicate the infinite mystery. Even God can only reveal Godself using a human language, and any language has its own limitations in articulating an experience. Whatever is revealed is understood and experienced and further articulated only in human language with all its limitations.

An Islamic theologian can show from the Holy Qur'an as well as from selected texts in the New Testament that Jesus Christ was not the Son of God as Christians would believe him to be. For him Jesus was only a prophet (*nabi*), an apostle (*rasul*), and a servant (*abd*). He can further show that Jesus was not crucified or resurrected, although Christians hold these as central to their faith based on the New Testament witness of the apostles and the apostolic community. For a Christian, the experience of God as Trinity as articulated in the creeds (Apostles' Creed and Nicene Creed) expresses the apostolic community's experience of God and Jesus Christ. Christian believers know the limitations of language for expressing the mystery of God. When they believe that God is one, they are aware that it is not a mathematical matter and that the threeness of God is not mathematical either. The three persons in the Trinity are not three individuals like individual human persons. If so, why should we complicate the understanding of an unfathomable mystery? It was the undeniable experience of the one God in threeness that compelled the apostles to proclaim what they had experienced. When they addressed God as Father, it was obvious to them that God was not a male, biological father—and when they proclaimed that Jesus Christ was the eternal Son who became human, they did not mean that God had a biological son. It is universally accepted that any religious language is symbolic, metaphorical, and as such evocative and descriptive. Though it is clearly written in the Qur'an that God "hears" (*as-sami*, Sura 2:121), "sees" (*al-bashir*, Sura 17:1) and that he has a "countenance" (*wagh*, Sura 28:88) and a "hand" (*yad*, Sura 38:75), would any Muslim, Christian, or anyone who understands religious language say that such anthropomorphic expressions about God must be taken literally? The Bible, too, abounds in such anthropomorphic expressions about God. Any articulation of the God experience requires symbols and metaphors. Symbols can unite, but dogmas can divide if dogmas are not understood in their symbolic function of giving an insight into the mystery that no human mind can fully comprehend. Towards the end of eighth century, when Caliph Al-Mahdi made a derogatory remark about the Fatherhood of God and the sonship of Jesus—asking the Nestorian Catholicos Timothy I whether God as the Father had biological organs to produce a Son—the caliph was showing his crass ignorance of the meaning of religious language, which is symbolic and evocative. However, Timothy I answered with all calmness, using metaphors to express that "as light is born of the sun and word of the soul, so also Christ who is the Word born of God" high above the times and before all the worlds.[5] Further, Timothy also pointed out

---

[5] J. Windrow Sweetman, *Islam and Christian Theology: A Study of the Interpretation of Theological Ideas in the Two Religions,* part 1, vol. 1 (London: Lutterworth Press, 1945), 74–78.

that God is not corporeal, so it is blasphemous to say that God has the physical function of "begetting a son." When the caliph accused Timothy I of tritheism, the Catholicos affirmed that while he believed in Father, Son, and the Holy Spirit, he still believed in one God. He further argued that just as heat and light cannot be separated from the sun, and they are not three suns, but one sun, likewise is the Trinity of the Father, the Son, and the Spirit. He gave further examples: the taste and the scent cannot be separated from the apple although they are distinct, yet it is one apple. The word of the Caliph clothes itself on the papyrus as a written word while his soul and his mind from which the word originated cannot be separated from the word, and both cannot be written like the word. Likewise is "the Word-God which clothed Himself with a body from among us without having been separated from the Father or the Spirit."[6] Timothy even makes a surprising statement to the caliph that three alphabets found at the head of some Suras of the Qur'an are mystical symbols of the Trinity. When the Caliph asked why the Prophet Muhammad did not affirm the Trinity plainly, the Catholicos answered that it was because of the polytheism prevalent in the Arab world and that the people would mistake the triune God for polytheism, so the prophet preached so strongly the unity of God.[7]

The Christian apologists had to defend their faith against the strict or radical monotheism of both the Jews and the Muslims. Patriarch Timothy I follows the tradition of Hilary, the Cappadocian Fathers, Tertullian, Augustine, and many others, using metaphors to explain the mystery of the Trinity. For Augustine, since human beings are the image of the Triune God, they have in themselves the reflection of the Trinity.[8] He gives the example of memory, understanding (intelligence), and will. Memory can

---

[6] Sweetman, *Islam and Christian Theology*, 75.

[7] Sweetman, *Islam and Christian Theology*, 75–76.

[8] Augustine of Hippo, *De Trinitate* X.14–15.

retain only what is understood and what is intended by the will. He gives another example of mind, knowledge, and love. Each of these implies others: mind knows and loves, knowledge implies mind and love, and love implies knowledge and mind. It was always a struggle to express the oneness and threeness of God at the time. Yet this mystery of communion—this God of communion—makes every human being an image of this communion and the source of one and many, individual and society, singularity and plurality. Whatever attempts are made to understand the mystery of the Trinity, it will always remain unfathomable for those who believe in this revelation. In a defense of Christianity composed by Paul of Antioch, a Greek bishop, around 1147 CE, to which famous Muslim theologian Ibn Taymiyya responded 170 years later with his work *The Correct Answer to Those Who Changed the Religion of Christ,* the bishop held the view that

> Were the Muslims to understand the Christian belief in the Trinity rightly, they would find nothing objectionable in it. By it the Christians are using three names to express that the One God is an existing Being … living … and speaking.… All the names and attributes of God stem from the three substantial attributes … of existence, speech and life. It is the second of these that explains the incarnation of the Word and the sonship of Christ.[9]

What is obvious to Christians may remain obscure to Muslims and vice versa. Going beyond the stage of condemnations like that of John of Damascus calling Islam a heresy like any other heresies or the Islamic condemnation of the Christian belief in

---

[9] Thomas F. Michael, ed. and trans., *A Muslim Theologian's Response to Christianity: Ibn Taymiyya's Al-jawab al Sahih* (Delmer, NY: Caravan Books, 1984), vii–viii, cited in John B. Carman, *Majesty and Meekness: A Comparative Study of Contrast and Harmony in the Concept of God* (Grand Rapids: Eerdmans, 1994), 337.

Jesus Christ and the Triune God as absolutely false and untenable in light of the Qur'an, there can be respect and understanding for each other's faith.

The foundation of the Christian faith is the experience of God's Word becoming human in Jesus Christ, his death and resurrection, and the transforming experience of the Holy Spirit. It would always remain a scandal not only to the Jews, as Paul would say, but also to the Muslims and a foolishness to the Gentiles. But for those who believe, Jesus Christ is the power and wisdom of God (1 Cor. 1:23–24). A Muslim or a Jew can never accept these faith affirmations without abandoning his faith. Is it still possible to have an interfaith dialogue? In the language of the Jewish philosopher Martin Buber, if the faith *in* Jesus Christ divides us, the faith *of* Jesus Christ can unite us. Jesus reveals in his person the same God of Abraham whom the Jews and the Muslims accept as the Beneficent and the Compassionate, whose children all humans are. Where interfaith dialogue fails or may not even take off, inter-hope dialogue can bring all God's children together to build a society where humans can live as brothers and sisters in harmony, equality, justice, peace, and reconciliation worthy of the One God, whose images they are. More than ever before, it is the need of the hour!

13

Christ beyond Postmodernism

Jesus Christ is the same, yesterday, today, and forever, but Christologies are many. How do all these Christologies authentically articulate Jesus and what he stood for as we read in the New Testament? The insights of postmodernism may be helpful to inquire whether various Christologies that emerged at different historical moments and in different contexts refer to the real Jesus Christ of the apostolic experience. All Christologies emerge from an experience of Jesus Christ as the absolute meaning of one's life and the expression of the same in a language meaningful to a particular context. It can so happen and it has already happened in the history of Christological reflections that a particular Christology is produced that does not refer to the real Jesus Christ of the apostolic experience.

In this chapter I attempt to understand how postmodernism challenges the traditional and historical articulations about the person and message of Jesus;[1] second, how the insights of postmodernism help us to delve deep into the mystery of

---

[1] Susan Brooks Thistlethwaite's insightful essay "Christology and Postmodernism" has been a great inspiration for the first part of my reflections in this chapter. Thistlethwaite, "Christology and Postmodernism: Not Everyone Who Says to Me, 'Lord, Lord,'" *Interpretation* 49, no. 3 (1995): 267–280.

Jesus Christ; and finally, how the person and message of Jesus go beyond the approaches of postmodernism in revealing the mystery of reality.

Postmodernism's Challenge to Christology

One of the notable contributions of postmodernism was that it challenged the settled foundations on which the social order, a state's governing principles, the rule of law, and so on are built and unsettled them. Postmodernism, first of all, challenged the contention of the modern period that humans are rational and coherent subjects. It showed that what was thought to be the natural product of human reason was indeed a product of social forces expressed through language. It affirmed that even our own self-understanding about ourselves is not something objective but is constructed by the way reality is named to us.[2] Understanding the significance of language is the key to understanding power structures, social organizations, social meanings, and individual consciousness. Philosophers like Jacques Derrida, Jacques Lacan, Julia Kristeva, Louis Althusser, and Michel Foucault contributed to the development of poststructuralist critiques of reality, significantly including the way we understand ourselves and our world. If this approach to reality leads us to better insights into the mystery of life and transforms our consciousness for the better, it can also challenge the foundations of our Christian faith—namely, our understanding of Jesus Christ as the center of our lives and our commitment to him. Everything that falls under the name of postmodernism or poststructuralism, however, may not lead to a transformative experience.

In his challenging and insightful book *Jesus and Postmodernism*, James Breech raised a rhetorical question: "What has Jesus to do

---

[2] Thistlethwaite, "Christology and Postmodernism," 269.

with postmodernism?" He says further, "Those of us entrusted with the resources and responsibility for generating knowledge and understanding of the Christian tradition can and should ask what relationship postmodernist theologies, which present themselves in Christian guise, have with the historical Jesus."[3] Breech's cautious remark about postmodernism and the historical Jesus points to the typical ambivalence of all that goes under the umbrella of postmodernism. However, certain challenges posed by some postmodernists like Michel Foucault can wake up theologians from their dogmatic slumber and give new insights into the inexhaustible mystery of Jesus Christ.

Foucault has shown convincingly that each system develops its own way of organizing concepts through language.[4] Each system has its own "discursive field," and the discourses in that particular discursive field will not have the same recognition and acceptance or power in another field. This may be obvious enough. Theological discourse will not have the same impact and acceptance in other discursive fields, like politics, economics, and other secular fields. Once the dominance of theology in all other fields suffered heavy battering during the Enlightenment and irretrievable loss of credibility during the periods of modernity and the advancement of science and technology, it became clear that theology could not answer all the questions raised about society and life. At this juncture, two options were open to theology. Fall back into fundamentalism and dogmatism, or discover the potentialities of the theological discourse to liberate religion from its obscurantism and exclusivism and release the innate power for integral human liberation.

Theology cannot be neutral. Theology is the articulation of faith in dialogue with the context of the theologian. The

---

[3] James Breech, *Jesus and Postmodernism* (Minneapolis: Fortress, 1989), 22.

[4] J. R. Carrette, ed., *Religion and Culture by Michel Foucault* (Manchester: Manchester University Press, 1999).

context of theological reflection itself is a complex web of power relationships, humanizing or dehumanizing structures, religious beliefs and practices, cultural elements, and sociopolitical and economic systems. A theologian, then, might support an existing oppressive system consciously or unconsciously while being immersed in their context if they have not transcended the context itself through a liberating experience of the *theos.* The Logos the theologian constructs can be prophetic and liberative or supportive of and justifying the existing structures of oppression. According to Foucault, words are the products of historical forces and functions in fields where meaning is made or not made.[5] If we analyze the context, content, and consequences of some of the Christologies of the twentieth century, it would become clear to us that Foucault's insight into the influence of historical forces and powers in the making of the language of a particular discursive field is valid.

We have already mentioned that Jesus is one, but Christologies are many. The prominent models of Christ in the twentieth century have included the Germanic Christ, the Latin Christ of France, the Anglo-Saxon Christ, the Afrikaner Christ, the Black Christ,[6] the liberationists' Christ, the feminists' Christ, the Brahminic Christ, and the Dalits' Christ. These have been sources of oppression and liberation.

The Germanic Christ emerged from a claim that the German people were the chosen ones through whom salvation is offered to all. Drawing implications from Luther's theory of the two kingdoms and the order of creation, the protagonists of this theology—namely, the German-Christians (*Deutsche Christen*)—attempted to make a synthesis of Nazism and Christianity. They

---

[5] Thistlethwaite, "Christology and Postmodernism," 272.

[6] Thistlethwaite, "Christology and Postmodernism," 267–268; Alan Davies, *Infected Christianity: A Study of Modern Racism* (Montreal: McGill-Queen's University Press, 1988), 72.

206   *Christ without Borders*

eliminated everything Jewish from the Bible and declared Germany as their holy land and Hitler as the embodiment of the law of God. Though the Confessing Church (*Bekennende Kirche*) movement led by Martin Niemöller and others valiantly confessed the Jesus Christ of the Christian tradition at the cost of their own lives, the Germanic Christ of the Nazi period prevailed over and supported an oppressive, racist, and tyrannical system until its collapse.

The royalist movement in France presented a Latin Christ whose atoning death was for the French race alone. Such an exclusive racial bias could also be clearly seen in the Anglo-Saxon figure of Christ, who was believed to be the greatest member of the great Anglo-Saxon race and was blond and Nordic like the Olympian gods. According to this understanding, Jesus was the white man par excellence.[7] For the Afrikaner, Christ became the symbol of racial superiority, an Aryan God. The Afrikaner Christ could be invoked by the white racists' regime to strengthen and support their brutal oppression of the Black majority. The Black Christ of James Cone and others can become the symbol of Black racism against white racism if this Christ is not recognized as the one who liberates both whites and Blacks from their dehumanizing prejudices, and discrimination against and hatred of one another.

The attempts at presenting a figure of Christ meaningful to the Indian context has produced the image of Christ as an *avatara* or incarnation like the other *avataras* of Vaishnavism. Those theologians who find the insights of *Advaita* or nondualism more meaningful for understanding the mystery of Christ understand Christ as *Isvara*, the link between the absolute and the relative. Both the avataric Christ and advaitic Christ can become the supporter

---

[7] Thistlethwaite, "Christology and Postmodernism," 268; Alan Davies refers to William C. Buthman, *The Rise of Integral Nationalism in France: With Special Reference to the Ideas and Activities of Charles Maurass* (New York: Octagon Books, 1970), 152.

and upholder of the dehumanizing caste system that condemns a vast majority of Indians to undignified and worthless human existence. S. Kappen observes, "Landed on the Indian soil, he [Jesus] took more after Vishnu than Siva. Like the former, he is solar (*sol invictus*), patriarchal, conservative, preserver of the world-order, proto-type of and protector of priesthood, patron of whoever happens to be in power."[8]

The Dalit-Christ of the victims of caste oppression can be liberative if while restoring the dignity of the victims he liberates the oppressors from being the victims of their dehumanizing religious system. If the Dalit Christ is presented as the one who supports violence and hatred of the victims against the upper castes, then he too becomes a victim of the victimized in their collective effort to justify their ideologies and actions.

Not only modern Christologies but also classical Christologies have their ideological underpinnings. Susan Brooks Thistlethwaite affirms that even the fundamental Christian affirmation that "Jesus is Lord" reveals a number of complex issues when submitted to poststructuralist analysis. When the persecuted Christians, who were only a minority, affirmed that "Jesus Christ is Lord," they were at the same time asserting that Caesar is *not* Lord. In this way the early Christian community subverted the hegemonic and military power of the Roman empire through a counterculture of love (1 Cor 13) and a life of living the Beatitudes (Lk 6:20; Mt 5:1–11).[9] As such, the faith affirmation in a subversive language was at the same time a political statement about the power of the powerless against the all-powerful Roman power structures. However, when Christianity became the religion of the Roman Empire, the same faith affirmation that "Jesus is Lord" assumed a new meaning of

---

[8] Sebastian Kappen, *Jesus and Freedom* (Maryknoll, NY: Orbis Books, 1977), 19.

[9] Thistlethwaite, "Christology and Postmodernism," 274.

power and domination. The Lordship of Christ was understood in imperial terms, and Christ therefore became the protector and supporter of the existing system of hierarchical order, the legitimizer of the divine right of kings. The kenotic image of Christ gives way to the kyriarchal figure of Christ. Consequently, the church of the poor and marginalized became the imperial church of domination and control. S. B. Thistlethwaite says,

> If traditional Christian doctrine was formulated at a time of imperial rule that invested its doctrinal language with militarism, hierarchy, and the reification of gender and race dominance, how do we reconstruct Christian doctrine to recover the critique of power and the communitarian vision of the first three centuries? The context of the first three centuries was one of resistance to oppression. The use of the political language of "lord" or "king" then produced a practice of subversion of dominant modes of authority. Hence, what we have to do to begin to reconstruct Christology is to put our feet somewhere else; we have to move our lives and our commitments away from authoritarianism to the road to Emmaus.[10]

Even the doctrine of the incarnation, that God became human, was construed to mean that God became male, to exclude women as if they were nonpersons. A sublime doctrine of faith could thus be manipulated to suppress the legitimate rights of women, who form 50 percent of all of humanity at a given time. Indeed, God becoming human means that, in Jesus of Nazareth, God became the flesh of *our* flesh, of every human being, male and female, the oppressor and the oppressed, the ruler and the ruled, the Black and the white, the Brahmin and the Dalit. The critique of postmodernism thus compels us to look into our fundamental faith

---

[10] Thistlethwaite, "Christology and Postmodernism," 276.

Christ beyond Postmodernism 209

affirmations, which we often take for granted, and challenges us to reconstruct them that they may be able to unleash their liberative potentialities to build true communities of authentic humans without discrimination or domination of any sort.

Postmodernism's Insight into the Mystery of Jesus

The irreverent iconoclasm of the poststructuralists is exhibited in their deconstruction of systems, dogmas, doctrines, and practices that claim to be absolute and terrorize humans to submit their lives to an illusion of certainty. Therefore, if there is an absolute dogma in postmodernism it is the doctrine of relativism. When such relativism becomes not only a creed but also an attitude toward the reality of life itself, it terrifies the guardians of public and private morality and traditional values, religious authorities, and structures and systems of power like that of governments. Obviously if nothing is certain or absolute, anything goes. No insistence on the practice of morality is possible as its foundations can be questioned and rejected or relativized. Morality may be only one possibility.

Nietzsche's announcement that "God is dead" seemed to have liberated humans from the tyranny of subjugation and enslavement that prevented them from becoming superhuman. One of the dogmas of postmodernism that "Death is God" seems to liberate humans from the inhibitions of responsibility and conscience. Mark C. Taylor, a self-proclaimed postmodernist theologian, says, "Postmodernism opens with the sense of irrecoverable loss and incurable fault. This world is infected by the overwhelming awareness of death—a death that 'begins' with the death of God and 'ends' with the death of ourselves."[11] For the New Testament

---

[11] As cited in Breech, *Jesus and Postmodernism*, 15.

scholar John Dominic Crossan, human life is a life toward death. His "theology of limit" allows the possibility of the experience of transcendence, the experience of God. Death being the final limit of life becomes the door to final transcendence, to God. Taylor's affirmation that "death is God" leads to the possibility of the destruction of traditional values and morality giving way to the growth of nihilism, profanity, and perversion. Through the theology of limit, Crossan also relativizes morality and affirms its subjective nature. However, this does not lead to anarchy and nihilism but promotes "freedom for human responsibility, personal and social decision, and the creation of those conventions that make us what we are." Breech, who refers to Crossan in his study *Jesus and Postmodernism,* seems to think that Crossan's approach to the reality of death is similar to Taylor's, though their implications of the same for morality are different. However, Breech and Crossan both reach almost similar conclusions at the end of their studies and analyses of the parables of Jesus. According to Breech, a closer look at those parables in the context of poststructuralism shows that they do not end with closure, although the evangelists present them as if they were stories with an ending. The parables in their original form, according to Breech, were not stories with an end. "In Jesus' parables we see a mode of being human, neither that of those who live episodically nor that of those who live in moralizing plots. Both these modes are imprisoned in time, in their own temporal sequences.... Jesus' characters transcend their own temporal sequences. In that sense, they are out of time."[12] The characters in the parables as well as Jesus himself transcend time, though they also exist to some extent within the bounds of time. Both Jesus and other humans are persons who live unending stories. John Dominic Crossan, at the end of his study of parable in contrast to myth, says that parable subverts myth's final word about reality and thus opens up the possibility of transcendence.

---

[12] Breech, *Jesus and Postmodernism,* 76–77.

Christ beyond Postmodernism 211

For Taylor, the reality of death as the end of everything explains postmodernism's predilection for a "de-moralized" world that repudiates traditional values and prefers nihilism, perversion, and so forth. However, for Crossan, the relativization of morality as a consequence of his theology of limit does not lead to anarchy or perversion but to freedom, responsibility, and transcendence. Taylor claims to be a postmodernist, while in Crossan one can detect the influence of postmodernism. Breech, who makes a critique of both, does not claim that he is a postmodernist but takes the challenges of postmodernism and almost follows poststructuralism's critique of language in analyzing Jesus's parables to arrive at a liberating vision of Jesus Christ and his message.

During his earthly life, Jesus resisted any attempt to categorize him. Even though the early church encountered Jesus as the absolute meaning of their life—therefore, their Lord and God—he can never be defined. Therefore, many Christologies are possible. None of them can exhaust the mystery of Christ, as he is that reality that surpasses every definition and system. Though it is unsettling for the believer not to have one clear picture of Jesus Christ, it leads to a realization that Jesus Christ is the mystery in which the believer is involved and is therefore a pole of the believer's own being. This awareness liberates humans from a narrow, limited, and static understanding of Jesus Christ and provides a refreshingly new and challenging awareness of one's own being.

Jesus beyond Postmodernism

The tendency of the human mind to define the indefinable, that it may be able to handle it, further develops into belief systems, dogmas, and institutions. What suffers in the process is insight into "the height and the depth, the length and the breadth" of the mystery that one encounters. If God's own definition of himself in Jesus Christ was to make humans recognize who God is and what humans are, the human tendency to define Jesus Christ makes him just another prophet, social reformer, or guru. Postmodernism challenges every system and structure that attempts to confine reality and manipulate it for justifying and promoting ideologies and power structures that in turn dehumanize humans. At the same time, postmodernism, by its very definition, accommodates all possible approaches to reality, sometimes even contradictory ones, letting each draw support for what a person is temperamentally attuned to—namely, despair or hope, anarchy or harmony, meaning or meaninglessness or everything together. Human life itself provides such a drama of contradictions. Such an approach to reality can be fascinating as it allows humans to be confronted with infinite choices. For postmodernists this infinite number of possibilities offers an opportunity to choose everything at once. How that is possible in actual life is another question. Do humans just live with such contradictions without taking decisions that make them authentic humans? There may be many who live a life as if they were condemned to a futile existence. For them, death is the end of everything. However, if transcendence is in humans' very nature, they take decisions that allow them to go beyond the temporal sequences of events. They do not react to the situations of life that try to control them. They pro-act to the situations through decisions that reveal their transcendence and influence the lives of others in such a way that they too are enabled to unfold their transcendence.

Breech raises a pertinent question: "Is there a mode of being human that can be grasped as inherently meaningful, and coherent, as grounded in the real in and of itself, without being evaluated in terms of some external norms?"[13] For Breech, T. S. Eliot's depiction of Thomas Beckett in *Murder in the Cathedral* offers a significant insight.[14] Eliot's Beckett is proactive and not controlled by the forces external to him, neither by his murderers nor by death itself. If results or consequences are the criteria to judge

---

[13] Breech, *Jesus and Postmodernism*, 55.

[14] Breech, *Jesus and Postmodernism*, 55–56.

Christ beyond Postmodernism 213

life and its actions, then they can be shown as both good and evil. A more stable criterion against which to judge life and its actions must be the case than merely the passage of narratives over time. Eliot's Beckett proclaims that his death shall be known "not in time," for "it is out of time that [his] decisions are taken."[15] Postmodernism, Breech claims, cannot explain coherently such moral decisions that are made in time and go beyond the limits of time. By referring to Beckett's decision to which his whole being gives entire consent, Breech suggests that "the mode of being human inaugurated by Jesus does not receive its coherence from bounded time and cannot be judged by its results. If closure and bounded time do not lend coherence to this way of living in story, what is its principle of coherence? What do Jesus' parables tell us are the truth and coherence intrinsic to a life lived in unending story?"[16] Only by recognizing the capacity of humans to transcend themselves and their history can one derive an insight into the mystery of human beings.

From his own long research on Jesus's parables, comparing and contrasting them with stories from extant literature of late Western antiquity, Breech concludes,

> Jesus' parables were dissimilar from all those extant to three hundred years before his time and three hundred years after him. This does not prove, of course, that Jesus was unique; that is a claim that can only be made from the viewpoint of Christian faith. But this research does prove in the scientific sense that Jesus' parables were dissimilar from all extant contemporary stories.[17]

---

[15] T. S. Eliot, "Murder in the Cathedral," in *The Complete Poems and Plays, 1919–1950* (New York: Harcourt Brace Jovanovich, 1952), 210–211, as quoted in Breech, *Jesus and Postmodernism*, 55–56.

[16] Breech, *Jesus and Postmodernism*, 56.

[17] Breech, *Jesus and Postmodernism*, 25.

214 *Christ without Borders*

Jesus's parables are dissimilar from Greco-Roman stories of antiquity and from rabbinic parables. How do Jesus's parables differ from other stories that end with a moralizing statement, either by an approbation or by a reprobation of the actions of the characters of the narrative? Jesus's parables in their original form do not have any ending or closure because he narrated without moralizing.[18] For example, we are not told whether the good Samaritan was rewarded for his actions, whether the elder son reconciled with the younger son who squandered his share of the father's property, whether the householder who hired workers for his vineyard at different hours of the day and paid everyone equally found a new way of making every laborer happy, and so on. The parables of Jesus are realistic, but they are also nondidactic, nonmoralizing, and fictional narratives.[19] The actions of the main characters in the parables are unmotivated. Yet their actions open new possibilities for others to act and react to what they have done.

At the end of his study of Jesus's parables, Breech concludes that there is a consistent relationship between Jesus's parables and his own story. As his parables had no ending or closure, his life, too, had no closure. The story of his life does not end with death. Death is not the God that winds up the reality of human existence, as some postmodernists would like us to believe. Resurrection appears to be the happy ending of the story of Jesus. "Rather in my view," says Breech, "the earliest Christians used their own culturally received concept of the resurrection appearances to reflect their conviction that Jesus's mode of being human cannot be judged by its results, that death did not hold the key to the meaning of his mode of being human. The clear implication of the resurrection experiences is that the personal mode is grounded in a reality which is ultimate, which engenders the lives of those who live in parabolic

---

[18] Breech, *Jesus and Postmodernism*, 35.

[19] Breech, *Jesus and Postmodernism*, 63.

story."[20] According to Breech, therefore, like the characters of Jesus's parables, Jesus lives in a story without end.

John Dominic Crossan seems to arrive at a similar conclusion at the end of his study of the parables of Jesus. "Jesus announced the kingdom of God in parables, but the primitive church announced Jesus as the Christ, the Parable of God."[21] Thus the parabler became the parable. Further, he says that the cross became the supreme Parable of the church, as Jesus died as parabler and rose as Parable. Unlike myths that establish the world, parables subvert the world; so there is a difference between mythical religion and parabolic religion. While mythical religion gives the final word about reality and thus excludes the authentic experience of reality, parabolic religion subverts the final word about reality and thereby opens up the possibility of transcendence.[22] Whatever Crossan's understanding of transcendence, from the context of his theology of limit, one can conclude that Jesus, the Parable, continues to subvert the human tendency to find false security in myths and systems that provide humans with an illusory comfort and prevent them to unfold their nature by transcending themselves.

The Christian experience of Jesus Christ cannot but repudiate the philosophical claims of postmodernism that death is God, or that the human story ends with death. What he reveals through his life and his teaching in parables is that though the human story has a beginning, it never ends. Paul seemed to have anticipated the postmodernists' claim that death is the end of everything. When he confronted it after encountering the risen Christ and became convinced of the resurrection, all he says is, "If the dead are not raised, 'Let us eat and drink, for tomorrow we die'" (1 Cor 15:32).

---

[20] Breech, *Jesus and Postmodernism*, 78.

[21] John Dominic Crossan, *The Dark Interval: Towards a Theology of Story* (Niles, IL: Argus Communications, 1975), 124.

[22] Crossan, *The Dark Interval*, 128.

However, neither death nor resurrection is the last word on Jesus. The last word then is a new beginning, when "God may be all in all" (1 Cor 15:28).

Admitting that there are different theoretical positions under the name of poststructuralism and its philosophical approach postmodernism, its insights into the significance of language open up new vistas for understanding the mystery of Christ. Poststructuralism has convincingly shown that historical and cultural contexts—with all their complex webs of power structures, human interrelations, social conditioning and cultural prescriptions—shape language. Words acquire oppressive or liberative meaning depending on the historical conditions and compulsions from which they have emerged. So the language of a particular culture at a particular historical period is not innocent, devoid of any ideological biases and interests. This applies also to religious language. If any Christology—whether orthodox, dogmatic, functional, ontological, universal, or contextual—does not allow humans to encounter the living Christ and experience true liberation it cannot be an authentic Christology. The Christ encounter mediated through the context needs to make humans more human, enabling them to transcend themselves to build a true community of all humans with right relationship among themselves and with the whole creation.

Postmodernism's insight into the significance of language can positively contribute to the understanding of the implications of various Christologies and to judge whether they are liberative or oppressive. However, the tendency of certain postmodernists to explain everything by appealing to the inevitability of death and by enclosing everything within the framework of bounded time goes against the fundamental human experience of transcendence and the Christian experience of Jesus Christ. In Jesus Christ, humans can encounter not only a timeless God who entered into time but also discover humans who are bound by time yet can transcend it to enter into timelessness.

14

From Christology to Christophany

Panikkar's Liberating Vision of Christ

One of Raimon Panikkar's (1918–2010) greatest contributions to humanity is his insight into the mystery of Christ, which is at the same time an insight into the mystery of humans and their world. His search for a meaningful Christology that is cross-cultural and interreligious leads him to an insight into Christophany that transcends all cultures and religions and at the same time remains at the heart of all cultures and religions because it is a transforming vision into the mystery of reality.

The identity of Jesus Christ remains always a mystery in spite of the authentic witness about his person and message. Dogmas and doctrines are formulated, historical and archaeological researches are made, and biographies are written to explain who he is. However all human *logoi* fail to articulate "the length and breadth, the height and depth" of this mystery whom we call Christ. The answer to the question "Who do you say that I am?" (Mt 16:8) is probably not meant to refer to the questioner but to the questioned. However strange it may seem to be, the answer to the question must refer to an insight into the identity of the one who answers, since the mystery of the questioner encompasses the mystery of the one who is questioned. "Who do you say that you are?" can be a direct question for which a direct answer can be given. But it will not reveal the existential reality of the person who answers the question. "Who do you say that I am" is an existential question. The answer cannot be articulated in words and formulas. It is an invitation to experience a transforming vision. It is an insight into the reality of oneself in relation to others, the world, and the ultimate other.

A Critique of Traditional Christology

A traditional Christology, with all its richness, is not intelligible outside the context in which it is articulated. It took shape when the Christian experience of Jesus Christ as the absolute meaning of one's life and as the Lord of the universe and history was articulated in dialogue with Judaism—the Greco-Roman world in the beginning and later with the German mentality and finally with Islamic culture. Christology was thus an interpretation of Christic experience conditioned by the life situation of those who interpreted their Christic experience. Such a ready-made Christology exported to other cultures—as a Western product often associated with the colonial powers—cannot communicate who Jesus Christ really is. This Christology cannot be catholic or universal. No Christology needs to be catholic. But any claim to catholicity for a limited and culturally conditioned interpretation of the Christic experience is a fragmentation of our knowledge of Christ. Further, traditional Christology does not seem to offer a credible image of Christ to those Christians who want to be open, ecumenical, tolerant, and fully committed without either diluting their Christian-ness or their commitment to Christ. Panikkar says, "In fact, from the Christian perspective, the entire modern problematic concerning intercultural and interreligious questions hinges upon the vision of Christ. Is he an Oriental Pantocrator? A Western divine prophet? The private God of Christians? The universal savior? A man for others?"[1] But for a Christian, Christ is

---

[1] Raimon Panikkar, "A Christophany for Our Times," *Theology Digest* 39, no. 1 (1992): 3.

the central symbol or icon that embodies the whole of reality, "the light that illumines everyone" (John 1:9), the alpha and the omega and all in between.

Christology, as a systematic reflection on the mystery of Christ, is an aggressive search by human reason to make this mystery intelligible or to categorize and define the reality that transcends all definitions and categorizations. All the discussions and disputes that led to the Chalcedonian Christological doctrine and the Christological reflections since then attempted to capture the mystery of Christ by making it a problem that humans can objectify, analyze, and reflect upon. However legitimate and laudable these attempts had been to develop a meaningful Christology, it was done within the ecclesial tradition without any dialogue with the religious traditions as if they did not matter. Though in the initial stages of the development of Christology, the Fathers of the Church entered into dialogue with the religious traditions and worldviews of the Greco-Roman culture to get an insight into the meaning of the mystery of Christ, with the ascendance of Christianity as the religion of the Roman Empire, Christology became an inner-ecclesial affair irrelevant to those who do not share the Judeo-Christian worldview. In order to liberate Christology from a narrow and limited understanding of the person of Christ and to open up the possibility for people of all cultures and religious traditions to encounter the mystery of Christ, Christology must further develop into Christophany. Panikkar takes the valuable insights of traditional Christology, goes further to develop a Christophany without supplanting it, and provides traditional Christology with new vistas and new possibilities to challenge all people with a transforming vision of Christ.

One can detect in Panikkar's Christology itself the seeds of a Christophany that further grows into a more systematic articulation of Christophany. In his earlier writings, Panikkar grappled with

220 *Christ without Borders*

the central question of Christology—that is, the identity of Jesus Christ—and approached the question from cross-cultural and interreligious perspectives.

The Identity of Christ

Christology raises the question "Who is Jesus Christ?" and reflects systematically to find an adequate and meaningful answer. The answer to the question addressed to Jesus by John the Baptist through his disciples, "Are you the one who is to come or are we to expect some other?" (Mt 11:3), is very precise, referring to the identity of his person in relation to what he is performing (Mt 11:5–6). This answer may look evasive if we are searching for a conceptual "who." But the "who" of Christ cannot be individualized by mere "here or there," as he is constantly "the coming one."[2] Here, according to Panikkar, the whole interest is centered not on the individual but on what he performs. To that extent the answer is appropriate as he is performing his messianic function. However, the question about his personal identity, his personhood, is unavoidable. For the Christian proclamation it is vital to communicate who he is. Peter, filled with the Holy Spirit, proclaims, "There is salvation in no one else, for there is no other name under heaven given among men by which we must be saved" (Acts 4:11). The name of Jesus Christ, in which alone there is salvation, is not a nominalist label, a magical formula, or a sign, because that cannot be a savior or mediator. This name that saves, according to Panikkar, is a real symbol. "It is a symbol, i.e., the very 'thing' as it appears and is in the world of our experience."[3]

---

[2] Raimon Panikkar, "The Meaning of Christ's Name in the Universal Economy of Salvation," in *Evangelization, Dialogue and Development: Selected Papers of the International Theological Conference (Nagapur, 1971)*, Mariasusai Dhavamony, ed. (Rome: Universita Gregoriana, 1972), 195.

[3] Panikkar, "The Meaning of Christ's Name in the Universal Economy of Salvation," 197.

A pure thing does not exist and nothing can exist without a name. Since any name with a meaning has an ontonomic constitution, it is neither purely subjective nor objective. The name is a real symbol because it is thrown between subject and object. If there is salvation in "no other name," only through the reality intended by this name is there salvation. It also implies that this reality can be encountered by people having other worldviews, cultures, and religious traditions that have another meaningful name for this reality that for Christians is constituted by no other name than that of Jesus Christ.

Mere lip service to the name Jesus Christ is not sufficient to lead one to the kingdom of heaven. The reality intended by this name must be encountered and proclaimed. Who is Jesus Christ? Panikkar says that Peter's answer, "You are the Messiah, the Son of the living God" (Mt 16:16), is perfect in the context in which the question is raised.[4] How can one translate this confessional statement in the way a Christian understands into the Indian context, for example, where there is no expectation of a Messiah but there is a strong belief that all are the sons of the living God? How can the answer of Peter to who Jesus is be meaningful outside the Petrine world? Panikkar asks whether those who do not share the Semitic worldview need to be circumcised in their minds to make this confessional statement intelligible to them. If the proclamation of Christ is to be intelligible to one who is outside the Semitic tradition, it really has to be translated and not transliterated. So the answer to the question "Who is Jesus of Nazareth, the Messiah, the Son of the living God?" is not to be answered through the principle of individuation, through what individualizes and distinguishes him from others. Rather, the question is to be answered through a principle of identity.

---

[4] Raimon Panikkar, "The Relation of Christians to Their Non-Christian Surroundings," in *Christian Revelation and World Religions,* Joseph Neuner, ed. (London: Burns & Oates, 1967), 163.

Panikkar distinguishes a double principle of individuation—namely, the principle of singularity which relies on external factors to distinguish a thing and admits plurality; and the principle of individuality which is grounded on the internal constitution of being that is capable of self-identity. In the context of Christian faith, we cannot apply both these principles to Jesus. In his person, he is not one among many, and so the principle of singularity cannot be applied to him properly. The principle of individuality would refer to what makes Jesus, Jesus—or the "what" of Jesus or the thing-in-itself. This will not answer the question of who Jesus is or of his identity as a living person. Panikkar is not saying that one cannot distinguish Jesus as a historical figure from James or John. But in traditional Christology, Christ is not a single individual in the sense of other historical personages, simply a member of the species. "Christ has human nature indeed, he is Man but he is not a human person. He is divine person, the second person of the Trinity having assumed human nature."[5] In this sense, following the Christology of Chalcedon, Panikkar says that Christ is man but not one man, a single individual, he is the divine person, incarnated, and is in hypostatic union with human nature.[6] But the presence of Christ for the believer here and now is the divine presence. Panikkar admits that if we push this doctrine too far we may end up in Docetism or dis-incarnationalism. The principle of singularity cannot be applied to Jesus because he is not simply a numerical exemplar of a species of human mortals. How, then, do

---

[5] Panikkar refers to Piet Schoonenberg's argument in *Ein Gott der Menschen* (Dubuque, IA: Benziger, 1969), where he discusses the problem of the unity in Christ as a person who is divine and human at the same time. Panikkar, "The Meaning of Christ's Name in the Universal Economy of Salvation," in *Service and Salvation*, ed. J. Pathrapankal (Bangalore: Theological Publications, 1973), 205.

[6] Panikkar, "The Meaning of Christ's Name in the Universal Economy of Salvation," 205.

From Christology to Christophany 223

we defend his true humanity? Panikkar says that if we insist that the humanness of Jesus has to be defended, this is to insist that the man Jesus has something peculiar, which, while not diminishing his humanness, transcends it in such a way as to make possible a sui generis relationship with him. This uniqueness of Jesus is the very negation of singularity and individuality. Panikkar affirms that the living Christ of Christian faith who is present in the sacrament and in others, who transcends time, with whom one can enter into personal relationship, does not fall in the category of individual in the philosophical and current sense of the word.

The important issue in any Christological reflection should not be the philosophical and theological problems concerning the unity of natures, namely, divine and human in Jesus Christ. According to Panikkar, the important issue is encountering him as true God and true Man. The encounter is possible only when identity can only be said to be real and thus true if we enter into a personal relationship with him. Only then may one discover "the living Christ of faith who lives in the interior of oneself."[7] In this experience one realizes that Jesus is the person who does not fall into the category of singularity or individuality, and his character is "not singleness but communion, not incommunicability, but relations."[8] So in Peter's confession of faith, that thou art Messiah, the Son of the living God, the only universal element, according to Panikkar, is *thou*. This *thou* is not the projection of one's own ego, and the issue is not to elucidate the predicate of this sentence but to discover this subject existentially. This *thou* cannot be and should not be pinpointed by an unequivocal means of identification as it would lead to idolatry, which is a sin against the Spirit. Therefore, according to Panikkar,

---

[7] Panikkar, "The Meaning of Christ's Name in the Universal Economy of Salvation," 212.

[8] Raimon Panikkar, *Salvation in Christ: Concreteness and Universality, the Supername*, Inaugural Lecture at the Ecumenical Institute of Advanced Theological Study Tantur, Jerusalem (Santa Barbara, CA, 1972), 32.

"The word Jesus has two basically different meanings: one as historical category and another as personal category. The former is reached by means of historical identification, which permits us to speak about Jesus and about the belief Christians have in and through him. The latter is reached by means of personal identity and allows us to discover him a 'part' or rather pole of our personal being, as one of the many traits that make our person."[9]

In his cryptic and often misunderstood statement "Christ is the Lord but the Lord is not only Jesus,"[10] Panikkar is trying to overcome the limitations of the understanding of Christ in the historical category. If we insist on understanding Jesus exclusively in historical categories, we will only discover him as a great man of history but we will not be moved to any personal relationship with him. "Jesus will appear as a historically relevant figure of the past, with a still uncommon influence on the present, but the only point of reference will be his historical coordinates and his impact on the lives of other men."[11] If Christology has to be true to its name, then it should not be satisfied with a Jesus-ology that, according to Panikkar, is the tendency of the contemporary European approaches to Christology.[12] The Christian who encounters the risen Christ in faith cannot but identify him with the historical Jesus. That is the guarantee that the person who enters into the very structure of his being had a human existence at a particular time of history. But then he knows too that it was a limited existence,

---

[9] Panikkar, "The Meaning of Christ's Name in the Universal Economy of Salvation," 212.

[10] Raimon Panikkar, "Have Religions the Monopoly of Religion?," *Journal of Ecumenical Studies* 15 (1974): 409.

[11] Panikkar, "The Meaning of Christ's Name in the Universal Economy of Salvation," 212.

[12] See Raimon Panikkar, *Die vielen Götter und der eine Herr: Beiträge zum ökumenischen Gespräch der Weltreligionen* (Weilheim Obb: O. W. Barth Verlag, 1963), 69–70.

even though it was of utmost importance that God became human in history.

The Christ of a believer's existential and personal experience transcends the historical constraints and limitations. Panikkar uses the example of the Eucharistic presence of Christ, which is the real living Christ whom one encounters in Communion. Here the real presence of Christ is not identified with the historical existence of Jesus. Separated from the faith dimension, outside this personal encounter with the risen Lord, Jesus would be as any other religious founder; he would be considered "a remarkable Jewish teacher, who had the fortune or misfortune of being put to death rather young."[13] Panikkar asserts that the living Christ of every Christian generation is invariably more than this description.

According to Panikkar, we can experience Christ within the limits of Abrahamic or Semitic traditions, the cosmic tradition of humankind, and in all authentic religious traditions. The expansive Christology he offers seeks integration as Christ is historical *and* transhistorical. Within the church, Christians can encounter the living Christ in the Sacraments and in fellowship with one another. Throughout the world, Christ can be encountered in the lives of each human person, especially in those who have been oppressed and deprived of abundant life. Christ is the most perfect expression of the cosmotheandric reality, weaving the divine, human, and cosmic in harmony and beauty.[14]

This person who makes human, divine, and cosmic communion possible cannot be thought of only in spatiotemporal categories. It is true that, in Jesus of Nazareth, a Christian encounters Christ, but the Christ of the Christian believer transcends the historical limitations of Jesus of Nazareth. Such

---

[13] Raimon Panikkar, *The Unknown Christ of Hinduism* (Maryknoll, NY: Orbis Books, 1981), 27.

[14] Raimon Panikkar, *Cosmotheandric Experience: Emerging Religious Consciousness* (Maryknoll, NY: Orbis Books, 1993), 121.

transcendence has been misunderstood as a separation of Jesus of Nazareth and Christhood; Panikkar's Christology does not separate these two. Christ is not some a-personal principle within the theological system or cosmic reality. Christ is at once the second person of the Trinity, the preexistent who reveals himself in Jesus of Nazareth, who is born of Mary, who "is the Bread as well as the hungry, naked or imprisoned," Panikkar writes.[15] In this nuance, Panikkar works to overcome the tendency to make Jesus an idol, failing to transcend Jesus as he himself did at his resurrection.

In the context of dialogue with other religions, Panikkar's approach is to deepen the understanding of the mystery of the person of Christ who is present in all authentic traditions because he is the Lord of everything that is and that comes into being. Traditional Christology is not able to present such an understanding of Jesus Christ as it attempts at an identification of *who* Jesus is rather than the identity of Jesus Christ. Therefore, Panikkar proposes a Christophany that leads to a vision of Jesus Christ's identity in which one gets an insight into the mystery of oneself, others, world, and God.

Christophany: A Disclosure of Christ

In his attempt to offer a credible figure of Christ to those Christians who wish to enter into dialogue with people of other religious traditions without diluting their Christian-ness or fidelity to Christ, Panikkar proposes a Christophany that transcends traditional Christology without supplanting it. In his Bellarmine Lecture of 1991, delivered at St. Louis University, Panikkar outlined a sketch of this Christophany, which I think recapitulates his Christological reflections of about half a century.

---

[15] Panikkar, *Cosmotheandric Experience*, 27–28.

From Christology to Christophany 227

For Panikkar, the Christophany that he proposes stands for the disclosure of Christ to human consciousness and critical reflection. Unlike Christology, from which Christophany does not totally depart, it emphasizes a more passive attitude of receiving the impact of Christ over against a more aggressive search by human reason for intelligibility. It reintegrates the Christ figure into a cosmological vision as well as integrates with critical discernment the homeomorphic equivalents of the same in other traditions where there is an epiphany of the sacred or the divine. Though Christophany does not claim to be universal, it does claim to offer a credible figure of Christ that enables Christians to enter into dialogue with other religious tradition and to remain open, ecumenical, and tolerant. Christophany develops in continuity with the traditional Christology and is a description of that epiphany of the real that Christians call Christ. Further, "Christophany is the fruit of dialogue with other religions as much as an interpretation of its own tradition over against a modern background."[16] Such a dialogue helps us to enter more deeply into the mystery of Christ. Christophany offers a way for Christians, together with people of other religions, to understand the figure of Christ.

Panikkar describes his Christophany in nine theses or *sutras*. The first of these *sutras* is the fundamental one, that is, Christ is the symbol of all reality. Panikkar uses the term "symbol" to express the experience of reality in which subject and object, interpreter and interpreted, phenomenon and its noumenon inextricably unite.[17] Christ is the symbol of reality because in him are enclosed not only "all treasures of divinity" but also "all Mysteries of Man" and all the density of the universe. Both the biblical and Christological affirmations about the person of Christ undoubtedly lead to this conclusion. He is the mediator and not an intermediary,

---

[16] Panikkar, "A Christophany for Our Times," 5.
[17] Panikkar, "A Christophany for Our Times," 6.

228 *Christ without Borders*

fully divine and fully human; the light that illumines everyone and everything is made by him and in him—the alpha and the omega and all in between. Therefore every being is a Christophany, and Christ is the symbol of the divinization of the universe.

A Christian knows Christ in and through Jesus. This is the second *sutra* of Christophany. The Christian discovers Christ *in* and *through* Christian revelation and experience. It is not a mere confession that Jesus is the Christ that saves one but the existential encounter with the reality that the name of Jesus Christ discloses. It is through the personal experience in communion with the community of believers—that is, the church—that Jesus is recognized, acknowledged, and believed to be Jesus Christ, through whom the universe was made, the Son of God, Light from Light, True God from God.

Panikkar repeats in his fourth *sutra* what he had already stressed in his earlier Christological reflections: Christ's identity is not his identification. Jesus can be objectively identified as being born and dying at a particular place and time. But this will not reveal his identity, which is not an objectifiable category. Christ's identity can only be encountered through a loving relationship, which is a gift from above. Christophany seeks to maintain the equilibrium between the identification and identity of Jesus, or between the Jesus of history and the Christ of faith. Since the identity of Jesus Christ transcends the spatial and temporal limitations and belongs to the mystery of person and personal relationship, Panikkar's fourth *sutra* of Christophany says that Christians do not have a monopoly on the knowledge of Christ. The Christian experience of Jesus Christ and the reflection on him do not exhaust the mystery of Christ. Many aspects of this mystery that surpass all understanding can be recognized in the insights of other religious traditions.

Christians need to study other religions for an adequate self-understanding of the Christian faith and to liberate Christology from its limitations. Therefore, the fifth *sutra* says that Christophany is the overcoming of a tribal Christology. It means that contemporary Christology must incorporate, as far as possible, the insights about the mystery that Christians call Christ as it manifests itself in other religions. Traditional Christology remained a tribal Christology because it did not take into consideration in its understanding of Christ all other religious experiences of humanity, concentrating almost exclusively on its own concerns. This Christology cannot address the ecological crisis and the human crisis of absolute poverty, injustice, oppression, wars, and religious fundamentalism and communalism. However, Christophany, by its very approach to the mystery of Christ and its openness to the manifestation of the Christic mystery in other religious traditions, can promote dialogue and collaborative action to face the ecological and human crises of our times.

Christophany considers that "protological, historical and the eschatological Christ is one and the same reality distended in time, extended in space and intentional in us." This is the sixth *sutra*, which expresses the unity of Christ as creator, redeemer, and glorifier. He is also one of the Trinity and the full manifestation of the Trinity. Christophany reveals to us the threefold tension in our awareness of reality. In the experience of temporal realities we get a glimpse of something not distended or timeless, eternal. In the experience of reality as spatial and material, we get a glimpse of something more than matter, that is, Spirit. Further, everything in us tends toward something beyond us, a transcendence, to God. Christophany shows that if Christ is not a dead symbol creation, then redemption and glorification relate to him. Creation is *creatio continua*, which is the foundation on which concrete time and the temporality of every instant rests. The protological Christ or the preexistent Christ is the same as the historical Christ, and the historical Christ cannot be separated from the Eucharistic Christ or the risen Christ. In the same way, the Christ of the Parousia cannot be separated from the Eucharistic and risen Christ. Christophany

230 *Christ without Borders*

thus helps us to integrate past, present, and future and thus to live consciously a tempiternal life.

For Panikkar, incarnation is also inculturation. It is the seventh *sutra* of his Christophany. According to Panikkar, incarnation is not only a historical event but also a cultural event intelligible in a particular cultural context. In the Semitic culture, it was intelligible because of its understanding of history. Outside the Semitic culture, its intelligibility depends on its transhistorical value. In Hindu India, the experience of the Christian Christ is better reenacted by the sacrifice of the Eucharist than by the narrative of Bethlehem. Incarnation is a historical act but is a temporally irretrievable event as it affects Man, who cannot be reduced to a mere historical being. Though Christianity is a historical religion, Christ in whom it believes is more than a historical reality, in the sense that the Semitic culture understood history. Since incarnation is already an inculturation in a particular culture, its acceptance in another culture transforms that particular culture that accepts this reality of incarnation. Therefore, we cannot absolutize one particular Christophany.

Christophany reveals to us the reality of a church that has no boundaries. According to the eighth *sutra* of Panikkar's Christophany, the church understands itself as the locus where incarnation takes place. The nature of the church, as the mystical Body of Christ—as *sacramentum mundi* or in Greek *mysteriou tou kosmou*—refers to a cosmic church. The ecclesiology of the Fathers must prevent us from a microdoxical interpretation of the church, reducing it to an official church and to a mere historical phenomenon. It is the church that exists throughout the universe as the locus of salvation. Man and the entire creation can reach salvation because at the very root of creation is the mediator, the link, the Christ, begotten by the source and origin of all divinity, who not only creates but also divinizes through his Spirit. The place where this takes place is the church. It is also the field where the

From Christology to Christophany 231

universe seeks its final destiny. Panikkar says that Man is the priest or the mediator in this divine cosmic struggle. Christophany is the epiphany of this and our own role in the universe.

In the final *sutra*, Panikkar affirms that Christophany is the manifestation of the mysterious union of the divine, human, and cosmic "dimensions" of reality. As Jesus Christ is pure transparency, whoever encounters him encounters the Father as well as the full Man and the cosmos. He is the living symbol of divinity, humanity, and cosmos. This experience, according to Panikkar, is the cosmotheandric intuition. Further, Panikkar says, "In Jesus Christ the finite and infinite meet. In him the human and the divine are united. In him the material and the spiritual are one—to say nothing of masculine and feminine, high and low, heaven and earth and, obviously, the historical and trans-historical, time and eternity."[18] Christophany shows that Christ cannot be separated from the Trinity, humanity, and history. If Christ is separated from the Trinity, he is just like any great teacher or prophet; if he is separated from humanity, he becomes another god. If his humanity is separated from his historical context, he becomes a Gnostic figure who does not share our limited human conditions.

Panikkar's Christophany is inseparable from his Christology. His Christology grows into Christophany, which offers a new, synthetic, and transforming vision of reality and its symbol, the figure of Christ. If Christology is the root, Christophany is the fruit. Christophany offers a challenging vision that liberates Christians from a narrow and sectarian understanding of Christ to a richer understanding and a better appreciation of the gift of the person of Christ in dialogue with other religious traditions and cultures and to work in harmony with them to face the ecological and human crises of the contemporary world.

---

[18] Panikkar, "A Christophany for Our Times," 20.

232   *Christ without Borders*

Panikkar's Christophany, though systematic in its articulation, transcends systems and particular ideologies and at the same time does not claim any universality. Since it is a vision and insight, each one is invited to enter into it and experience the fullness of life. It offers a figure of Christ who manifests who God is, what the world is, and what we are, and what we can become. It may take time for Christians as well as the followers of other religious traditions and cultures to understand, appreciate, and accept the richness, depth, and value of Panikkar's intuition. But when it happens, it will certainly affect and transform those who are open to responding to their innate nature of transcendence and communion.

Index

Abelard, Peter, 38
accommodationist theology, 93
adoptionism, 28–29, 123, 124, 154
   advaita (nondualism), 180
   advaitic Christ, 206–7
   advaitic intuition, 45, 48–52, 181
   on nonduality of suffering, 183–84
   Upadhyaya, response to, 113–14,
      159–60
Ai, Emperor, 108–9
Akbar, Emperor, 112, 135
Aleni, Giulio, 109
al-Mahdi, Caliph, 198
Alopen (Nestorian missionary), 107–8
Amaladoss, Michael, 98, 168
androcentric theology, 85–86
anhypostasis doctrine, 74
Animananda, Rewachand, 166
Anselm of Canterbury, 37–38, 39
Aphrahat the Persian, 31–32
apocrypha, 191, 193
Apollinarianism, 30, 46, 163–64
Apology (Tertullian), 91
Apostles' Creed, 197
Appasamy, Aiyadurai J., 114
Arabic Infancy Gospel, 191
Arianism, 2, 28–29, 51, 56, 188
Athanasius of Alexandria, 4, 26, 37,
   51, 100–101
Athenagoras of Athens, 25
atonement doctrine, 37–38, 39, 164
Augustine of Hippo, 35–36, 37, 39,
   95, 97, 133, 190, 199
Avalokitesvara, 107–8
avatara theology, 140, 177
  as docetic, 47–48
  Jesus the *avatara,* 114–15, 131, 135,
    164–65, 179

mystery of Christ, understanding
   via, 206–7

Babi the Great, 32
Barth, Karl, 60, 69–70, 72
Beckett, Thomas, 212–13
Ben Dosa, Hanina, 66
Bevans, Stephen, 108
bodhisattvas, 107–8
Boff, Leonardo, 79–80
Book of Heracleides (Nestorius), 34
Bornkamm, Günther, 61
Boyd, Robin, 167
Brahman
   maya, contrasting with *Brahman,*
     159–60
   Nirguna Brahman, 114, 156–57,
     161–62, 165–66
   Saccidananda Brahman, 114, 155–58
Breech, James, 203–4, 210, 211, 212–15
Buber, Martin, 201
Buddhism, 41, 43, 81, 107, 108, 136,
   141, 177
Bultmann, Rudolf, 60, 70–71
Byung Mu Ahn, 118

Carr, Anne, 84–85
Chakkarai, Vengal, 115, 154
Chenchiah, Pandipeddi, 115
Cheng Tang, Emperor, 109
China, 12, 107–9, 110, 142
The Christ (Schoonenberg), 73–74
Christ and Culture (Niebuhr), 90
Christography, 87
   Christographical outsiders, 54–58
   contemporary Christographies,
     64–69
   in quest for historical Jesus, 58–64

234 *Index*

Christology
  Alexandrian Christology, 28, 29, 46, 47, 56
    divinity of Jesus, emphasizing, 2, 4–5, 30, 87, 188
    paradigm shift to Antiochene Christology, 4–7, 11, 87
  Antiochene Christology, 2, 4–7, 11, 27–29, 31, 47, 87, 188
  Asian Christologies, 92, 142
  Asia in Christ-of-culture view, 93–94
    Asian experiences of Christ, 121–22, 124, 129–30, 145
    diversity of Asian Christologies, 105–7, 120
    East Asian faces of Christ, 107–12
    Jesus of Asian women, 119–20
    normative Christology in the Asian context, 39–43
  below and above Christologies, 73, 123–24, 130–32, 154
  Black Christology, 3, 205–6
  Catholic Christology, 11, 12, 14
  Christological heresies, 17, 56
  contemporary Christologies, 217, 229
    anthropological Christologies, 70–77
    Christocentric Christologies, 69–70
    cosmic Christology, 86–88
    Dalit Christology, 3, 82–83, 170
    feminist Christology, 83–86
    liberation Christologies, 77, 78–82, 131–32, 170
    postmodernist challenge to Christology, 203–9
  contextual Christologies, 11–13, 19–21, 216
  cosmic Christology, 86–88, 180
  functional Christology, 76–77, 130, 132, 172, 184, 216
  Indian Christologies, 136, 143, 147–50, 179, 181
  of insiders and outsiders, 54–58
  Kyrios as a Christological title, 174
  of liturgy and piety, 13–15
  normative Christology, 18, 150
    in the Asian context, 39–43
    of Hellenistic Christians, 23–27
    of the Jewish community, 22–23
    in Latin tradition, 35–39
    in Syrian Christianity, 27–35
  ontological Christology, 77, 124, 132, 184, 216
  paradigm shifts in Christology, 4–10, 13
  of the poor, 122–23, 130, 184
  sectarian Christologies, influence on Islam, 192–201
  theophanic Christology, 57, 70
  traditional Christology, critique of, 218–26, 227, 229
  of Upadhyaya, 152–53, 154–66, 168, 170
  variety of Christologies, 1–4, 55
Christology at the Crossroads (Sobrino), 78–79
Christophany, 48, 51, 181
  as a disclosure of Christ, 226–32
  Panikkar's insights into, 217, 219
  totality of Christ, recognizing, 52
Church Dogmatics (Barth), 69–70
Clement of Alexandria, 26, 94, 167
Collyridianism, 188
Cone, James, 206
Confessing Church, 206
Confucianism, 108–9, 110, 141, 142
Cooke, Bernard, 12
Correct Answer to Those Who Changed the Religion of Christ (Ibn Taymiyya), 200
Council of Chalcedon, 3, 8, 31, 46, 57, 76, 95, 145
  Christological Formula, 2, 14, 26, 30, 32, 36, 45, 47, 48, 50, 72, 84, 162
  Christology of, 15, 57, 70, 73–74, 78, 124, 219, 222
  vere Deus/vere homo statement of, 69–70
Council of Constantinople I, 131
Council of Ephesus, 30
Council of Nicaea, 2, 25, 29, 56, 76, 123, 131, 188
Council of Seleucia Ctesiphon, 32
countercultural movements, 92

Index

Crossan, John Dominic, 61, 68–69, 210–11, 215
The Crucified God (Moltmann), 77
Cyril of Alexandria, 4, 30, 32, 34

Dalits, 208
  Christ of the Dalits, 132, 186, 205, 207
  Dalit Christology, 3, 82–83, 170
  Jesus the Dalit, 117–18
  as oppressed, 3, 130, 182
Daly, Mary, 86
Daniel, Monodeep, 82
De Nobili, Robert, 112, 135
Desert Fathers, 91
Diatesseron (Tatian), 192
Diodore of Tarsus, 27
Dionysius the Areopagite, 33
Dioscorus of Alexandria, 32
Discourses on Monotheism (Alopen), 108
divine sonship, 33, 37, 51, 66
  in Alexandrine Christology, 2, 4–5, 30, 87, 188
  Bultmann on, 70–71
  in Chalcedonian Christology, 2, 26, 47, 48, 50, 56–57, 72, 73, 84, 124
  in Christ above culture view, 94–95
  in contextual Christologies, 11–12
  Kappen on, 81–82
  New Testament references to, 195, 196
  Sen on Divine Humanity in Christ, 112–13, 141
  unity of divine and human natures, 2, 45–46, 162–64, 222–23, 231
Docetism, 2, 46, 47, 56, 94–95, 124, 154, 183, 188, 222
Does God Exist (Küng), 76
Duffy, Stephen J., 7
dynamic monarchianism, 189

Eastern Christianity, 13, 27, 32, 111, 183
Ebionites, 55–56, 187
Elias of Nisibis, 32
Eliot, Thomas S., 212
enhypostasis doctrine, 74
the Enlightenment, 58, 204
Ephrem the Syrian, 32
Epiphanius of Salamis, 188
Eutyches of Constantinople, 30, 188

Fitzmyer, Joseph, 66
Foucault, Michel, 203, 204, 205
Francis, Pope, 87
Francis Xavier, Saint, 112, 135
Funk, Robert, 61, 68

Gandhi, Mahatma, 137–38
Gaudium et spes pastoral constitution, 11
German Christians, 205–6
Gnosticism, 46, 56, 93, 95, 99, 183, 187–88, 231
God is dead concept, 209–10
Gogarten, Friedrich, 71
Gold-Crowned Jesus (Kim), 116, 127
Goreh, Nilakantha, 135–36
Gospel of Pseudo-Matthew, 191
Gospel of Thomas, 191
Gregory the Great, Pope, 37
Guan Yin, 108

Harmony (journal), 153
Harnack, Adolf von, 59
headship, 84–85
Hegel, G. W. F., 59
Heiler, Friedrich, 167
Hellenistic Christianity, 40, 59, 143, 169
  Arius as interpreting, 28–29
  Hellenistic Christology, 23–27, 76, 93
  Indian thought, seeking complementarity with, 131, 170
  Jesus as a Hellenistic Jewish sage, 61–62, 68–69
  Latin theology, influence on, 35, 36
  testimony of Hellenistic believers, 64–65
heresies and false doctrines, 17, 141, 200
  adoptionism, 28–29, 123, 124, 154
  apocryphal writings, finding expression in, 190–91
  Chalcedon as safeguarding against heresies, 2, 45
  Docetism, 2, 46, 47, 56, 94–95, 124, 154, 183, 188, 222
  modalism, 155–56, 158, 189
  monophysitism, 30–31, 32, 33, 34, 50, 56, 188, 191
  tritheism, 158, 189, 199

236 Index

Hinduism, 41, 112, 117, 177, 182, 207
- Christ, interpretation of, 113, 131, 134, 135–37, 145, 150, 178–79, 230
- *Isvara,* considering Christ as, 131, 165–66, 206
- Jesus, viewing as a yogi and sannyasin, 138–40
- Sen, articulating Hindu views on Christ, 140–42
- uniqueness of Jesus, considering, 142–43
- Upadhyaya on Christianity for Hindus, 151, 152–54, 154–66, 167–70
- *See also advaita; Brahman*

historical Jesus of Nazareth, 8, 13, 45, 55, 71, 87, 125, 171, 177, 204, 208
- Boff on, 79–80
- Christhood of historical Jesus, 20–21
- historical limitations, Christ as transcending, 179–80, 225–26
- identity of, 19, 55, 175
- in the Indian context, 81, 147, 148, 178
- Jesus as the Lord of history, 144
- mystery of the historical Jesus, 46, 50, 54
- Pannenberg on, 72–73
- Panikkar on, 115–16, 221–22, 224–25, 228–30
- the poor, linking with, 122–23, 128, 132
- as a prophet, 54, 67, 173–74
- quest for the historical Jesus, 58–64, 65
- Schillebeeckx on, 75–76
- unity of divinity and humanity in Christ, 47, 56

Hopkins, Julie M., 129
Horsley, Richard, 67–68
hypostatic union, 2, 30, 32, 162–64, 222

Ibn Taymiyya, 200
Ignatius of Antioch, 16, 56, 95, 144
incarnational Christology, 26, 28, 57, 72
inclusive Christocentrism, 3, 8
inclusive transcendence, 180, 182
India, 47, 135, 140, 221

advaitic intuition, Indian concept of, 45, 48, 49
Christic identification in the Indian context, 176–81
Dalit Christology, 82–83, 117–18, 132
Gandhi as a reformer of Indian society, 137–38
Indian Christian theologians, 130–31, 147, 148
Indian Christologies, 12, 136, 143, 145, 147–50, 160
Jesus as liberator of Indians, 80–81
Jesus of the Indian subcontinent, 112–19
normative Christology, developing for India, 22, 150
principle of identity, emphasizing, 49–50
suffering Christ of the Indian subcontinent, 182–86
Upadhyaya on Christ in the Indian worldview, 151, 152–54, 161, 163, 167–70

Infancy Gospel of Thomas, 191
In Memory of Her (Schüssler Fiorenza), 84
Introduction to the Incarnation of the Lord of Heaven (Aleni), 109
Irenaeus of Lyons, 56, 95, 100, 189
Islam, 17, 191, 218
- monotheism of, 137, 189, 199
- Muhammad as prophet for, 142, 177, 191, 199
- sectarian Christologies, influence on, 192–201

Jainism, 136
Jesuits, 107, 108, 112, 135
Jesus and Freedom (Kappen), 80
Jesus and Postmodernism (Breech), 203–4, 210
Jesus Christ
- as alpha and omega, 17, 23, 51, 54, 87, 99, 173–74, 219, 228
- as ascetic, 138–40, 142
- Asian experience of, 121–22, 124, 129–30, 145
- avataric Christ, 47–48, 114–15, 131, 135, 164–65, 177, 179, 206–7

Index

237

baptism of Jesus, 21, 123, 190, 196
body of Christ, 33–34, 87, 129, 230
Christ as Messiah, 54, 58, 59, 66, 125, 128, 129, 144
   the expected Messiah, 19, 55, 175, 177, 182
   Islam on Jesus as Messiah, 194, 195
   of Jewish expectations, 16, 19–20, 22–23, 175
   Messiah as a Christological title, 81, 137
   Peter on recognizing Jesus as Messiah, 221, 223
colonizers, associating Jesus with, 106–7
cosmic Christ, 86, 102
cosmotheandric Christ, 115–16
crucifixion of Christ, 77, 123, 126, 129
   as abhorrent in Confucian culture, 108–9
   Jesus as crucified for the values of the kingdom, 85-86, 85–86
   Jesus as the crucified and risen sage, 110–11
   suffering of Christ on the cross, 130, 182, 183, 186
as a Cynic, 65, 68–69
death of Jesus, 26, 35, 75, 82, 144, 177, 190, 201
   Christian belief on death and resurrection, 196–97
   Islam, interpretation of, 195, 197
   postmodern view on, 214, 215–16
   resurrection of Jesus from death, 28, 73
faith in Christ, 14, 18, 31, 49, 51, 67, 70, 83, 91, 142, 195, 201
   articulation of faith, 55, 57
   Christ of faith and Jesus of history, 58–59, 63, 71, 87, 175, 224, 228
   early church, faith experience in, 45, 46
   faith affirmations, 45, 50, 57–58, 66, 147, 148

living faith in Christ, 6, 15, 42, 223
Godhead, Jesus as part of, 157–58, 162
as guru, 137, 147, 212
humanity of Jesus, 6, 13, 77, 123, 201
   in Chalcedon Formula, 47, 48, 50, 72, 73
   in contemporary Christologies, 69–74
   in contextual Christologies, 11–12
   denial of the humanity of Jesus, 2, 46, 56, 183, 231
   early Christian views on, 5, 33, 37, 56–57, 94–95, 100–101, 217
   false doctrines on, 188, 190
   Indian understanding of, 45, 112–13
   Jesus as model of what it is to be human, 76, 99
   Logos, incarnation in human Jesus, 26, 70, 87, 141
   the maleness of Jesus, 83–86
   New Testament references to Jesus as human, 195, 196
   Panikkar, in Christology of, 51, 222–23
   the poor, recognizing Jesus the human, 116–17, 129, 133
   in Syrian theology, 29–30
   Upadhyaya, in Christology of, 162–64, 168
identity of Jesus, 53, 171–81, 179, 180, 182, 186, 217, 220–26, 228
Islamic understanding of Christ, 192–93, 193–201
Jewish origins of Jesus, 65–66, 101
kenotic Christ, 42, 43, 120, 208
kingdom of God, proclaiming, 7, 66, 67–68, 75, 79, 80, 125, 132, 215
as liberator, 18, 41–42, 78–80, 82, 106, 116–17, 119, 121–22, 150
as mediator, 24, 33, 36, 76, 120, 181, 230
mission of Christ, 22, 28, 41, 55, 58, 68, 78, 134, 147
   Boff, Christological reflections on the mission of Jesus, 79–80

238 *Index*

Jesus Christ *(continued)*
colonial powers as associated with, 178–79
commitment to mission in contextual Christologies, 6, 15
in contemporary Christographies, 64–66
mission command of Jesus, 27, 145
women as sharing in Christ's saving mission, 86
moral teaching of Jesus, 112, 137
nondualistic relationship with culture, 100–102, 103
nonviolence, associating with, 137–38
as normative, 7, 8–9
obedience of Christ, 23, 28
as One, 1, 13, 55, 56, 57, 74, 205
as Pantocrator, 106, 182, 218
parables of, 210–11, 213–15
preferential option of Jesus for the poor, 111, 130, 183
resurrection of Jesus, 55, 58, 62, 100, 175, 195, 201, 224, 229
in Chinese context, 108–11
Christologies, explaining resurrection through, 19–20, 42
in feminist Christology, 85, 86
New Testament witness to, 188, 190, 196–97
Panikkar on, 225, 226
the poor, meaning of resurrection to, 132–33, 174
postmodern view of, 214–16
recognition of Jesus before and after resurrection, 20–21, 73, 172
as redemptive, 26, 87
Schillebeeckx stance as controversial, 75–76
as vindication of Jesus's life, 28, 79
as sinless, 36, 38, 74, 164
sinners, dying for, 62, 68–69
as a social reformer, 59, 63, 65, 67, 186, 212

as Son of Man, 26, 81, 113, 142
sonship of Christ, 21, 23, 26, 73, 76, 89, 124, 133, 177, 196, 228
Council of Chalcedon on, 57, 74
Hindu understanding of, 139–40, 153, 178
honorific title, Son of God as, 28, 81, 137, 188, 195
human, Son of God becoming, 72, 97
as identity of Jesus, 123
inability to accept concept, 66, 119
Islam, understanding of, 197, 198, 200
Peter, recognizing Jesus as Son of God, 221, 223
Sophia, Jesus identified as, 86, 158–59
suffering of, 38, 78, 79, 109–10, 126–30, 133, 182–86, 188
as a teacher, 51, 63, 65, 108–9, 180, 225, 231
Trinity, as second person of, 39, 57, 74, 116, 124, 142, 161, 222, 226
uniqueness of, 3, 10, 16, 60, 76, 81, 146, 148, 171, 177, 223
Brahman, Christ as unique incarnation of, 164–65
Christ as unique savior of humankind, 4, 150
Christian believers, insistence on Christ's uniqueness, 179, 213
death and resurrection as making Jesus unique, 110
Mozoomdar on Jesus as a unique incarnation, 113, 142–43
women, openness of Jesus with, 84, 85
as Word, 16, 26, 28, 94, 96–97, 101, 115, 134, 135–37, 144, 158, 159, 188, 190, 192, 194, 201
as yin and yang, 111–12
as a yogi, 138–40
See also divine sonship; historical Jesus of Nazareth; Lordship of Christ; mystery of Christ; prophetic Christian tradition; salvation; sin
Jesus Christ Liberator (Boff), 79–80

Index

Jesus in the World of Judaism (Vermes), 66
Jesus-Messiah Sutra (Alopen), 108
Jesus Seminar, 61–62, 68
Jesus the Jew (Vermes), 65–66
John of Antioch, 27
John the Baptist, 21, 67, 124–25, 172, 220
John of Damascus, 200
John of Montecorvino, 107
Johnson, Elizabeth, 85–86
Joseph, father of Jesus, 55, 187
Julianism, 188
Jüngel, Eberhard, 77
justification, 36, 38, 39
Justin Martyr, 24–26, 94

Kant, Immanuel, 59
Kappen, Sebastian, 80–82, 116, 207
Käsemann, Ernst, 60
Kasper, Walter, 72
Katholikos Iso'yabb III, 32
Kelly, John N. D., 26
kerygma, 41, 60, 71, 73, 106, 122, 123
Kim Chi Ha, 116
kingdom of God, 7, 66, 67–68, 75, 79, 80, 93, 96, 125
Knitter, Paul F., 9
Korea, 12, 110, 118–19
Krishna, 115, 142, 164, 165, 177
Küng, Hans, 76–77

Laudato Si' encyclical, 87
Lee, Jung Young, 111–12
Leo I, Pope, 31, 32, 36, 39
Lessing, G. E., 58
liberation theology, 77, 78–80, 116
Lipner, Julius, 169–70
Logos, 2, 14, 57, 70, 74, 97, 131, 153, 205
  faith in Christ as Logos, 64
  Greek Fathers as developing concept, 24–26
  incarnate Logos, 162, 164, 168
  Jesus as dwelling in the Logos-God, 163–64
  John, Logos Christology of, 21, 73, 102, 180
  as known and unknown, 42, 122
  Logos-*anthropos* Christology, 28, 29, 37

Logos-*sarx* Christology, 28, 30
  preexistent Logos, 29, 123, 141
  Upadhyaya, Logos in Christology of, 158–59, 161
Lordship of Christ, 1, 31, 64, 93, 118, 177, 197, 224
  confession that Jesus is Lord, 54, 56, 62, 75, 144, 175
  in early Christologies, 211, 218
  in fundamental Christian kerygma, 41, 106, 122, 123
  Hindu view of Jesus as Lord, 134, 150, 178, 179
  identity of Jesus as Lord, 174–75
  Jesus as Lord at resurrection, 126, 172, 189
  the Risen Lord, 190, 196
  Roman Empire, accepting Jesus as Lord, 145, 207–8
  Upadhyaya on Jesus as Supreme Lord, 158
Luther, Martin, 38, 95–96, 205

Mack, Burton, 68
Mahavira, 136, 177
Manicheism, 191
Maranatha Christologies, 75
Maréchal, Joseph, 47
A Marginal Jew (Meier), 67
Massey, James, 82, 83
maya (illusion), 159–60, 165
Mehta, Ashok, 129–30
Meier, John P., 62, 66, 67
Mencius, 110
Mennonites, 92
The Message of Christ (Gandhi), 138
Minjung of Korea, 118–19
modalism, 155–56, 158, 189
Moltmann, Jürgen, 77–78
monism, 49
monophysitism, 30–31, 32, 33, 34, 50, 56, 188, 191
Mozoomdar, Pratap Chander, 113, 142
Mudaliar, Umapati, 136
Muhammad, Prophet, 142, 177, 191, 195, 199
Murder in the Cathedral (Breech), 212

240 *Index*

mystery of Jesus Christ, 2, 17, 19, 54, 106, 111, 132, 150, 171
  advaitic intuition into, 44–45, 48–52
  in Chalcedon doctrine, 57, 219
  Chinese minds, preparing to receive, 108–9
  diversity of Christologies as a dimension of, 1, 11, 12–13, 88, 143
  in Indian thought, 169–70, 206
  Panikkar, insight into, 115, 180–81, 217, 226–29
  postmodern approach to, 202–3, 204, 209–11, 216
  search for understanding of, 46–48, 63
  speculation on, 123, 147–48

Nestorianism, 30, 32, 33, 34, 46, 50, 56, 107, 188, 191, 198
Nicene Creed, 14, 197
Niebuhr, H. Richard, 90, 93, 99
Niemöller, Martin, 206
Nietzsche, Friedrich, 209
nondualism, 49, 100–104, 113, 114, 138, 139, 183–84, 206
Nostra aetate declaration, 7–8

Ohlig, Karl-Heinz, 37
On Being Christian (Küng), 76
On Idolatry (Tertullian), 91
The Oriental Christ (Mozoomdar), 113, 142
Origen of Alexandria, 26, 100, 167

Panikkar, Raimon, 49, 131, 168
  Christophany of, 51–52, 217, 220–32
  on the cosmotheandric Christ, 115–16
  on the identity of Christ, 180–81
Pannenberg, Wolfhart, 72–73
pantheism, 86. 177
parabolic religion, 214–15
Patterson, Stephen J., 68
Paul of Antioch, 200
Paul of Samosata, 28
Peter the Fuller, 31
Philippines, 12, 117
Philoxenus, Patriarch, 31
Pieris, Aloysius, 94, 116

the poor, 78, 79, 81, 83, 117, 172, 174, 208
  in Asia, 40–42, 105, 121–22
  Christology of the poor, 122–23, 130, 184
  Jesus of the poor, 126–30, 185
  liberator of the poor, Jesus as, 106, 117, 119
  the poor of India, explaining Jesus to, 168, 169, 182
  preferential option for the poor, 85, 111, 183
  sufferings of the poor, 116, 130, 132, 133, 182–83
positivist school of historiography, 60–61
postmodernism, 202–3
  Christology, challenge to, 203–9
  Jesus beyond postmodernism, 211–16
  mystery of Jesus, insight into, 209–11
poststructuralism, 203, 207, 209, 210, 211, 216
Prabhu, George Soares, 116
principle of identity, 49–50, 111, 147, 221
principles of singularity and individuality, 222–23
"The Problem of Historical Jesus" (Käsemann), 60
prophetic Christian tradition, 20, 54, 81, 123, 174, 187, 191, 218
  Jesus as an apocalyptic prophet, 41, 66–67, 105, 121
  Jesus as an eschatological prophet, 61, 65, 67, 75
  Jesus as a prophet among others, 147, 177, 194, 197, 212, 231
  Jesus as a prophet of social change, 67–68
  Nestorianism, prophetic role of Christ as neglected in, 34–35
  the poor, accepting Jesus as a prophet, 122, 125, 132
  the suffering prophetic image of Christ, 129, 185
Protestants, 3, 57–58, 59, 60, 69, 91–92, 115, 154, 167
Proto-Evangelium of James, 191

Index

Quakers, 92
Quest for the Historical Jesus (Schweitzer), 59

Radhakrishnan, Sarvepalli, 138–39
Rahner, Karl, 2–3, 8, 47, 71–72
Raja, A. Maria Arul, 118
Rama, 115, 164, 177
Ramanuja, 114–15
Rayan, Samuel, 116
Regulae fidei (Irenaeus), 189
Reimarus, Hermann Samuel, 58
relativism, 209
Religion of Jesus the Jew (Vermes), 66
restitution, 36, 37, 39
Ricci, Matteo, 108
Ritschl, Albrecht, 59
Robinson, Neal, 192
Roy, Ram Mohun, 112, 137, 140
Ruether, Rosemary Radford, 86

Sabellius, 189
salvation, 8, 22, 29, 41, 69, 73, 80, 106, 145, 163, 190, 196, 218
    Christian claim of Jesus as savior, 88, 122, 150, 197
    heresies as endangering salvation, 155
    Hindu mind as grappling with, 178
    Jesus as a personal savior, 23
    mission of proclaiming Jesus as savior, 4, 5
    name of Jesus Christ, salvation in, 220
    in pluralistic approach, 9–10
    Upadhyaya on true salvation through Jesus, 158, 160, 168
    in Wisdom Christologies, 75
Samartha, Stanley J., 131
Sanders, Ed P., 67
Sankara, 159
satisfaction doctrine, 38–39
Schillebeeckx, Edward, 61, 75–76
Schleiermacher, Friedrich, 59
Schmidlin, Josef, 167
Schoonenberg, Piet, 70, 73–74
Schroeder, Roger P., 108
Schüssler Fiorenza, Elisabeth, 84
Schüssler Fiorenza, Francis, 13
Schweitzer, Albert, 59–60, 66

Second Vatican Council, 2, 3, 13, 131–32
    liberation Christology after, 78–79
    paradigm shift in Christology, causing, 4, 5
    seeds of truth, recognizing in other religions, 7–8
Sen, Keshub Chunder, 113, 140–42, 154, 155–56, 158
Severus of Pisidia, 31
She Who Is (Johnson), 85–86
sin, 27, 36, 50, 79, 93, 97, 126, 138, 223
    forgiveness of sins through Jesus, 23, 117, 174
    Jesus as dying for sinners, 62, 68–69
    Jesus as saving humans from sin, 80, 165, 177
    Jesus as sinless, 36, 38, 74, 164
    liberation from sin, 80, 147
    original sin, 35, 69
    the sinful in culture, 95, 96, 101
    Upadhyaya, sin in theology of, 160, 161
    in yin and yang system, 112
Sobrino, Jon, 77, 78, 79–80, 125
Society of the Four Vedas, 136
Song, Choan Seng, 116, 128
Sophia (Wisdom), 86, 158–59
Strauss, David F., 58–59
subordinationism, 189
Suh, David Kwang-sun, 119
Syrian Christian tradition, 29, 35, 40, 42
    Arabic world as influenced by, 191, 192–93
    East Syrian church, 27, 31, 32, 34, 107
    West Christian church, 27, 28, 30, 32, 34

Taoism, 111–12
Tatian of Abiabene, 192
Taylor, Mark C., 209, 210–11
Teilhard de Chardin, Pierre, 86–87, 140–41
Tertullian, 50, 91, 190, 199
Theissen, Gerd, 67
theocentrism, 7–9, 72, 90
Theodore of Mopsuestia, 27, 29–30, 34
Theological-Historical Commission, 11
theology of limit, 210, 215

242 *Index*

Theophilos of Antioch, 24–25, 151
Thistlethwaite, Susan Brooks, 207–8
Thomas Aquinas, 37–38, 39, 84, 94, 152, 159, 167
Thomas, Madathilparampil M., 131, 168
Tillich, Paul, 71
Timothy I, Patriarch, 198–99
Transcendental Christology, 3, 14
transcendental Thomism, 71
Transforming Grace (Carr), 84
Trinity, 32, 50, 59, 137, 180, 187, 189, 190, 229, 231
   intra-Trinitarian relationship, 77, 114
   Muslim understanding of, 195, 197–200
   patristic theology of, 52, 181
   second person of Trinity as Christ, 39, 57, 74, 116, 124, 142, 161, 222, 226
   Upadhyaya as interpreting, 155–58
tritheism, 158, 189, 199
True Meaning of the Lord of Heaven (Ricci), 108
The Twentieth Century (journal), 162–63
typological exegesis, 193

Unitarians, 137, 156
Unitatis redintegratio decree, 7

Upadhyaya, Brahamabandhav, 151
   advaitic philosophy of, 113–14, 159–60
   appraisal of approach, 166–70
   Christological reflections, 154–66
   Greco-Scholastic thinking, rejecting, 113, 131
   theological method of, 152–54

Vaishnavism, 48, 115, 136, 162, 164–65, 177, 206, 207
Väth, Alfons, 166–67
Vedanta, 114, 140, 153–58, 162, 165–66, 167, 169, 170
Vermes, Geza, 65–66
Virgin Mary, 136, 191
   goddess, viewed as a, 188, 190
   in Islam, 192–95
   Jesus as born of, 52, 55, 142, 181, 187, 226
Vivekananda, Swami, 138–39

Weiss, Johannes, 66
Why God Became a Man (Anselm), 38
Wisdom Christologies, 75
Wolfenbüttel Fragments (Reimarus), 58

yin and yang, 111–12
Yun-ka, Jonathan Tan, 110